CI/SfB
Project Manual

organising building project information

by Alan Ray-Jones BA (Arch) FRIBA and Wilfred McCann BA BArch

Incorporating the authoritative United Kingdom version of the international SfB classification system as it applies to project information.

The Architectural Press on behalf of RIBA Services Ltd

85139 123 0
First Published 1971
© RIBA Services 1971

Printed by Diemer & Reynolds Ltd., Bedford

Preface

This manual is about methods of data co-ordination which incorporate CI/sfB, the UK version of the international sfB classification system. CI/sfB is already used extensively in building industry office libraries, and was recommended to architects as an aid to the organisation of project information by the RIBA Council in April 1969. This recommendation makes possible a further step towards the convergence of methods of data co-ordination which has recently been encouraged throughout the construction industry by the efforts of the National Consultative Council Working Party on Data Co-ordination. The activities of the working party stem from the BRS *Study of coding and data co-ordination for the construction industry** which sets out the criteria which an eventual national system would have to meet. It has been predicted that such a system will come about largely through the gradual convergence of existing systems rather than through the creation of something new.

The manual describes the organisation and arrangement of design team project information and documents, as distinct from the arrangement of general information which is explained in the RIBA *Construction indexing manual** and *The organisation of information in the construction industry**, or the description of the administrative processes which are the subject of the RIBA *Job book**.

It advises architects and others on how to provide contractors with the co-ordinated information they need in order to build efficiently, and uses the experience of individuals and professional offices who have tried to bridge the gaps in the techniques evolved by architects, quantity surveyors, engineers and others over the years for the presentation of information. These offices have endeavoured to provide integrated information, fully signposted and cross-referenced. All owe a considerable debt to Professor Bjorn Bindslev of Denmark, who has done much work in this field since 1962 through the development of the CBC system. He, in turn, built on the work of Lars Magnus Giertz, the Swedish architect who was mainly responsible for the invention of the sfB system of classification as a 'standard list of contents' for national and job specifications, price books and building product catalogues in Sweden in 1951.

Until recently these offices worked independently. But some time before the RIBA Council recommendation of CI/sfB as the basis of a system of data co-ordination they met together at the RIBA as the sfB working group of offices (chairman W. R. V. Ward FRIBA) to exchange and pool the experience which has led to the production of this manual by RIBA Services Ltd.

Part I provides offices with a basis for making informed decisions on the best methods to adopt in their own circumstances. It begins by explaining the system in general terms and then describes various ways of applying it to the work of the office. Office policy makers are advised to read section 1: policy. In some circumstances it may not be necessary for them to read more than this. Those with a special responsibility for data co-ordination should read the whole manual, and all other users should begin by reading the section dealing with the application which is of particular relevance to them as shown on the list of contents on pages 5-6, and refer to other sections only where necessary.

Part II, on the other hand, provides a detailed 'off the peg' set of definitions and methods, as a drawing board aid for use by all offices who feel able to accept it as it stands. As far as possible, the definitions should be regarded as standard.

When further experience is available of applying the manual in varying ways to projects of different sizes and types, in a variety of contractual situations and with and without the use of computers, the advice and definitions given in this manual will be reconsidered and, where necessary, improved upon by RIBA Services Ltd. This manual should not be regarded as fixed for all time, nor should the system be rigidly or thoughtlessly applied. For example, suitable CI/sfB based methods of organising information on a large hospital project may be quite different in detail from those which it would be sensible to use for a small house. What suits one office may not suit another, and building and management techniques inevitably change as time goes by. Systems of data co-ordination must reflect these changes.

Experience in applying a system provides important pointers to its development, and RIBA Services will be glad to have users' comments on the manual.

*See bibliography, appendix D

Foreword by Sir Robert Matthew

It is appropriate that this manual, the first project which RIBA Services has completed, aims to assist practising architects and their professional colleagues to do, more effectively, the sort of work which occupies most of their time. All will agree with some of it; few will agree with all of it; but none should ignore the possibility it opens up of providing more effective project information.
I warmly commend it to the critical consideration of every architect.
Sir Robert H. Matthew,
Chairman, RIBA Services Ltd
August 1970

Authors' Foreword

Alan Ray-Jones BA arch (UCL), FRIBA, born in London in 1930, has worked in several architectural offices.
Served on RIBA Technical Committee in 1964; became head of RIBA Technical Section in 1965; appointed Technical Director of RIBA Services in 1969

Wilfred McCann BA BArch, aged 26, received BA in Architectural Studies (Newcastle University) in 1966, and BArch in 1970. Has 2½ years experience in architects' offices, and spent 2 years doing work on SfB for RIBA. Is now a member of staff with A. Rossi, Consett

It has only been possible to write this book because of the generous way in which quantity surveying and architects' offices (from the largest to the smallest), contractors and others, have pooled their experience and contributed to the development of CI/SfB.
We owe much to all those who have taken time and trouble to comment on the manuscript through several drafts, and particularly to W. R. V. Ward FRIBA as Chairman of the SfB working group of offices, and to individual members of offices represented on the group, particularly Wallace Cuthbertson FRICS, Stuart Hendy FRIBA, David Keate FRIBA, J. Powell FRICS, Malcolm Talbot ARICS and Roger Thorpe FRIBA, each of whom has given helpful and detailed comments on one or more sections of the final draft. We are also grateful to Jack Mills FLA for reading the drafts and advising on classification.
Part I sections 1, 2, 3, 4 and 6 are based entirely on present-day use of CI/SfB. Section 5 was almost entirely rewritten in the third (final) draft. It stems from present practice in specification arrangement in a number of offices, but so far as is known no office is using in their entirety the methods set out in the section.
Section 7 has been produced in conjunction with CBC LTD. Sections 8 to 13 are all introductory and experimental to a greater or lesser degree.
It will no doubt be thought by many, including some talented designers, that the subject of this book is entirely divorced from the real business of architecture, and even that it is an impediment to it. We emphatically disagree with this view and believe, on the contrary, that systematic methods of organising the information they receive and produce, help designers to produce better buildings. More often than not, the best architecture comes from the best organised offices.
But we also know that readers unfamiliar with the SfB 'language' will find parts of the manual indigestible, and even alarming, however sympathetic they may be to its aims. To such readers we can only say first, that the book will make more sense when they have learnt the language at least a little, and that it is not a difficult language; secondly, that they should go slowly and not at a gallop; and lastly, that they should not take too much on trust. If after reading the manual they can find other, simpler, and better ways of achieving the same aims, the manual will still have served its purpose.

Contents

Other applications of data co-ordination

PART 2

Part I Explanation

An explanation of CI/SfB based methods of data co-ordination and their application to project documents. Part I of the manual provides offices with a basis for making **informed decisions on the best methods to adopt in their own circumstances. Part II provides a detailed specimen set of methods and definitions.**

Introduction to data co-ordination and CI/SfB

Section 1: Policy

This section is concerned with non-technical aspects of data co-ordination

1.1 Why use data co-ordination?
1.2 Why use methods based on CI/SfB?
1.3 Introducing CI/SfB-based methods
1.4 Effect on the office

1.1 Why use data co-ordination?

Traditional Methods

When, in 1966, the Tavistock Institute of Human Relations published a digest of their earlier report to the Building Industry Communication Research Project, they entitled it 'Interdependence and uncertainty—a study of the building industry'. The reasons are not hard to find.

Over a period of many years the building process has become increasingly complex, and the standards of performance expected of the participants have risen constantly. In contrast, the pattern of communications within the industry has changed little since the introduction of the Standard Method of Measurement in 1922, and is based on an out-dated concept of building.

Evolution of the detailed design of a building remains dependent upon a lengthy process of question and answer at each stage, amethod ill-suited to the pace and complexity of modern building, and both private and public clients now

expect a prediction of final costs more accurate than intuitive methods will allow.

At the beginning of the process, client and architect usually communicate by means of sketch drawings, supplemented by approximate estimates based upon inadequate feedback of cost information from previous projects. Most of the decisions which will have a material effect on the ultimate cost will be made at this stage, although frequently neither client nor architect will be aware of their significance.

Equally serious is the lack of any disciplined method of ensuring that information collected from a variety of sources at briefing stage will find its way to the production information and thus be reflected in the completed building.

Later, the vital interaction between architect and consultants is frequently bedevilled by poor communications, with boundaries of responsibility ill-defined in consequence. In particular, time rarely allows the architect to provide the qs with complete and detailed information at taking-off stage, with the result that it is customary for the qs to contribute much of the specification, and in many cases a considerable proportion of the detailed design, both of which are properly the responsibility of the architect.

At no stage is there any agreed method of co-ordinating the output of the numerous organisations contributing to the production information.

In consequence the contractor's site agent, frequently a man with no formal training in management techniques, is obliged to put together sets of drawings from the architect, consultants and subcontractors (with no obvious relationship between them), and to co-ordinate them with an apparently unrelated specification/bill of quantities, itself in a form unsuitable for ordering materials or for control of site operations. While doing so, he is bombarded with revised and additional drawings, letters, instruction sheets, minutes of meetings and verbal instructions, without any clear indication of how to relate them to the tender documents. Quite apart from the lack of co-ordination between the sets of documents produced by the many participants, only the bill of quantities can be said to have a format which will help the contractor to find information without a lengthy search. The documents produced by the architect are usually particularly defective: there is no clear distinction between the functions of drawn and written information; the drawings themselves, usually regarded as the primary means of communication, are not organised to any particular pattern, and do not bear any relation to the sequence of operations on site. They are not even in a form which will suit the architect's convenience by allowing him to re-use information on future projects, thus saving time and offering an opportunity for the progressive improvement of details. Not surprisingly, contractor's costing systems stemming from this state of affairs are unreliable, resulting in defective feedback to the architect and qs, and thus to the next project. Errors and omissions abound, contractor's claims multiply, and architects' indemnity premiums rise constantly.

Systematic and unified methods

Left to itself, without attempt at improvement, the situation described above would continue to deteriorate, because the number of people and organisations contributing to project documents is steadily increasing as time goes by, because of the increasing complexity of the building process and the continuing pressure towards specialisation.

'*Fragmentation occurs when architect, structural engineer and qs are jointly involved in design . . .*'

A typical example of the fragmentation which results from this occurs when architect, structural engineer and qs are jointly involved in designing and specifying roof construction. Without some commonly accepted framework or guidance, each will have his own view of what constitutes the 'boundary' of the subject.

The word 'roof' will have a slightly different meaning to each of them (is the eaves part of the wall or part of the roof? Or is it a subject on its own account which must be dealt with separately?) and methods of presentation will vary. The architect may show roof details on the same drawing as the floor slab because there is sufficient space on the sheet; the engineer may disperse information on roof and other building parts over several sheets to get all sections on one sheet and all plans on another; the qs may present roofing as a work section in the bill of quantities, between asphalt work and carpentry, and may also include some relevant information in work sections for concrete or structural steelwork.

Inconsistency in *defining* subjects, and *arranging* them in relation to one another, inevitably makes it difficult to find information on them, and this is a root cause of poor communications in the building industry.

There is no doubt that this need for consistency in dividing information, especially if it is accompanied by the need to code it, will be irksome to some people—architects and other designers perhaps more than others. However, experience suggests that systematic methods, used intelligently, actually assist good designers to produce better design. They may even, in some respects, lead to greater freedom in the presentation of information.

Advantages and disadvantages Perhaps the best answer to the question 'why use a system?' is given by the list of claimed advantages for data co-ordination which are given below, taken from replies to questionnaires completed by offices using sfB-based methods.

In the opinion of these offices sfB-based data co-ordination:

● Provides a common 'language' for use between team members, reduces the risk of errors or misunderstandings

● Makes possible more effective co-ordination of effort, both within the office and between different offices

● Provides a design check list, helps ensure that no requirement is missed

● Makes it possible to compare past and present projects more accurately from viewpoints of performance and cost

● Assists programming, design, and document production

● Makes it possible to build up libraries of standard or 'type' details (drawings) and clauses (specifications), to help ensure that work is not duplicated and that experience—good or bad—is not lost or ignored

● Provides a search pattern, makes finding quicker

● Acts as an incentive to providing the contractor with comprehensive information (because gaps show up)

● Provides a ready-made index to project information

● Facilitates the use of computers and makes it possible, even without them, to sort information in different ways to meet different needs

● Permits complete cross referencing between all documents, making it less likely that information will be duplicated or varied without reason.

Many or all these advantages should apply equally to any system of data co-ordination and should lead to:

1 A reduced time for the design/build process and greater likelihood of completion within target time and cost

2 Better feedback of experience and tried details, resulting in more trouble-free construction and buildings and increased opportunity for the architect to concentrate on major aspects of design

3 More versatile documentation, giving the contractor a chance to organise his own precontract planning and contract administration more effectively.

These are considerable claims and it would be misleading to pretend that improvements can be gained without difficulty or effort on the part of offices introducing data co-ordination. The list of possible difficulties below, taken from the same inquiry, shows the other side of the coin—though it is fair to add that none of the offices concerned declared any intention of reverting to traditional methods; also that they had been working without benefit of any centrally produced manual or set of definitions. Some offices felt that:

● Revision of the system may necessitate modifications to drawings libraries, or even cause details to be redrawn

● The system may increase the number of drawings and thus lead to increased costs for prints and postage

● Use of copy negative techniques, which data co-ordination methods tend to encourage, increases the difficulty of making revisions

● If drawings suitable for re-use are to be produced, more time has to be taken initially over their preparation

● It is sometimes difficult to achieve collaboration from consultants, and difficulties are caused if team members are not willing to abide by the rules of the game

● New methods lead initially to extra work

● Good definitions are essential.

The primary users of project documentation are of course the contractor, his estimator, buyer, production manager and site staff. It is an important part of the job of any system sponsor to gather user reaction and meet user demands. The comment below is from a contractor receiving sfB-based documentation. It may not be typical, and any other properly designed system would probably have evoked a similar response.

'A system of this type, if adopted by all architects, qs and contractors, would lead to a saving in time and money, because it appears to help reduce the amount of preparation required after the contract has been let, when the contractor may already be on site. In particular it could lead to: quicker turnover of capital, reflected in lower prices; shorter site supervision period for the architect; fewer variation orders; more comprehensive proposals to the client; easier cross reference between drawings, specification and bill (thus helping site staff); more accurate and earlier material ordering, and reduction in the waste factor; fewer mistakes due to discrepancies between drawings; more accurate labour planning well in advance of progress on site.'

1.2 Why use methods based on CI/SfB?

The merits of CI/sfB which need to be considered when comparing it to other potential classification systems are:

First, it is very closely related to international sfB, a system which was originally developed by a group of people representing a wide range of building industry interests, for use as a means of arranging specifications rather than library information.

Second, it has the backing of the RIBA, both for office library (*general* information) and for *project* information use. This provides security against sudden changes or wholesale abandonment. It also provides centralised administration and development, and reduces the need for a lot of expensive development work within individual offices.

Third, it is already extensively used in building industry office libraries in this country, and the RIBA is providing publishers with a prepublication classification service to achieve maximum consistency in classification. Therefore it provides a potential link, particularly important to designers, between library information and project information.

Lastly, it has already been through many of the sorts of teething troubles that any system almost inevitably has to face.

It can be used with computers. It forms a compact language consisting of a limited number of codes and headings, and the main classes or groups of concepts are few enough in number to be readily memorised by those who use them at all often.

sfB, CBC and CI/sfB, all closely related systems having a great deal in common, have been thought useful by many people for a gradually extending range of purposes. The main reason for their popularity may be that they all consist basically of three 'tables' (lists of codes) which are of considerable relevance and importance to most members of the building team for a large part of their work.

The tables are: *elements* or building parts (eg 'walls'); *construction forms* (eg 'blocks'); and *materials* (eg 'clay').

1.3 Introducing CI/SfB based methods

CI/sfB may be brought to the attention of the office in the first place through the initiative and enthusiasm of only one or two people but it is essential that the office as a whole (including senior management) is satisfied that its use— even on a limited scale—is worthwhile. Use of CI/sfB may eventually affect almost every activity in the office and careful planning and staff education are necessary.

The following suggestions, made in the light of experience, show how it may be introduced one step at a time. It cannot be assumed, of course, that the particular sequence shown below will always be the best, and in most small and medium sized offices this recipe for step by step introduction may seem over elaborate and unnecessary.

1 Convert library to CI/sfB

Most published information is now classified by CI/sfB. If a self-service library is set up at an early stage using CI/sfB

'*Use of* CI/SfB *may eventually affect almost every activity in the office . . .*'

classification this will help staff to become familiar with codes and headings like those shown on the CI/SfB wall chart*, and this in turn will greatly ease the introduction of coding techniques. The work involved in setting up or changing over an office library to CI/SfB is not dealt with in this manual but advice and assistance is available from RIBA Services Ltd. It will become progressively easier and cheaper for offices to run CI/SfB arranged libraries as more trade and technical information is classified centrally for manufacturers and other publishers by RIBA Services SfB Agency Reference Service.†

2 Delegate a responsible member of staff

Ideally, one member of staff should be delegated to read available information*, on data co-ordination generally as well as on CI/SfB, and it may be helpful to go on suitable courses such as those arranged by the RIBA management advisory officer. During the early stages of introducing CI/SfB methods this person should remain responsible for implementation. It seems important that the job should be carried out by someone well respected and with sufficient authority, who is prepared to listen and learn as well as persuade.

3 Give staff lecture

It is important to keep the office as a whole properly informed of new developments. If work is delegated to one or two people everyone should know what these people are doing and any conclusions and proposals made by them should be discussed openly before being put into practice. An introductory lecture is one way of achieving this, although some of the claimed advantages of data co-ordination will have to be taken on trust at this stage.

4 Set up a pilot project on the organisation of drawings

It is essential to gain experience using the system on a pilot project before applying it throughout the office.

The following should be considered in selecting and setting up a suitable project:

● The project chosen should not be likely to raise any particularly difficult constructional or organisational problems. Ideally it should include an element of repetition

● A small or medium-sized project will provide quick feedback of the experience gained on it and allow some degree of experiment without the risk of a lot of abortive work

● The programme and allocation of time to be spent on the project should not be too tight, since those working on it will be learning how to apply CI/SfB methods in addition to running the job

● If CI/SfB is to be applied in the first place to production drawings and schedules at RIBA plan of work stage F‡, all or most design work should be completed before stage F begins. If design and production overlap badly, abortive work may result and this will discourage staff

● Confidence and experience in using CI/SfB methods should be established within the office before attempting to bring in outside consultants (structural, H&V, etc), unless they are already familiar with CI/SfB. It may be best to choose a project which requires a minimal contribution from consultants

● It is best not to be too ambitious. Coding of specification items on drawings and elsewhere, for example, should normally be tackled only after the arrangement and coding of drawings and schedules has become second nature§

● Whenever new persons or organisations outside the office are asked to examine the project documents, they can be sent a copy of an explanatory leaflet (like the 'Brief explanation of CI/SfB' in part II) and asked to comment

● The almost universal tendency, when first using CI/SfB and other similar systems, to produce many more drawings than usual should be strongly resisted. Use of CI/SfB does *not* necessitate production of very large numbers of drawings.

5 Assess the pilot project

Even if the pilot project has gone very well it is a good idea to look at the finished documents and try to draw comment from those in the office who have not been directly involved.

Criticisms must be answered and the approach modified, if necessary, to take account of them, although uninformed comment from people without practical experience should not be allowed to carry too much weight. The documents produced will establish guidelines for those using the system on future projects and help to make the next stage of implementation as smooth as possible.

* See bibliography, appendix D
† Further information and copies of leaflets describing the service are available free, from RIBA SfB Agency Reference Service, c/o RIBA Services Ltd.

‡ See para 3.5 'Plan of Work'
§ See para 4.2 'Sheet structuring and coding' and para 4.3 'Item-type coding'

'The project chosen should not be likely to raise any particularly difficult constructional or organisational problems . . .'

6 Use on all jobs

Full advantage will not be gained from the application of CI/SfB methods to drawings until they are used on most or all projects in the office. Use of the system should however not be extended until contractor's site staff have had a few weeks to assimilate and comment on the pilot project drawings.

More extensive use can clearly be assisted by dividing members of the pilot project team among other groups. Regular meetings and discussions during the early stages will be needed if all work is to be co-ordinated, and an office manual may be needed at this stage unless part II of this manual is used as it stands.

7 Other applications

As soon as the office has gained confidence in using the system for drawings production, other applications can be introduced, adopting the same approach as that used for drawings: test first on one relatively simple project; draw comments from staff; apply the conclusions on other projects. It is difficult to suggest a sequence of applications because the most convenient order will be determined by many factors such as availability of projects, availability of staff, attitude of consultants, etc. A possible sequence is shown below:

1 Library
2 Sheet structuring of production drawings and schedules, *architect only* (plan of work stage F)
3 Sheet structuring of production drawings and schedules, *with consultants* (plan of work stage F)
4 Brief collection (plan of work stages B, C)
5 Cost planning (plan of work stages B to E)
6 Coded specification and item type coding on drawings (plan of work stage F)
7 Bills of quantities including quantities on drawings (plan of work stages F, G)
8 Feedback reports from previous projects (plan of work stage M)

9 Correspondence filing, quotations etc (plan of work stage A onwards)
10 Job product filing (plan of work stage E)
11 Drawings programming (plan of work stages E to F)
12 Design details (plan of work stage E)

1.4 Effect on the office

Finance and quality of service

The experience of a wide range of sizes and types of multi-disciplinary and architects' offices, public and private, indicates that data co-ordination methods on the lines suggested in this manual are not—as many offices fear they may be—a means of spending a lot of money over many years on development work which shows no real benefit.

Some offices have claimed a cost saving of anything up to 10 per cent or even 15 per cent, but most are unwilling to give a figure, because they say much of the hypothetical cost benefit is used to provide a higher standard of service to clients and, through better documentation, to contractors. If CI/SfB methods are introduced in the first place on a broad front, or for some of the most complex applications, they will almost certainly lead to increased costs over one or more projects.

All kinds of organisational patterns are to be found in operation in offices using CI/SfB methods. Some, for example, have job architects who are responsible for projects at all stages and others have separate divisions for design, design production and supervision. However, it is not the purpose of this manual to discuss advantages and disadvantages of different types of organisation except to record that success or relative lack of success in using CI/SfB seems to depend more on personalities and on individual enthusiasm and accomplishments than on the organisational structure of the office.

Small offices, particularly if they are multi-disciplinary, can often move very much faster than big ones. A two-man office which habitually prepares its own quantities from its own drawings was using CI/SfB for all production drawings, schedules, specifications and bills of quantities within three months of first hearing about the system, and reported both cost benefit and improved documentation.

Quantity surveyors

Some quantity surveyors are among the most enthusiastic advocates for CI/SfB based methods. But others are inclined to be wary of new forms of documentation, and architects need to remember that to qss, who receive information from many architects in many forms, CI/SfB arranged documents are at present just one more variety to be tolerated.

Experience shows that few qss are critical for long; they usually appreciate the fact that use of the system by architects seems invariably to lead to more complete documentation being provided at an earlier stage. Many qss take off by 'elements' in any case, and find that receipt of drawings already arranged this way (by CI/SfB Table 1) enables them to rationalise and speed up their procedure for bill production. Bills of quantities arranged by Table 1 can be produced at more or less normal costs. If a qs is asked to take-off so that the information can be used to produce various different arrangements of the bills to suit the contractor at different stages of the job, he will almost certainly be committed to increased production costs: initially this will be due in part to lack of familiarity with the system but even when this stage has passed the production of several arrangements will inevitably involve more effort than the production of a single arrangement. However, against this must be set the advantage to the contractor of having available the bill arranged in ways which can save him considerable time and effort in the ordering of materials, site programming and costing. This suggests that a contractor who is organised to take advantage of the increased accuracy and flexibility of the information provided should be prepared to pay for any additional cost of taking-off and billing. He would thereby be saved the remeasurement and reclassification of project information which he more often than not has to do at present simply to rearrange it in a form which he can use.

Consultants

It is impossible to generalise about the reactions of consultants, which vary widely according to the discipline (services consultants may react differently from structural engineers), the particular firm concerned, and its working relationship with architects. However, many consultants have shown a remarkable willingness to collaborate in the production of integrated documentation on all matters from the use of common paper sizes and copy negatives to the acceptance of common classification systems. Many have been impatient for the architectural profession to adopt consistent methods so that they do not have to vary their methods unnecessarily to meet the needs of different firms of architects.

Contractors

Architects often underestimate the ability of those who use their drawings and specifications to assimilate new methods; if it is remembered that traditional documentation has no formal structure (except that information is grouped roughly by scale of drawing), and that practice differs from one architect's office to another, it will more readily be appreciated that even a first unsophisticated attempt at structured information, based on a consideration of site requirements, is likely to represent a substantial improvement from the contractor's point of view. In practice, most contractors find that the ease with which they can find information is ample compensation for becoming familiar with the codes and their associated headings. It is important to give contractors an early opportunity to ask questions about the arrangement of the documentation.

Computers

Information on the availability of computer programs can be obtained from RIBA Services. Computer processing is likely to be economic in the immediate future only on fairly large projects, whereas experience can be gained with use of manual data co-ordination methods on projects of any size including very small ones.

An important point to note about computer operation is the need for strict discipline, accuracy and checking techniques which may come fairly readily if the office is already well acquainted with the information system, but may be difficult to achieve if the whole thing is new. However, some offices have dived in at the deep end and have used computers straight away on large projects with fully coded schedules or bills of quantities.

Section 2 Basic Principles

This section describes the requirements for an information system for the construction industry, and the way these may be met. It inevitably introduces a number of new terms and these are marked with an asterisk and explained in the glossary (appendix C). Users should not feel, however, that it is necessary to absorb the section in detail at first reading

---

2.1 Requirements for an information system
2.2 Classification and coding
2.3 Identification and coding

2.1 Requirements for an information system

BRS *study*

The Building Research Station *Study of coding and data co-ordination for the construction industry*† states (chapter 7) that an information system and its associated code must:

1 *Classify information* in sufficient categories for users' needs and . . . allow data to be retrieved . . .

2 *Identify* and describe resources* (identify uniquely commodities, equipment, etc)

3 *Describe projects* (eg describe their form by co-ordinates or other methods)

4 *Foster the development of procedures* (eg flow charts, sequences of operations, preferred vocabularies)

5 *Support information flow* (eg identify for various users the way they should 'structure' the information they put out; provide cross referencing between documents)

These criteria may be summarised in three basic requirements. A system must:

1 Give quick, easy access to information (by a *search pattern**)

2 Relate (*cross reference**) the individual contributions of those providing information

3 Divide information in a way which meets the needs of individual users (*by sortation**)

In addition it must be acceptable to architects and other producers of information and be usable with computers.

Taking the three basic requirements one by one.

Search pattern

The general arrangement of a document or set of documents (eg chapters in a book, or drawings in a set of drawings) should positively help the reader to decide where to look for the information he wants.

There are two ways in which documents may be used: they may be read from start to finish (so that nothing is missed),

* See glossary, appendix C
† See bibliography, appendix D

or they may be used like a dictionary (by a user who wants to look up a quick answer to a particular question). In either case, the user will be helped considerably by a simple, readily understood and remembered arrangement or 'search pattern' which will put first (ie at the top of the pile, or at the left-hand end of the shelf, or on the first page), the subjects which he expects to find first, and then lead him on naturally to more and more detailed information.

For example, the contractor having his first sight of drawings for a new project is helped if he finds first a drawing showing the layout of the whole project, followed by drawings showing subsections of the project in an increasing degree of detail. For example:

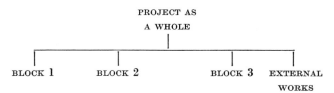

Most 'traditional' documentation is in fact arranged this way. A new user would not be much helped by finding first (say) a drawing showing a staircase or a concrete slab.

One possible form of assistance for a user searching for information is an alphabetical index, which should ideally take him straight to the right place. In some circumstances this may do away with the need for a search pattern. Unfortunately, however, the cost of preparing a comprehensive alphabetical index for each individual building project would be quite prohibitive. A standard (preprinted) index may be some help but will usually not include the one item which the user wants to find. (A standard index, which may be bound in with project documents, is included in part II.) The difficulty is that an alphabetical index is (or should be) a list of 'known subjects' in a known order. There is no difficulty about the order, which is simply A-Z, but there is no agreement at all on which words to use for subjects. For example, someone searching for information on fixing two pieces of wood might look under *wood*, *softwood*, *hardwood*, *timber*, *nail*, *wire*, *planks*, *sections*, *boarding*, *adhesives*, or *jointing methods*.

Another form of assistance which is much easier to produce and should always be provided, is a list of contents such as a list of drawings or specification sections. A list of contents shows the whole search pattern in a compact way.

Cross reference

A further, valuable form of assistance to searching for information is a proper scheme of cross referencing from each item of information to closely related items, as shown in **1**. This may be done using codes, or words, or both together.

1 *Cross referencing from general technical information to project information, and between different types of project documents*
2 *Same set of books sorted in three different ways; by series, by author and by subject. French books have been shaded, to show the effect of alternative sortations*

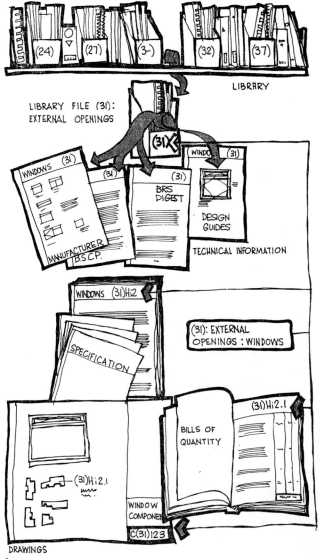

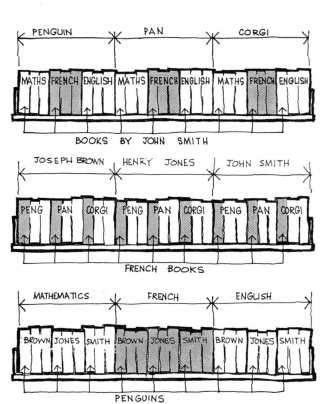

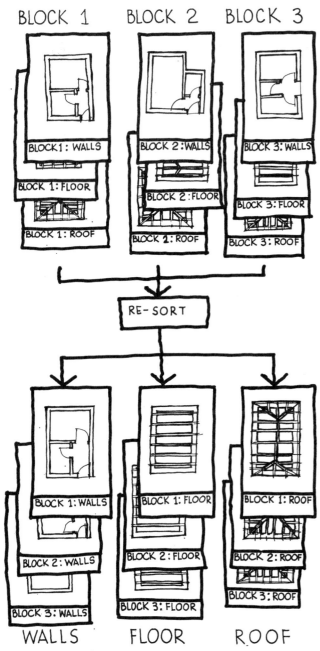

3 *Drawings showing building elements for different blocks of a project sorted by block and by building elements*

Sortation

No search pattern, however good, is likely to seem perfectly natural, logical and effective to all users for all purposes. Three possible sortations of the same set of books are shown in **2**, and it is easy to imagine circumstances in which users would prefer the third sortation by subject to the sortation by author, or vice versa.

Similarly, the contractor may want an arrangement of drawings or pages (eg in bills of quantities) that bring together in one 'set' information on all the elements or parts (eg external walls, roofs, etc) that make up *block 1*. On the other hand, he may want brought together, as one set, all information on *roofs* (and on no other parts), for all blocks including block 1. He will only be able to achieve both arrangements if the architect has drawn the roof for each

block on a separate sheet of paper, so that the sheets can be shuffled or sorted like playing cards **3**.

But he cannot expect to sort *drawn* information in too many different ways, for this would involve having a very small amount of information on each drawing, and would defeat the purpose of the drawings, which is to give a general picture of the project and the parts of which it is to be formed.

Fortunately, it is possible to provide more than one arrangement of *written* information (in the form of schedules or bills of quantities) particularly where computers are used. The use of classification systems such as CI/sfB facilitates sortation.

2.2 Classification and coding

Classification

Classification provides a search pattern by relating similar items of information and separating those which are different. The enquirer is helped to the extent that examination of the structure of the classification will establish where a given item is likely to be found.

Many classification systems are organised primarily by facets*. A facet is an identifiable concept that groups together items of information which are alike and separate from other groups. A faceted structure provides flexibility in manipulating information into different forms. In the example below the random list of terms on the left has been rearranged on the right into three groups of similar terms which have been given titles as independent facets.

	building types
secondary schools	secondary schools
windows	offices
offices	primary schools
steel	universities
roofs	hospitals
primary schools	*elements or parts*
universities	windows
copper	roofs
wood	*materials*
hospitals	steel
	copper
	wood

If further subdivision within a facet is required a hierarchy of terms may be developed according to a series of characteristics such as 'primary function' in the example below:

building types (divided by primary function, eg administration)

    administrative
      offices
    health and welfare
      hospitals
    educational (divided by stage of education)
      schools
        primary
        secondary
      universities

In diagrammatic form, the hierarchy would look like this:

* See glossary, appendix C

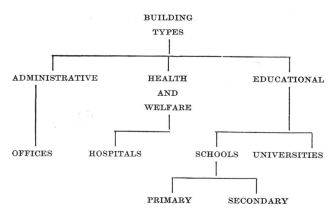

Each concept* in the hierarchy above forms a class* of the classification. It is important that the concepts at each level in a hierarchy should mutually exclude one another, and that concepts should be entirely divided by one characteristic before being divided by another.

It is important that the classification system be related closely to the use which will be made of it. There is no point in classification for its own sake and it is altogether irrelevant if all that is needed is a method of identifying and labelling individual items, eg the serial number of a £1 note. However, classification is essential if relationships between items are to be shown. For these reasons most classification systems represent a compromise between detail for the advantage of specialists, and simplicity for the advantage of the general user.

The way in which a classification scheme assists sortation and provides various search patterns is apparent from the example shown in **3** in which the facets used are Project division (eg *Block 1*) and Building element or part (eg *Roof*). The facets relating to the CI/SfB methods described in this manual are as shown in the table below.

Coding

No mention has been made so far of codes and coding. The use of codes as 'labels' for concepts is not an essential feature of a classification scheme, and codes should never be used unless they are useful. They are often used in conjunction with headings in classification schemes, for practical reasons:

1 It is difficult to be consistent in the use of words and too easy to write 'wall' where 'external wall' is meant. Where class definitions are important (see above) the use of codes in addition to headings, eg: '(21) External wall', provides a valuable precaution against error. It works the other way too, of course: codes should not normally be used without words. Codes usually stand for carefully defined

* See glossary, appendix C

concepts, and most users appreciate the need to adhere to the definitions implied by them. But terms such as 'External wall' used without an accompanying code appear self-explanatory and users are apt to put their own interpretations on them.

2 Codes provide a shorthand symbol which assists the economical storing, transmission or manipulation of information.

3 The use of codes facilitates grouping in accordance with principles of classification and makes it possible, for example, to keep together terms such as tin, copper, lead, etc, which are related to each other yet have different initial letters. They would be scattered if arranged in alphabetical order.

4 If codes are alphabetic (A . . . z) or numeric (1 . . . 9) they place the concept in a particular position amongst other concepts, to provide a consistent and memorable sequence of terms:
e Stone
f Concrete (formed)
g Clay
h Metals
i Wood

The commonest reason for a long code is the amount of detail it represents; the more precisely the information is described, the longer the code will be; eg

Roof—Timber = (27)i
    (27)   i
Roof—Truss—Timber—Softwood = (27)Gi2
    (27)   G   i   2
or
Block 1—External wall—bricks—clay—heavyburnt
    1   (21)   F   g   2
                    = 1(21)Fg2
Block 1—External wall—bricks—clay—heavyburnt
    1   (21)   F   g   2
—brickfacework   = 1(21)Fg2G14
    G14

How far coding is taken depends on the circumstances. But two points perhaps need to be stressed:

First, the general rule may be to keep codes as short as possible; but the result of doing this may be a slight lengthening of the time needed to find an item—and when this is multiplied by the number of searches made it could eventually outweigh the initial inconvenience of using a longer code.

Second, looking forward to mechanized sorting, machines are far less worried by long codes than humans. The more precisely an item is described the more easily it can be

Table—Bold headings give classification facets relating to CI/SfB methods; these are further explained in section 3 of part I of this manual

Process	**Project division**	**Element or part**	**Construction form/material**	**Project type**	**Work stage**	**Work section**	**Operations**
		(CI/SfB Table 1)	(CI/SfB Table 2/3)	(CI/SfB Table 0)	(RIBA plan of work)	(SMM)	(CI/SfB Table 4)
eg: Building work Manufacturing work	eg: Building works External works Block Level Zone	eg: Substructure Superstructure Services Fittings	eg: Brick or brickwork Clay	eg: Hospitals	eg: Stage F	eg: Concrete work	eg: Placing

separated from the rest when required. Against this must be balanced the likelihood that the number of human errors in coding (because of incorrect typing, etc) increases in proportion as the length of codes increases.

If facets are used to identify items to enable them to be sorted, either by means of the computer, or manually as bits of paper, it is more than likely that codes of some kind will have to be used. But if facets are used in a static way to subdivide a large volume of material, as with chapters and paragraphs in a book, it may be sufficient to use words alone.

Concept analysis

It has so far been assumed that what is to be classified and coded is quite clear, and that all that needs to be done is to allocate the appropriate code and word to it. But this may not necessarily be so, for two reasons:

In the first case it may not always be clear whether a particular thing falls within one class or another. For example, large tiles (coded s) may be very similar to sheets (coded R). When in doubt, there are a number of guide lines which can be applied in making decisions as to how to code in such cases.

For example, the item can be classified according to whatever may be regarded as 'dominant' about it. Natural language description will be a good guide. A window with an aluminium frame will of course include glass at some stage, but if it is given a single material code to distinguish it from a timber framed window it might usefully be coded as aluminium, to match the natural language description of it as an 'aluminium window'.

Also, the point of view of the user should be considered. Under what subject would he *expect* to find the item?

The other possible cause of difficulty is that a document such as a drawing may include two concepts from the same facet, such as:

SPACE HEATING SYSTEMS *in* FLOOR BEDS
(56)   (13)
(both codes from Table 1 of CI/sfB)

If both concepts *have* to be shown on one drawing (and one should always ask: do they?) and if only one code is to be used to code it, which should be suppressed? Or if both codes were to be used (dual coding is *not* recommended for most applications in this manual)—which code should come first? Users of Part II will find they are given a lot of help, and again there are in any case guidelines that can be followed. For example:

Ends should be cited* (and thus coded) before means, the whole before its parts. In the case above the space heating system almost certainly becomes part of the floor, not vice versa, and drawings showing both should therefore be given the code for the floor bed rather than the code for the heating system **4.**

Operationally, the space heating system probably cannot be installed before some part of the floor is there to receive it. Again, the drawing should be given the code for floor beds rather than the code for heating systems.

* See glossary, appendix C

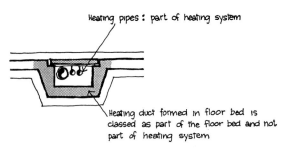

4 *Heating pipes (56) in floor bed (13) raises question of how drawing is to be coded*

Because of the way that Table 1 of CI/sfB is constructed this means that—where in doubt—the *lowest* of the two codes should be generally used rather than the other one.

Natural language is a guide. The use of the preposition *in*, in the example above, indicates subordination of one concept to another.

Again, the point of view of the user should be considered. But far more important than getting the code 'right' is the need for consistency throughout the project documents. In the last event, it is better to be consistently wrong than to be inconsistent!

2.3 Identification and coding

Whereas classification codes tell one in which *class* an item belongs, identification codes merely *identify* particular items, without necessarily classifying them at all, eg:

1 = PROJECT NO 1

But identification codes frequently do include symbols used for classification purposes. For example:

41.1 = HOSPITAL PROJECT NO 1

In this case the whole code 41.1 uniquely identifies a particular project, but the code 41 (from CI/sfB Table 0) classifies it as a hospital.

A more general example, which might clarify the distinction, is the motorway code M6. The M is a classifier, telling one what *kind* of road it is; the 6 identifies the road within this class.

Identification codes may be used to identify things as various as complete projects, door openings, components, details, specification clauses, drawings, items on drawings or in bills of quantities.

Section 3: Facets in use

The last section outlined the requirements for an information system and described the purpose of classification and identification. This section briefly describes the main classification facets and gives prominence to the four which are used most extensively. The full code structure for CI/SfB Tables 1, 2 and 3 is given later, in Part II. Later sections in Part I show how they may be used in conjunction with one another for various purposes

---

3.1 Process facet
3.2 Project division facet
3.3 CI/SfB Table 1 facet
3.4 CI/SfB Table 2/3 facet
3.5 Other facets
3.6 Conclusions

3.1 Process facet

Scope

The RIBA *Handbook of architectural practice and management** refers to three types of basic information which need to be given to the contractor. These are:

(*a*) information on COMPONENTS and COMMODITIES of all kinds (eg bricks, windows, etc), *whether made on or off site;*
(*b*) information on ASSEMBLIES of these components and commodities (eg brickwork or windows in position) built *on site;*
(*c*) information on the LOCATION of these assemblies as part of the finished building. The three types are shown diagrammatically in **5**.

* See bibliography, appendix D

5 *Need to arrange information by 'process' has been recognised for some time. A clear distinction can be made between 3 categories: 'location' information, which shows where work is to be located without necessarily showing how it is to be carried out; and the two basic types of work information—on-site building ('assembly') work and on or off-site manufacturing ('component') work*

Definitions

Location information Location information is directed particularly at the people responsible for the overall co-ordination of work on site. For example it may be necessary to indicate the precise geographical location on the project of a particular wall opening and its relationship to neighbouring parts of the building. Locational information is inevitably tied to a particular project, and there seems to be little doubt that drawings are at present usually the best medium for showing such information. Drawings can show complex relationships between parts of the building which are difficult or impossible to convey using words alone. In present drawing practice much location information is shown with detailed assembly information.

Assembly information* On-site assembly information is often muddled up in present practice with detailed information about individual components, products and materials which make up the assembly, and which may or may not be made on site. Assembly information is potentially re-usable from project to project, although assemblies are normally less likely to be repeated without alteration than are components.

Commodity (component) information* Manufacturers, including contractors' workshops, do not normally need information on where a component is to be located in a building (except for the purpose of delivering it), or even necessarily on how it is to be assembled in relation to other components. But they do need full information on the component itself, including information on the assembly of the materials and products of which it is made. Component information is often re-usable.

Applications

In the case of *drawn* information these three categories may be best kept on separate sheets, since they are used, on the whole, by different people. In the case of *specification* and *measured* information, items describing commodities can be separated from items dealing with assemblies (building workpieces or constructions). Traditional *bills of quantities* may, for example, have a schedule of commodities at the end for ordering purposes. Operational bills include separate pages for 'production work', meaning commodities and other resources which are bought in by the contractor, as distinct from those which he creates on site as an integral part of the building assembly process.

This distinction between Process types is important for the organisation of project information. Some offices recognise more than three basic categories, for example:

* See glossary, appendix C

COMPONENT   LOCATION   ASSEMBLY

LOCATIONS, divided into blocks etc

ASSEMBLIES

COMMODITIES, divided into components; sub-components; accessories; products; materials

However many categories are to be recognised, a firm decision will need to be made by each office using CI/SfB based methods on the place of Process type in the search pattern. For various reasons which will be discussed in later sections, it is assumed throughout the manual that the location drawings and schedules will act as the 'way in' (at least for new users) to much of the information provided to the contractor:

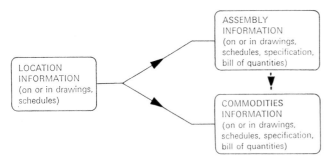

Coding

The coding methods adopted for coding Process type on documents will depend to some extent on the number of categories recognised. There are several possibilities, for example:

1 It may be sufficient in some applications to use *words* eg:
LOCATION, as eg: EXTERNAL AND INTERNAL OPENINGS:
  LOCATION
ASSEMBLY, as eg: ROOF: ASSEMBLY
COMPONENT, as eg: DOOR: COMPONENT

2 Each category may be given a simple *code*. Possible codes are:
L LOCATION
A ASSEMBLY
C COMMODITY (or COMPONENT)

3 The first digit of the identification code (the *drawing number*) for each drawing or schedule may be used to indicate whether the sheet is showing location, assembly or commodity information, so that, for example:
Sheets no 001 to 199 could show location information
Sheets no 200 to 399 could show assembly information
Sheets no 400 to 599 could show component information

4 Assembly and commodity information can be coded A or C as appropriate, but location information need not be given a process code at all. It can be given the appropriate physical division (location) code as described below.
The specimen documents in Part II use methods 1, 3 and 4.

3.2 Project division facet*

Scope

All projects need to distinguish for some purposes between different *physical* divisions—such as particular blocks, floor levels, zones, rooms, etc; and between different *functional*

* This term is also used in the *Building Industry Code*

spaces and divisions and groups of these—such as department types (eg 'Outpatients'), house types, room types, etc.

Physical divisions A classification of physical divisions is shown below:

PROJECT

  BLOCKS, eg:
    Block 1 (building works 1)
    Block 2 (building works 2)
    Block 9 (external works)

  LEVELS, eg:
    Level 1
    Level 2

  ZONES, eg:
    Zone 1
    Zone 2

  ROOMS, eg:
    Room 1
    Room 2

Functional divisions Many classifications of functional spaces exist for particular building types, and the division of information according to the way space is used is needed particularly at *briefing* stages, so that data on user requirements for spaces such as kitchens and bathrooms can be brought together.

Definitions (physical divisions only)

Project The entire project, comprising building works and external works up to and including the site boundary **6**.

Blocks Any section of the works which needs to be separately identified, either because it differs from other sections in physical shape or constructional character, or because it will be constructed at different times and will therefore be referred to separately in project documents, can be given a unique block number; **7** shows five blocks.

Blocks may be of any size (the tank room is given a block number in the diagram), and need not be physically separate from other blocks. Where blocks are joined together the decision on what should be allocated to one block and what should be allocated to the other can be made on building operational grounds **8**.

The dividing line between building works and external works (which are often treated as a separate 'block' or 'blocks') is usually the external face of the external wall, so that the work in the ground below the building is included with building works **9**. This definition is used by the Building Cost Information Service* of the Royal Institution of Chartered Surveyors for cost analysis purposes.

Fixtures such as canopies attached to the buildings are regarded as part of the building. Patios are normally regarded as external works.

Levels The project can be divided in levels, ie *horizontal* divisions **10**. Usually it is convenient to number levels within blocks, and block 3 level 2 may therefore differ from block 4 level 2. The distance between levels is not necessarily

* See section 8: Cost planning, later in this manual

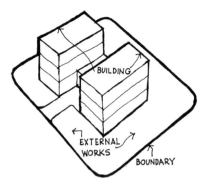

6 *Project (building works and external works)*

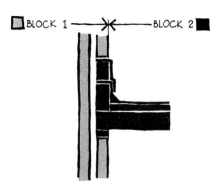

8 *Boundary between blocks (Section)*

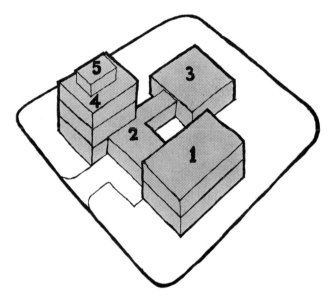

7 *Example of a project divided into five blocks*

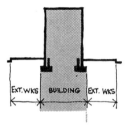

9 *Boundary between building works and external works (Section)*

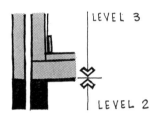

10 *Boundary between levels (Section)*

storey height. The ground below the lowest floor slab will need to be coded as a 'level' if all work is to be given a project division code.

Zones The project can be divided into zones, ie *vertical* divisions. Zones are usually numbered within levels and may consist of groups of rooms with some common characteristic. The location of services can be indicated approximately by zone coding as an aid to finding information on them. See **11** to **13**.

Rooms Zones can be divided into rooms or, if zones are not given, levels can be divided into rooms.

Applications

Physical divisions Codes or words for the different physical divisions of projects are already used throughout project documents, though the only division recognised, in the simplest case, is the one between *building works* ('the building') and *external works*.

Drawings, cost analyses, and bills of quantities will usually need to keep within the boundaries implied by the definitions given above, particularly when copy negatives are being used. For example, a drawing showing building works should not show part of external works too unless there is a good reason for doing so. Consistency in this respect will simplify checking and co-ordination of information. Codes for physical divisions will be put on all location drawings and schedules but should not be used on assembly commodity drawings and schedules, unless this can be done temporarily, in the cases in which it would be useful, by using stickers or copy negative techniques. If stickers are used, they should be removed at the end of the project so that the drawing is re-usable for future projects.

Functional divisions Housing projects, involving the repetition of many units of accommodation of a limited number of types, will make considerable use of codes for house types, as groupings by function. These are quite distinct from the physical division codes which indicate particular houses or groups of houses irrespective of type.

Coding

Physical divisions It is not possible to recommend a single form of coding suitable for all projects. The example below uses one digit for projects with only a few divisions and two digits for those with more. The codes marked with asterisks will not be much used in practice:

For projects with few divisions	For projects with more divisions	
_*	__*	Project (two or more blocks)
0*	00*	Building works blocks
1	01	Block 1
to	to	to
8	89	Block 8 or 89
9	90	External works blocks
	91	Block 9 or
	to	Blocks 91
	99	to 99
_*	__*	Project (two or more levels)
0*	00*	Level 0 (below lowest floor level)
1	01	Level 1 (lowest floor level)
to	to	to
9	99	Level 9 or 99
_*	__*	Project (two or more zones)
1	01	Zone 1
to	to	to
9	99	Zone 9 or 99
__*	___*	Project (two or more rooms)
01	001	Room 1
to	to	to
99	999	Room 99 or 999

Application of Coding: A simple way to show physical divisions on location drawings and schedules or against items in briefing information or elsewhere is to use an oblique stroke to separate each code from the next:

    1   Block 1
    1/1   Block 1, level 1
    1/2   Block 1, level 2
    1/1/1   Block 1, level 1, zone 1
    1/1/2   Block 1, level 1, zone 2

This is the method used on the specimen documents in Part II and it is shown diagrammatically in **11**.

Unless it is considered important for the second digit in the example above to be used for LEVEL on all projects throughout the office, it may be preferable to use it to indicate ZONE instead on projects such as lock up shops, where the building type and the method of construction (eg cross wall construction) create vertical divisions which run through all levels **12**. In such a case the *third* digit would indicate LEVEL.

Search pattern: To retrieve all information on a particular location it is only necessary to find its code and from it, automatically, the codes of all larger spaces which may also contain information on it. For example, the only sheets, items, etc which could possibly include information on:

Block 1, level 1, zone 2, = code 1/1/2

apart from any sheet or item with that code, would be sheets or items coded:

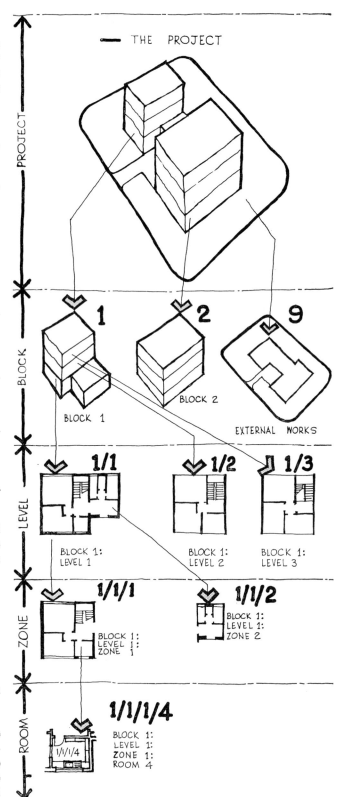

11 *Project division coding using first digit to indicate block, second digit to indicate level, third digit to indicate zone, and fourth digit to indicate room. See also* **12, 13**

Block 1, level 1, = code 1/1
or
Block 1, = code 1

These codes can be used on a small key plan or axonometric to go on all location plans to show how one part of the project relates to another **14**.

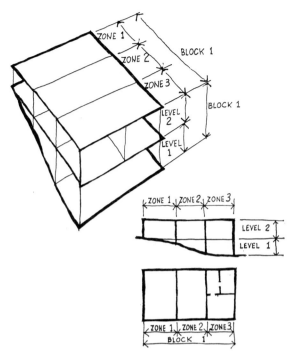

12 *For some cellular building types such as houses and lock-up shops it may be better to use second digit of project division code to indicate zone, rather than level*

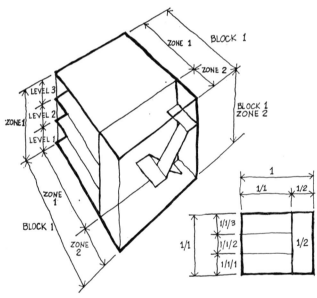

13 *Example of block divided first by zone, second by level. In this case the stairway is treated as a zone*

Physical division codes showing location may also be given in title boxes on drawings, schedules, etc if required:

BLOCK	LEVEL ZONE	ROOM
2	**4/2**	**19**

Functional division These codes may also be given in title boxes on drawings, schedules, etc if required.

The use of these codes in conjunction with other facets is discussed in later sections

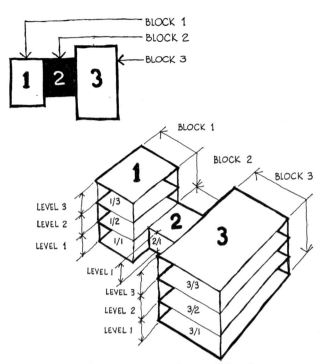

14 *Use of key plans or axonometrics on all location drawings for large projects helps users to find the drawings they want quickly*

3.3 CI/SfB Table 1 facet: Elements*

Scope

This is in some ways the most important facet for many purposes since it provides a spine code which runs through most applications of CI/SfB. All projects need to distinguish between major parts of building and site such as substructure and superstructure; between walls, floors, roofs, etc; or between many smaller parts, for a wide variety of purposes. The classification of parts provided by the CI/SfB is as follows:

PROJECT

SUBSTRUCTURE

SUPERSTRUCTURE
 Primary elements (walls, floors, etc)
 Secondary elements (door openings and doors, window openings and windows, etc)
 Finishes (wall finishes, floor finishes, etc)

SERVICES
 Mainly piped (heating, hot water, etc)
 Mainly wired electrical (power, lighting, etc)

FITTINGS
 Fixtures (fixed benches, etc)
 Loose equipment (tables, chairs, etc)

The full classification is given in Part II.

Definitions

These will be given in Part II. The illustration **15** shows the distinction which is made in Table 1 between site and building as compared with that in **9**.

---

* Elements are parts of a building or site, as defined in Table I of the CI/SfB *Construction indexing manual*. See bibliography, appendix D

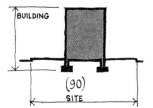 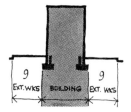

15 *Building, external works and site*

Applications

Guidance on the use of Table 1 for particular purposes is given in later Sections.

It is recommended that Table 1 should be used for the classification of Elements (ie parts of building or site) on most or all project documents. The table is used at present in rather different ways by different offices to meet their own needs. For this reason, the particular methods set out in Part I of this manual are intended only to illustrate points which need to be considered, not to lay down hard and fast rules. The specimen documents in Part II show typical applications of Table 1.

Coding

The code consists of two digits which are enclosed in brackets to distinguish them from other numeric codes which may be used—eg project division and other facets.

Examples of two-digit codes from Table 1 are:

(– –) PROJECT IN GENERAL (two or more main group parts)
(2–) MAIN GROUP PART (eg primary elements of superstructure)
(21) EXTERNAL WALLS

If, in other words, one wishes to assign a code from CI/SfB Table 1 to a drawing containing information exclusively on external walls, the appropriate code would be (21). If the drawing describes both external walls (21) and stairs (24), it would have to be coded (2–), which includes within itself the whole group of codes (20) to (28).

In addition, one or two very large organisations may use the letters A to Z (not part of the CI/SfB system) to provide a very detailed division of types of parts; for example:

(21A) EXTERNAL WALL PART A (which could be a wall tie, a prefabricated wall unit, or any other part of an external wall).

It is likely that this most detailed level of coding will, however, only be thought necessary by industrialised building systems or client organisations using computers to control very large building programmes. It is strongly recommended that this sort of development work should *not* be undertaken by offices until they are thoroughly familiar with the use of Table 1, as it stands, for project information. All the codes at present in general use are shown in the matrix in Part II.

Search pattern

To retrieve all information on a particular element or part (eg external walls) find its code, by reference to Table 1, in Part II of this manual.

Then (See **16** below):

1 Search first for any drawings, schedules, specification or measured items with that specific code, eg:
(21) EXTERNAL WALLS

2 Then, if the required information has not been found, search sheets or items having a main group code with the same initial digit, ie:
(2–) PRIMARY ELEMENTS

3 Lastly, if necessary, search sheets having the code for parts in general, ie:
(– –) PROJECT IN GENERAL

If the information required has not been found by this point it is not in the document(s) at all.

The use of Table 1 codes in conjunction with other facets and its use for finding information is further discussed in later Sections of this manual.

Table 1 codes should be given in title boxes on drawings, schedules, etc. The example in the box below is the code for External Wall. The plain language counterpart of the code (ie external walls) should normally be included elsewhere in the title box.

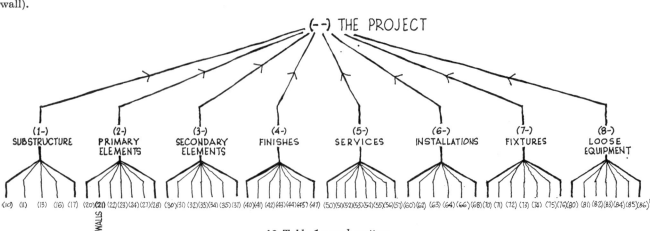

16 *Table 1 search pattern*

3.4 CI/SfB table 2/3 facet: construction form/material

Scope

This table consists of two major facets, each of which may be used separately:

Construction form is used to classify products according to their physical form at the point of application, a characteristic which affects method of handling and skills required on site, etc.

Material or 'substance' is used to classify products according to the material of which they are made, another characteristic which affects methods of handling and skills required on site.

The combined Table 2/3 provides a useful classification of general building products. The full classification is given later in this manual in Part II.

Definitions:

Table 2 Construction form classifies products by their form either individually or as the 'dominant' products in building assembly work (eg in the sense that brick is dominant in brickwork).

Table 3 Material Products are normally classified, where only one material code can be given to them, by the dominant material of which they are made. This is not necessarily the principal material in terms of quantity but is the one most likely to be referred to in natural language. For example, an 'aluminium' window may eventually include more glass than aluminium but since all or most windows include glass it is natural for users to refer to windows by the more varied materials of which their frames are made. The *Construction indexing manual** gives (p74) some guidance on the classification of products with no obviously dominant material. The classification code on trade literature can safely be used when it has been given by the RIBA Services sFB Agency Reference Service.

Applications

Guidance on the use of Table 2/3 in conjunction with other facets for particular purposes is given in later Sections; see para 4.2 *Facets in use.*

Coding:

Table 2 uses capital letters, eg:
  F   Blocks
  R   Rigid sheets

Table 3 uses lower case letters for materials, as follows:
  f to o materials in formed products, eg: g clay
  p to s materials in formless products, eg: s asphalt
  t to v materials by function, eg: t fixing and jointing
          materials: u protective materials
  v   painting materials
  w   chemicals
  x   plants
  y   materials, general

Each letter can be followed by a numeral to give a more detailed breakdown (see *Construction indexing manual* pages 81 to 86 and Part II of this manual).

*See bibliography, appendix D

Application of coding

Typical examples of codes made up of Tables 2 and 3 in combination are given in section 5.

Search pattern:

To retrieve all information on a particular construction form find its code by reference to Part II then:

1 Search first any sheets or items with that code, eg:
  Gf2   Large units (structural): heavy concrete

2 Then, if necessary, any sheets or items with the code of the wider class concerned:
  Gf   Large units (structural): concrete, etc

3 Lastly, if necessary, any sheets or items with the Table 2 code only:
  G   Large units (structural)

Table 2/3 codes may be given in title boxes on drawings, schedules, etc if required (see also para 4.2 *Title box*). The plain language counterpart of the code (eg large concrete units) should normally be included elsewhere in the title box.

3.5 Other facets

Project code

Every project must be identified by a project code, but no recommendation is made for standardising the form of the code at present, since standardisation would serve no useful purpose except amongst offices working in consortia or group practices.

However, it may be useful to include, as part of the project identification code, one or more classifying digits for *building types* from CI/sFB table 0, to facilitate feedback of information from the project to the library. For example:

  41 Hospitals
   3 Identification code for the third hospital project

If this is done it is important, to avoid any possibility of confusion, that either the number of digits from table 0 should always be the same, or that a point should be introduced before the identification code, eg:

  41.3 third hospital project (2 digits from table 0)
  413.2 second mental hospital project (3 digits from table 0), *not* the thirty second hospital project.

Because the project code will appear on every document associated with the project, it will not help users to find their way around the project information. Therefore it should not be given any great prominence in the title box or elsewhere, and should not conflict with consultants' needs to give the project their own project code for identification within their own offices.

Plan of work code

The RIBA *Handbook of Architecture practice and management** identifies the following stages of work:

A Inception
B Feasibility
C Outline proposals
D Scheme design
E Detail design
F Production information
G Bills of quantities
H Tender action
J Project planning
K Operations on site
L Completion
M Feedback

Some offices have used plan of work codes on project documents to link them with the RIBA Management Handbook*, the RIBA Job Book*, and the internal office procedures which have been developed from these two books; and to identify the stage at which they were produced. For example: outline design drawings can be prefixed C; production drawings can be prefixed F.

Use of these codes has been found to assist the planning and control of work within architects' offices, and between architects and consultants, because they can be used—like Table 1 codes—to relate to networks of the Precedence Diagram type. They help to make a clear distinction between (for example) design details for internal doors, stage E (32), and production drawings for internal doors, stage F (32).

However, the codes are of no use or interest to the contractor and should not normally appear in the title box on production information issued to site.

If the codes are used, care needs to be taken to ensure that they cannot be confused in any way with the similar Table 2 codes or Process codes.

Standard method of measurement (SMM) code

SMM is used by the building industry not only as rules for the measurement of building work but as a format for bills of quantities, which helps contractors' estimators who need to physically dissect the bills they receive for tender purposes, in order to send them to their sub-contractors and suppliers to get prices. For this reason, some offices who have produced project documentation using CI/sfB based methods have used the SMM groupings in conjunction with CI/sfB Table 1, although so far few attempts have been made to provide cross reference between bills of quantities and drawings by coded annotations on drawings using SMM codes. This may be partly because the SMM is not an easy classification to use without constant reference to an index, and because it does not provide a predictable search pattern.

Methods of collating CI/sfB-arranged bills of quantities into SMM order for estimating purposes, are further discussed in Section 6 of this manual.

A list of SMM work sections and main subdivisions in relation to CI/sfB Tables 1, 2 and 3 is included in appendix B and

the Table 2/3 definitions in Part II facilitate cross reference to relevant work sections in the SMM.

Operations code

In order to plan the best sequence of building operations on site and organise his labour, plant and material resources, the contractor first needs to abstract relevant information from the production documents.

The Building Research Station, in conjunction with other organisations, has undertaken a number of projects in which the design team considered these operations from details on the drawings, and constraints generating from the client, so that the drawings and bills of quantities could be organised in a way meeting, as far as possible, the contractors' needs in this respect.

It may clearly be difficult at present for the design team to define the extent of each operational 'package' with certainty if the contractor has not been appointed when the production information is prepared, but once each has been identified (whether by the contractor or the design team) operational drawings and bills can be produced.*

Most operations are related to a particular type of building part (such as those in Table 1) and a particular construction form (as in Table 2/3), in a particular Project division (location). Because of this, project information arranged by these three facets appears to go a long way towards meeting contractors' needs for defined operations, although the operational packages thus identified will normally be arranged in an order that makes for easier retrieval and does not vary from project to project; rather than in the order in which operations may be carried out on a particular project.

Item identification

Reference has already been made, above, to the need for a project code which can be given to all items of information (drawings, etc) connected with a particular *project*. But it is equally necessary to identify each individual *item* separately from every other item. Item identification can be regarded as a facet, and is further discussed in Section 4.3.

3.6 Conclusions

This section has given details of eight facets which may be used for the organisation of project information. If this seems unduly complicated it is worth remembering that one facet (Project Code) is already in general use; that three (Plan of Work, Standard Method of Measurement, and Operations) are certainly not vital to early use of CI/sfB based methods; that Process type, although important, may not always require coding and that Table 2/3 will not need to be used by most offices until they are thoroughly familiar with Table 1. It is therefore necessary to use only Project code and two of these facets, Project division and Table 1, in addition to a drawing identification number, for coding when using the system for the arrangement and definition of drawn and scheduled information at stage F (Production information) of the Plan of Work. There is no need to start with this application, but most offices have found this a satisfactory way to introduce CI/sfB (see Section 1 para 1.3). It is fully described in the next Section.

* Operational Bills and Drawings are discussed in Bills of Quantities or the operational bill [(A4s)] (AJ 28.1.70), which also contains a full list of references to the subject

* See bibliography, appendix D

Application of data co-ordination to drawings, specifications and bills of quantities

Section 4: Drawn and scheduled information*

This section of the manual is concerned with the application of the principles set out in Section 2 Basic principles (using some of the facets described in Section 3 Facets in use), to drawn and scheduled information and particularly to the sort of information produced at Plan of Work stage F (production information), as defined in the RIBA Handbook of Architectural Practice and Management†, and the RIBA Job book†.

This is described first partly because it is likely to be the first application of CI/SfB-based methods of data co-ordination in most offices (see para 1.3), and partly because it is difficult to explain or understand techniques which may be used for the arrangement of specification and measured information, unless the arrangement of the *drawn* information from which the latter derive is described first. Examples of typical documents are given in Part II

4.1 Introduction

4.2 Sheet structuring and coding

4.3 Item type coding

4.1 Introduction

Function of drawn and scheduled information

Words such as 'drawings' and 'schedules' are used so loosely that it is important to define the way that these and other key terms are used in this manual.

Drawn information is simply information in graphic form, whether it is given on individual sheets of paper as 'drawings' or as illustrations bound in with specifications or bills of quantities. *Scheduled information* is information in tabular form, whether found on 'drawings' or elsewhere. Specification items and measured items in bills of quantities are special forms of scheduled information which are described later.

Wherever possible, the word *drawings* has been used to indicate sheets of paper consisting largely of graphic information, and *schedules* to indicate sheets of paper consisting largely of lists of items. *Sheets* has been used where necessary to cover both 'drawings' and 'schedules' and to distinguish them from bills of quantities and other information in book form.

---

*A note about BS 1192: 1969 BUILDING DRAWING PRACTICE
BS 1192: (1969) includes, on page 43, a brief note on the use of CI/SfB for coding drawings. This section may be regarded in a sense as an extension of that page, giving more detailed advice. As far as possible it complements, rather than overlaps, the remainder of the BS. On a very few subjects (eg title box arrangement), this section gives advice differing to some extent from that given by the Standard, usually because experience of using CI/SfB has shown that some change is necessary. Where possible, readers should look at the two documents together before deciding on their own methods
† See bibliography appendix D

Location drawings are any and all drawings which are permanently tied to a particular project by showing room names, door numbers, etc or in other ways. The basic module grid, which helps to define the exact positions of components and elements in the building (see BS 1192:1969 para 5·5), can of course be shown on assembly drawings as an aid to users. But any locational references, such as grid numbers or letters, or levels in relation to datum, will then need to be removed before drawings are re-used on other projects. *Assembly drawings* are any other drawings showing building work (ie construction work in its final position); and *component drawings* show components which may be manufactured on or off site. *Details* are parts of any of these three types of drawings. Location details, for example, are the individual elevations and sections through the building which make up many location drawings.

The relationships between some of these terms are shown diagrammatically below.

Potentially reusable information about work carried out in its final position (building work)	Information special to the particular project	Potentially reusable information about work which might be made on or off site (manufacturing work)	
Assembly drawings and schedules	Location drawings and schedules	Component drawings and schedules	Information often in sheet form
Specification and/or bill of quantities		Specification and/or bill of quantities	Information often in book form

In traditional practice and on small projects, location drawings (as described above) are the only drawings produced and show component and assembly as well as location information. The penalty paid for this compression of information is that the drawings cannot be used again. But however the drawings are arranged, they provide the natural 'way in' to a search of project documents for most users. This is because of the power of graphics to give an overall picture of construction (at any level of detail) by conveying information about complex relationships of building parts (the shape and nature of the roof in relation to the wall, or the construction of the eaves) in a way that cannot be matched by words alone. Because of this key function, two of the basic requirements which should be met by an information system—that a clear search pattern or arrangement should be provided (para 2.1), reinforced by adequate cross referencing (para 2.1)—are especially important in the case of drawings. The third requirement, for information sorted in different ways to meet different needs, should be met increasingly effectively in future by schedules—including bills of quantities—because these documents normally consist entirely of written information and can thus be sorted readily by computer.

Introducing CI/SfB *based methods*

Most offices already using CI/SfB have used it for the arrangement, coding and cross referencing of drawings and schedules *before* using it for the arrangement of specifications or bills of quantities, or for cross referencing to these documents from coded specification notes (annotation) on

drawings and schedules. The remainder of this section is therefore divided into two stages or parts:

STAGE I Sheet structuring and coding (deciding what goes on each sheet and cross referencing between sheets by means of codes) para 4.2.

STAGE II: Item type coding (fully cross referencing from coded annotation on drawings and schedules, specification and measured information) para 4.3.

4.2 Sheet structuring and coding

4.21 Search pattern

There are two main ways in which drawings may be read or searched:

1 *Like a story:* They may be read like a continuous story, where the object is to provide the reader with a gradually unfolding picture of the whole subject. The natural progression is from the general to the particular, from a 'bird's eye view' of the whole scheme right through to large scale details of very small parts of it.

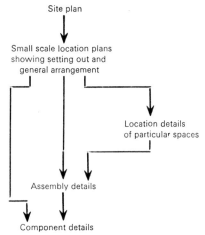

At every stage in examining the sheets, the 'whole' has to be examined before its 'parts', if the parts are to be understood in the context of their surroundings. An eaves detail, for example, will be almost meaningless unless read in the context of the roof of which it forms part. Each sheet looked at should provide a key to the next one(s).

2 *Like a dictionary:* Drawings may also be used like a dictionary by a reader who already knows the project and wants to go straight to the right place for quick answers to particular questions. In this case, there are two apparently conflicting requirements, which may seem difficult to reconcile on drawn information. The first is the need to divide the information up into individual units which can be sorted (para 4.26) in different ways to meet the particular needs of individual users. The second is to keep the number of sheets of paper which need to be examined to a minimum. Inevitably, the more facets are used to meet the needs of different users at different times (see below) and the more that information is subdivided, the more individual pieces of paper will be produced, making search more tiresome and difficult for users who need to be able to grasp the project as a whole.

Fortunately, it is possible to go a long way towards providing for the dictionary requirement adequately (of the two it is by far the most difficult to satisfy) without producing a welter of sheets. This is because:

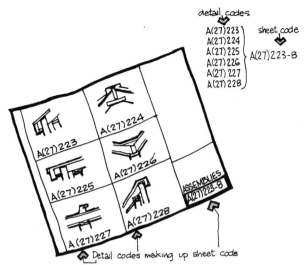

17 *Retrieval of drawings is simplified if the detail number or code automatically calls up the drawing number. In the example, A is the code for assembly information (building work rather than manufacturing work) and (27) is the code for roof structure*

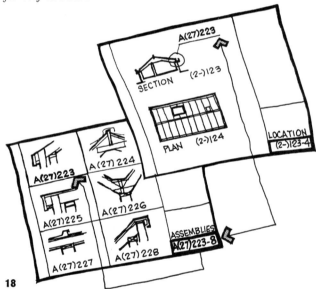

18

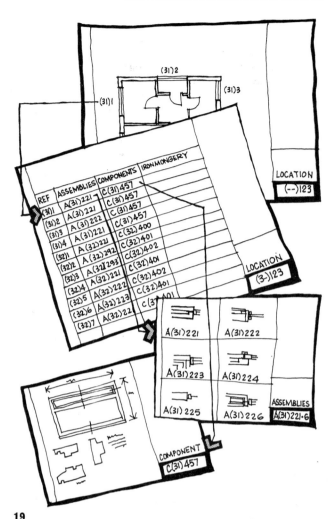

19

18 *Cross reference from one drawing to another to help the user to find typical assembly or component details. (2–) is the code for superstructure*
19 *Cross reference from one sheet to another to help the user to find detailed information on items*

1 An adequate search pattern can be obtained by the use of only three facets, each of which is recognised as important and useful by both designers and constructors. These are: (*a*) *Process type*—location, assemblies and commodities (see Section 3 para 3.1 and the introduction to this section); (*b*) CI/SfB *Table* 1 (see Section 3 para 3.3); (*c*) *Project division* (see Section 3 para 3.2).

2 These facets are designed so as to avoid unnecessary duplication of sheets.

3 The extensive use of cross referencing makes it possible to provide easy-search facilities, while dividing up information for sortation very much less than would otherwise be necessary.

4.22 Cross referencing

Cross referencing techniques based on the use of codes for Process type and Table 1 are shown diagrammatically in **17** to **19**. The methods illustrated have been used throughout the specimen documents shown in Part II. These codes will usually be accompanied in practice by brief notes or headings, but there is insufficient room to show these on the diagrams. There are three basic cross referencing situations:

1 Cross reference between the codes given to *details* and the codes given to the *sheets* containing these details **17**.

A link between these two types of codes can be made as shown above, so that any reference to a detail code from another sheet automatically gives the code for the drawing on which the detail is to be found.

2 Cross reference to *other sheets and details* **18**.

3 Cross references to full information on *particular items* such as individual windows or external wall openings **19**. The aim is to provide a comprehensive system of cross references so that wherever the user may look first within the search pattern he will know precisely where to look next for an answer to his question.

4.23 Facets in use

This section describes the way in which the facets in Section 3 may be used for sheet structuring. The three types of sheets involved are discussed in detail in section 4.25: *Location, assembly and component drawings and schedules,* and some users may find it easier to read that section before reading *Facets in use.*

Process facet

The introduction to Section 4 has already made the essential distinction between the types of drawings required for the basic processes of co-ordination (*location* drawings); on-site building work (*assembly* drawings); and on- or off-site manufacture (*component* drawings). Possible methods of distinguishing between these three types of information were described briefly in Section 3. The use of mnemonic coding (A = ASSEMBLY) for this purpose is illustrated in the specimen documents in Part II. Some offices use the first digit of the drawing or schedule identification code ('drawing number') instead of, or as well as, mnemonic coding, and

20 *Sheets coded at three levels. Those coded (21) etc show details of particular elements or parts. Those coded (2–), (3–) etc show element groups, and sheets coded (– –) show the project as a whole*

recognise more than the three basic categories, for example:

CATEGORY	IDENTIFICATION CODES
Layout drawings	001, 002 etc
Block drawings	101, 102 etc
Other location drawings	201, 202 etc
Assembly drawings	301, 302 etc
	401, 402 etc
	501, 502 etc
Component drawings	601, 602 etc
Sub component drawings	701, 702 etc
Item drawings (showing eg basic timber sections) or accessories drawings	801, 802 etc
Spare	901, 902 etc

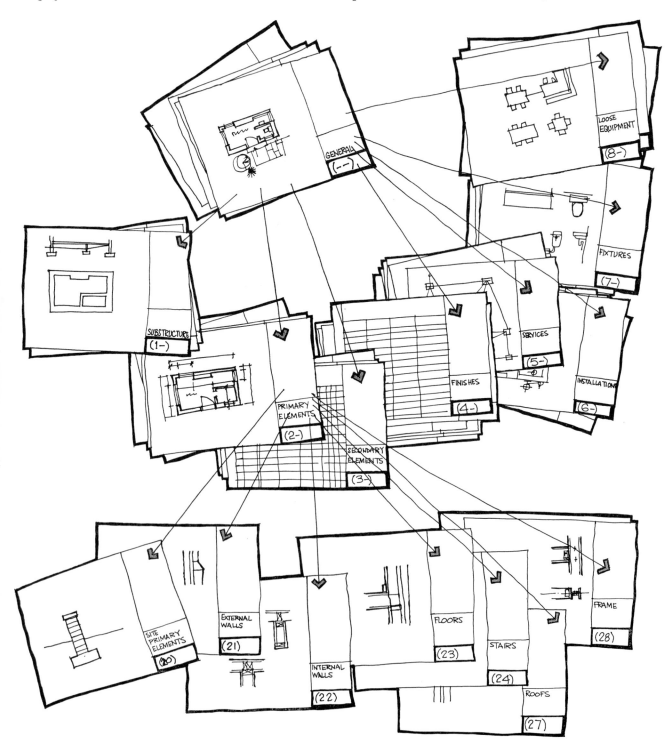

Table 1 facet

Table I is used to code all drawings and schedules, and was briefly described in section 3. Offices already using CI/SfB-based methods for sheet structuring use CI/SfB Table 1 in one of two ways. Both use the same codes for all the specific elements (or parts) such as (21) external walls, or (56) space heating; but they differ in the codes used for details, drawings etc which combine several specific parts.

The first method uses codes ending in 9 as 'summary codes' covering two or more elements in any particular group. For example, (21) and (23) will be summarised by (29). The disadvantage is that summary drawings (which are frequently location drawings and are therefore 'key' drawings) do not come at the top of sets of drawings, where they would be most helpful, since they have codes ending in '9'. This method has *not* been followed in this manual; it is however the basis of the CBC system explained in Section 7, and is further described there.

The second method, which is followed throughout this manual, uses codes ending in – (spoken 'dash') to summarise two or more elements in any particular group. This is indicated by the solid arrow in the diagram below. Codes ending in 9 are used as summary codes *for cost accounting purposes only*, as indicated by the open arrows.

in –, at the beginning of each group of elements, as summary codes (but not for cost information). (2–) summarises elements (20) to (28); (1–) to (8–) are summarised by (– –).

Details or sheets that relate to two or more main groups (1–) to (8–) are coded (– –) PROJECT.

The effects of using this method are that:

1 Key location drawings for the project are rather more likely to come at the *beginning* of sets of drawings.

2 It corresponds closely with the CI/SfB codes used in library practice, except that (90.1), (90.2) etc are used in library practice instead of (10), (20) etc.

3 The summary codes (19), (29) etc; (99), (90) and (9–) may be used as building cost summaries if required for all purposes involving cost accounting since they facilitate adding to totals (ie adding to the end). Similarly, codes ending in – (a symbol without numerical value), may also be used to identify totals when necessary.

Project division facet

This facet was briefly described in Section 3. Its use in conjunction with the second method of using Table 1 described above is demonstrated below and on the specimen documents in Part II. In every case Project division coding is used on location drawings and schedules only, not on assembly or component drawings.

Other classification facets:

Codes for other classification facets, particularly PLAN OF WORK and CI/SfB TABLE 2, may be used for coding sheets, but their use is less essential than the facets discussed so far.

Plan of work codes may be used with advantage on prints or negatives circulated internally in the office as a means of distinguishing (for example) between component design drawings produced at stage E and final production drawings of the same components produced at stage F. These codes will not usually be helpful to contractors, quantity surveyors or other users of production stage information and may be confused with Table 2 codes. They should therefore probably not be included in the title box, and should be removed from negatives before taking prints for external issue.

(1–) SUBSTRUCTURE	(2–) PRIMARY ELEMENTS	(3–) SECONDARY	(4–) FINISHES	(9–) BUILDING & SITE COST SUMMARY
	(20) SITE PRIMARY ELEMENTS	cost →		(90) SITE COST SUMMARY
	(21) EXTERNAL WALLS			
	(22) INTERNAL WALLS			
	(23) FLOORS			
	(24) STAIRS			
	(25) VACANT	cost ↓		
	(26) VACANT			
	(27) ROOFS			
	(28) FRAME	cost →		
(19) BUILDING SUBSTRUCTURE COST SUMMARY	(29) BUILDING PRIMARY ELEMENTS COST SUMMARY	(39) BUILDING SECONDARY ELEMENTS COST SUMMARY	(49) BUILDING FINISHES COST SUMMARY	(99) BUILDING COST SUMMARY

Using this method, (2–) PRIMARY ELEMENTS is used as a main code for any detail that has to do with two or more of the parts coded (20) to (28) on the matrix. This method, unlike the previous one, relies on the project division code to make the distinction between sheets showing external works, and those showing building works.

The diagram **20** shows the method of using codes ending

CI/SfB *table 2 codes* are used by some offices as a means of subdividing Table 1 codes in the title box on drawings and schedules. They give a broad indication of type of assembly (building work) according to the 'dominant product' used, and may also provide a helpful subdivision of assembly drawings. The codes most likely to be used are:

E Concrete work
F Brickwork, blockwork
G Work with structural units
H Work with sections, bars
I Pipe work

Table 2 may also be used to code component drawings. SMM *codes* can be added in the title box to drawings and schedules to assist cross reference to conventionally arranged bills of quantities and specifications.

4.24 Identification coding

The function of identification coding was described in Section 2 para 2.3. Apart from identifying the project each office needs a method of allocating identification codes to particular drawings or schedules to follow the classification codes in the title box. The following factors are among those which need to be considered before deciding what methods to adopt:

Details on drawings Individual details on particular drawings can be numbered in the traditional way, as 'detail A' 'detail B' etc, or the code for the drawing as a whole and the codes for individual details on it can be related by making the identification code for the drawing as a whole a summary of codes for the details on it, as already described previously, and shown on **17**. For example, four details of foundation assemblies coded (16) 221, (16) 222, (16) 223, (16) 224 can be grouped together on a drawing which would, by this method, be coded (16) 221–4. This method is used on the specimen documents in Part II.

Coding by process type and origin Part of the identification code can be used to classify process type as well as, or instead of, using mnemonic coding as described previously. Some offices use the first digit to distinguish between location, assembly and component information as described in para 4.23. For example, location details may be coded by using codes 001 to 199, eg (16) 135, assembly details by using codes 200 to 399, eg (16) 221, and component details by using codes 400 to 599, eg (16) 453. In some circumstances it may be necessary to use four digits as below, and allow a much larger block of codes for each process type, but the same principle can be applied:

second digit to classify producer, and the third and fourth digits to identify the particular drawings.
If the identification code is structured for each project in this sort of way it is clearly important to ensure that enough codes are available to meet future needs. The code structure shown below allows the architect 998 codes for assembly details (at four details to a sheet that is about 249 drawings), for *each* Table 1 code.

Library of details A library of standard details can be built up from details produced for individual projects. Each detail will need to be coded for future retrieval using either the identification code allocated to it during the project, or a special library code which can be allocated to it for indexing purposes when it is placed in the library, as described in Section 13. Some offices use the sort of code structure described above as a means of allocating detail codes quite independently of project codes, and in this case the detail carries the same code throughout its life, whether it is in the library or is being used on a project. Other offices have found it simpler to allocate new codes for the library and for each project on which it may subsequently be used. The methods selected by each office will vary according to its size, the nature of its work and other factors. There is no single ideal universal method. Far and away the most important thing is to avoid unnecessary complexities.

Amendments The entire identification code can be changed every time a drawing or schedule is amended after the contract has been let. Some offices do this instead of using traditional 'amendment' or 'revision' letters, partly to discourage frivolous amendments. Amendments are dealt with in more detail later in this Section.

Table showing how part of identification code can be used to classify drawing by process type and producer

First digit		Architect	Structural engineer	H & V engineer	Electrical engineer	Landscape architect	Spare for other specialists and suppliers
		Second digit 01234	5	6	7	8	9
Location	0	0001–0499	0500–0599	0600–0699	0700–0799	0800–0899	0900–0999
	1	1000–1499	1500–1599	1600–1699	1700–1799	1800–1899	1900–1999
Assembly	2	2000–2499	2500–2599	2600–2699	2700–2799	2800–2899	2900–2999
	3	3000–3499	3500–3599	3600–3699	3700–3799	3800–3899	3900–3999
Component	4	4000–4499	4500–4599	4600–4699	4700–4799	4800–4899	4900–4999
	5	5000–5499	5500–5599	5600–5699	5700–5799	5800–5899	5900–5999

Location details	0001–1999
Assembly details	2000–3999
Component details	4000–5999
Spare	6000–9999

This sort of code structure may be combined with a *producer* (eg architect, engineer) identification code to enable each consultant to allocate identification codes to the drawings and schedules he produces. If the particular Table 1 codes used by consultants are *never* used by the architect, of course, it may not matter if precisely the same identification codes are sometimes used by both, since (56) 411 will clearly refer to a very different sort of detail from (16) 441. But it will help to avoid any possibility of confusion if (say) the second digit of a four digit identification code for details is used as a classifier, to identify the producer. This can be done in various ways: the table above assumes a four digit identification code in which the first digit is used to classify process type, the

4.25 Location, assembly and component drawings and schedules

The following paragraphs show how the facets described above can be used for the arrangement of location, assembly and component drawings and schedules. Definitions of these three categories were given in Section 3 and in the introduction to Section 4 and examples of them are included in the specimen documents in Part II.

Location drawings and schedules

Typical location *drawings* show layouts, elevations and sections. They include dimensioned setting-out drawings and general arrangement drawings showing few dimensions but much other information. Even large scale details showing assemblies will be treated as location drawings if they include information which ties them to a particular location on a particular project (see para 4.1). Location sheets may be coded by any of the facets described above. On a very small and constructionally simple project **21, 22** it may be possible to show all general arrangement and setting out information for both Building Works and External Works on one or more sheets (depending on the geographical extent of the project), coded

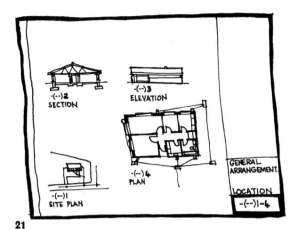

21

    –   (– –)
Project   Table 1
division

In practice, of course, the project division code at least may be omitted in such a case. If the project is larger but is still constructionally simple the project division code can be used to split up the general arrangement and setting out drawings according to the project division dealt with in **23**. For example:

Building + External Works: plan
(key layout drawing)   – (– –)
Block 1: plans, sections, elevations   1 (– –)
Block 2: plans, sections, elevations   2 (– –)
External Works: plans   9 (– –)

Any one of these classification codes can, if necessary, be used on two or more drawings. The project division codes— and 0, may usually be omitted without causing difficulty.

If the project is shown in more detail still (if, for example, it is not really possible to show adequately the whole of superstructure setting out, substructure setting out, and all services and fittings together in a clear fashion on the same series of general arrangement and setting out drawings), then Table 1 main group codes (1–) Substructure, (2–) Primary elements, etc can be used to split up the information in a more formal way between different sheets.
This may be done to a very limited extent (eg by splitting off services only, but putting all other information on general arrangement and setting out drawings) as shown in **24**. Or it may be done to a greater depth as shown in **25**.

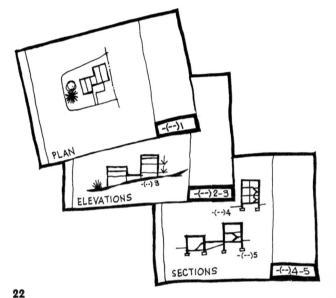

22

21, 22 *Small or simple projects. not requiring a detailed breakdown of information. In practice, all the — (dash) symbols and the brackets could be omitted. They are only given here to show how they fit into the general framework provided by the coding system.*

Lastly, any of the specific codes from Table 1 may be used. For example, it may be necessary to show a plan of the roof on a separate sheet from the other primary elements. In this case a roof layout (location) drawing can be produced, titled and given the specific element code (27), eg:

Block 1: Roof   1 (27)

in addition to a primary element main group drawing:

Block 1: Primary elements setting out   1 (2–)

which will still be required.

This explanation should make it clear that the system leaves the producer freedom to decide exactly what degree of breakdown will suit any particular project. It is, of course, the subject of the particular, self-contained pieces of drawn or scheduled information (ie 'details') on sheets which dictate the code they are to be given. If, for example, details and specification information about a roof and a pipe layout for the hot water service are both shown on the same sheet of paper, it can only be coded (– –) even if the pipe layout takes only a small fraction of the sheet.

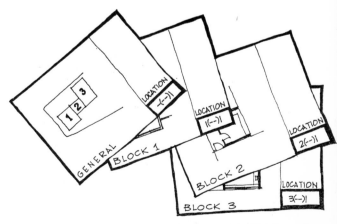

23 *Breakdown of drawn information by project division code but not Table 1. Again all the — (dash) symbols and the brackets could be omitted.*

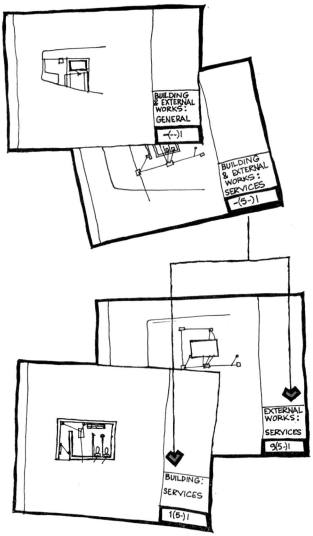

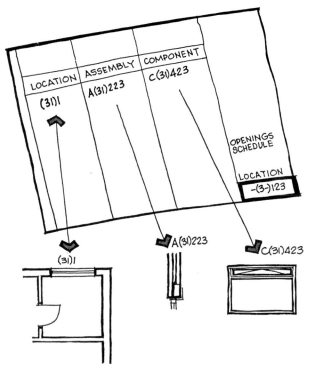

26 *The function of location schedules, to co-ordinate information*

24 *Breakdown of drawn information by Project division code and Table 1 main group codes. The − (− −) symbol on the first drawing and the − on the next one could be omitted without affecting the search pattern.*

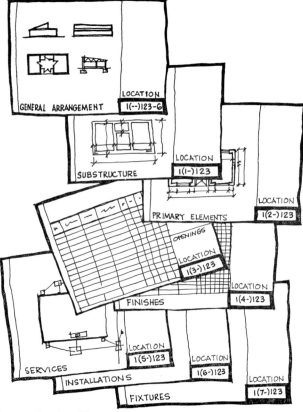

25 *Further breakdown by Table 1 main group codes*

Finally, the word LOCATION should normally be included in the title box for drawings or schedules showing locational information, as on the examples in Part II. Typical examples of location *schedules* are window and door schedules which describe head, jamb and sill conditions, lintel, window type for, say, 'window opening 29' or (using Table 1 cross reference methods) for '(31)29'. Location schedules have the same function—of co-ordination—as location drawings as shown in **26**. The reason for using schedules is usually the practical one that space on the location drawings is often too limited to show clearly the numerous cross references which are otherwise needed around window and door openings. In designing schedules, it may be useful to begin always as in **26** with headings for location information followed by headings for assembly information, and end with details of the components to be assembled.

Assembly drawings and schedules

Typical assembly *drawings* consist of one or more relatively small scope, large scale details—with perhaps as many as four, five or six details on one A3 sheet—showing how components and products are to be brought together and fixed in position. They will not include locational information (eg room names) of a kind which restricts their use to a particular project. They will frequently include specification information relating to two or more Table 1 elements or parts.

This may happen in either of two ways:

1 Elements from different main groups: First, a detail may need to cover two or more Table 1 elements (parts) which are not in the same vertical column on the matrix in Part II of this manual, for example methods of fixing (68) Hose reels to (22) Partitions, or (56) Heating pipes in (13) Floor beds. In this case, Section 2 (Concept analysis, para 2.2) gives guidance on which of these parts should take precedence

and how, therefore, the detail should be coded. The detail should include specification information only on the 'primary' part and on the junction between the two parts, but not on the other one. In the example **27**, the detail could be coded (13) Floor beds, (1–) Substructure or (– –) Project. It will not include notes on the types of heating pipes to be used unless this information is in any case repeated on the drawing for the heating system or if the detail is coded (– –). Details coded (– –) may, or course, include any information about the project.

2 Elements from the same main group: In this case, a detail may need to cover two parts which are related vertically on the Table 1 matrix, as when floor structure is shown on a detail in conjunction with wall structure. If specification information is given on both wall and floor, and on the junction between them, the detail *must* be coded (2–) if it is to fall within the search pattern **28**.

However, a great many details may then appear to require this main group code and some of the benefit of Table 1 coding may be lost if the number is too large. Offices using the system have dealt with this in a number of ways. For example:

1 Each element is shown twice over, on separate details, each of which can then be given a specific Table 1 code **29**. If this is done, complaints from contractors on the inevitable proliferation of drawings will almost certainly follow, and *the method is not recommended*.

2 Information on the junction between two elements may appear only on the detail showing one of them. A cross reference to this detail using the symbol shown in Part II of this manual can then be given on location or assembly drawings or schedules. In the example **30**, the detail includes specification information on the floor assembly but *not* information on the external wall, except where it meets the floor. The detail need not, therefore, be coded (2–), but can be coded (23) Floor. Specification information on the external wall will then be shown on the general external wall drawings, coded (21).

If this method is used, some rule or guidance is needed to help producers of information who will need to decide (for example) whether wall/floor junctions should be shown on wall details coded (21) or on floor details coded (23).

The diagram **31** should establish consistent practice for primary elements. It is based on the easily remembered principle that the element which takes precedence and provides the code for the detail showing the junction, shall always be the one with the *highest* code. For example, information on junctions between (23) Floors and (24) Stairs shall always be shown on details coded (24), not on those coded (23).

3 The method suggested above will often ensure automatically that the way the junction information is given reflects operational logic—that is, that the information will be shown on the sheets or details in use when the junction is made.

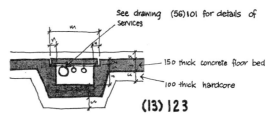

27 *Heating duct in (13) floor bed. (56)101 is a location drawing, since it is not prefixed A (Assembly) or C(Component)*

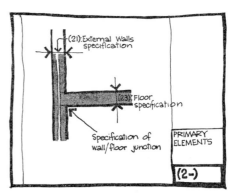

28 *Specification of (21) External walls + specification of (23) Floors + specification of junction = (2–) primary elements*

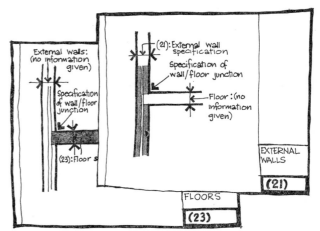

29 *Proliferation of drawings showing junctions between elements*

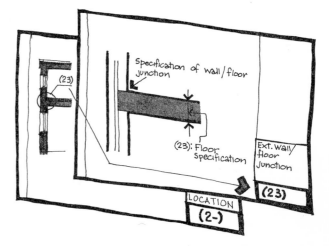

30 *Specification of (23) Floors + outline of (21) External wall + specification of junction = (23) floor*

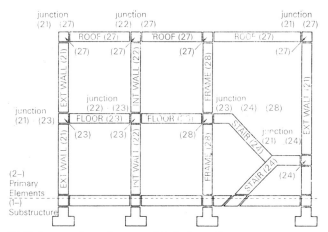

31 *Code precedence for assembly information*

However, this will not always happen. For example, in the case of a detail showing a floor unit resting on a steel angle fixed to a stanchion, all junction details between frame and floor unit will be shown on the frame drawing because (28) is a higher number than (23). But the contractor will require information on the method of joining floor unit to frame at the time that he fixes the floor. It might help him more to show it on the (23) drawing rather than on the (28) drawing.

Probably the strongest argument for using operational logic to determine where and how information is shown is that operational thinking by designers helps towards better constructional design. On the other hand, the rule suggested at 2 above has the merit of CI/sfB as a whole, namely that it serves as a standard which will apply to all situations.

4 All sheets showing two or more primary elements can be coded (2–) and Table 2 can be used to subdivide them. Any method adopted will be strengthened considerably if location details and sheets include adequate cross rererence to assembly information.

Whereas precise cross reference to assembly drawings and schedules can be provided from the location drawings, it cannot be provided in the opposite direction. This is not usually a disadvantage, since users will normally refer from location to assembly information, not vice versa. It may sometimes, however, be necessary to refer from an assembly drawing to a location drawing. The fact that the Table 1 code on the assembly drawing is clearly related to the Table 1 code on the location drawing—in the sense that information relevant to an assembly drawing coded (21) can only be found on location drawings coded (21), (2–) or (– –), will help this search.

As an additional aid, some offices add project division codes on self-adhesive *removable* title box labels, to show where in the project the assembly is to be constructed.

Assembly *schedules*, like assembly drawings, include no reference to location or particular items on a particular project. They will give details of standard assemblies such as 'Bay *type* (21)04' or 'Floor finish *type* (43)01', which may recur on future projects.

Component drawings and schedules

Component (commodity) *drawings* show information needed for the off- or on-site manufacture or production of a particular type of commodity (see glossary appendix c), which may be anything from a timber section to a complete

prefabricated room unit. Like assembly drawings and schedules they often consist typically of several relatively small scope, large scale details. They must not, if they are to be suitable for re-use, show the component in position, or include any dimensions other than those within the boundaries of the component itself. Specification information may very well be included on component drawings as on those shown in Part II, and quantities have also been shown on them by offices in which architect and qs are able to work closely together.

Component drawings showing quantities have been included by some offices in 'production bills of quantities'.

Schedules showing drawn ranges of similar components (for example doors or door frames of different sizes) can be useful in the office as a visual index for designers and quantity surveyors to types and sizes available; but should not usually be sent out of the office, since only a few of the sizes shown will normally be used on any one project. The contractor will however require—for each component to be used on the project—sufficient detail for pricing and manufacturing purposes, with a location schedule showing how many units are needed and where they are to be.

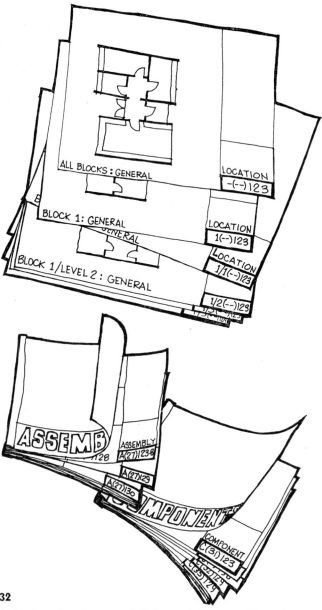

32

If location drawings are of different size to assembly and component drawings, first sortation by process type is easiest arrangement to follow

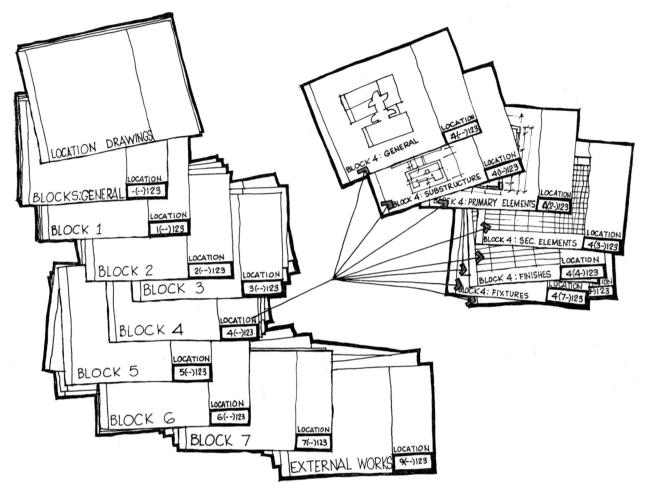

Ready-made components taken from manufacturers' catalogues need not be drawn (unless manufacturers' catalogues lack information in the right form for the contractor's use), but can be scheduled or included in the bq.

4.26 Sortation

It has already been suggested (see para 2.1) that drawn sheet information cannot be sorted as readily as written information. This is largely because the increased difficulties caused to users when they have to try to get an overall picture from the many small pieces of paper that sortation necessitates, more than outweigh the advantages of being able to get different arrangements of them. The use for drawn and scheduled information of the three facets Process type, Project division and Table 1 Element means that the following sortations are theoretically possible:

1 Process type ÷ project division ÷ element **33**
2 Process type ÷ element ÷ project division
3 Project division ÷ element ÷ process type
4 Project division* ÷ process type ÷ element
5 Element ÷ process type ÷ project division
6 Element ÷ project division ÷ process type

In fact, however, for the reason already given, drawn and scheduled information is not usually divided to a sufficient degree to enable these sortations to be achieved.

The first obstacle to sortation is the *size* of location drawings. If they differ in size from component and assembly drawings (they are often larger because of the need to get complete plans on to them) then the only primary arrangement possible is by process type **32**.

* or house type, room type.

33 *Process type ÷ Project division ÷ Table 1 Element (location sheets only)*

The second obstacle: there is often no point in supplying five identical copies of an assembly detail, one for each block of a project, merely because it is repeated in all five blocks. For this reason arrangement by project division will often only be possible or necessary for sheets showing location, as shown above.

It is certainly possible to arrange assembly and component drawings primarily by Table 1 elements. But if *all* sheets are sorted overall by Table 1—as they can be if they are all the same size—the key (location) drawings will be scattered among assembly and component drawings. Sortation by Table 1 may be the most suitable primary arrangement for drawings for a single block project but will otherwise be limited to assembly and component drawings, and to location drawings for individual blocks, zones or rooms.

Drawings and schedules can also be sorted by producer (architect, structural engineer and the like), if this seems useful, particularly if they are identified by a classifying symbol incorporated in the identification code and if consultants have agreed to use the same sheet sizes **34**.

4.27 Lists of drawings and schedules

The search for information will be much helped if the user can have lists of available drawings. It will be easier to keep drawings lists in different sortations up to date if the drawings register for each project is in card index form. Information on the cards can be photo-copied from time to time on to A4 sheets for general use **35**.

4.28 Sizes, title box, key diagram, amendments

Sizes On many projects all drawings and schedules can be produced on a single size of sheet and A3 is being used increasingly. Most offices using CI/SfB are building up

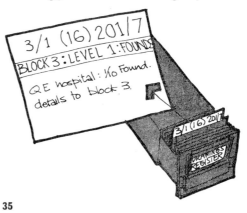

35

libraries of standard or type component and assembly drawings and schedules. They have found it convenient to use this size for these types of information even on larger projects where it may be necessary to introduce A1 for location drawings. A3 size sheets can conveniently be used flat on site in A3 size covers, or simply slid into plastic slides. If A3 sheets are folded to be made part of an A4 size document, as component drawings will need to be if included in bills of quantities, an allowance must be made for a filing margin. This gives the sheet size **36**.

Title box

Information given in title boxes is of two main kinds:

1 Information about the content of the drawing or schedule which distinguishes it from another within a single collection for a particular project. This is information which users need day by day to help them find the particular sheets they want, and it needs to be most prominent on the sheet. It consists principally of the sheet code and title.

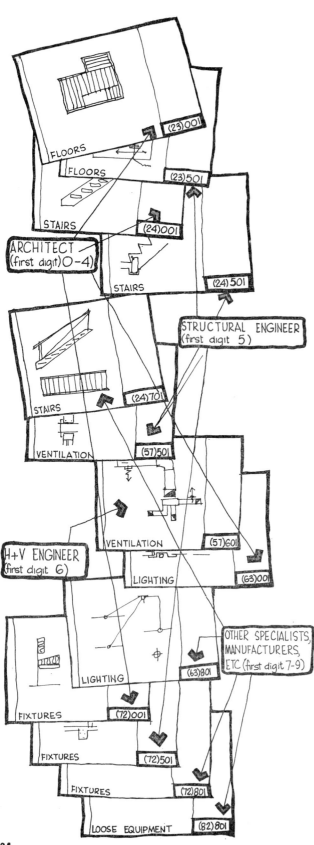

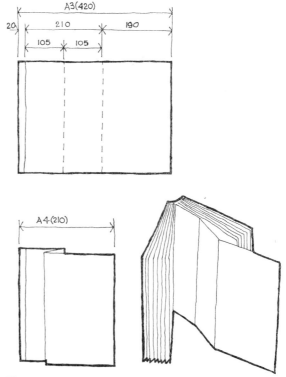

34

36

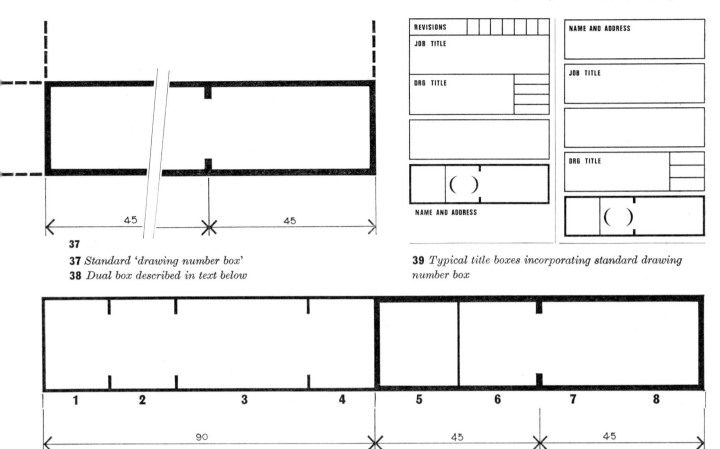

37 *Standard 'drawing number box'*
38 *Dual box described in text below*

39 *Typical title boxes incorporating standard drawing number box*

2 Information which does not help users to find the sheet. Much, though not all, of this information may be of use mainly to the office which produced it.

● First, information on sheet content.

SHEET CODE(S):
The sheet code should be the most prominent piece of information in the title box, since it is used to find the sheet and to keep it in the correct order among other sheets. It will be employed increasingly (instead of the sheet title) as users begin to memorise the codes.

Because of the code's importance for retrieving information easily, it is recommended that a standard form of 'drawing number box' should be used, in much the same way, and for the same reasons, as a standard CI/sfB classification box is used on trade and technical literature **37**.

The sheet code should always be kept in the right hand corner for easy retrieval—whether drawings are folded (as prints) or stored in binders or plan chests. Sheets stored in racks or plan cabinets may need to have the sheet code repeated on the top edge of the sheets.

Use of the box will improve consistency and recognition and will be a sign to contractors and others receiving information that the documentation has been organised in accordance with CI/sfB, as set out in this manual.

The dual box shown above **38** includes the standard box referred to in the last paragraph. This dual box can be used within various title box arrangements on many sizes and shapes of sheet, **39**. It makes the important distinction between location (project division) codes which identify

information which is inevitably quite specific to a particular project, and other codes (eg Table 1) which identify subjects which apply to projects in general and form the sheet code. If the box is on a two part 'sticker' attached to the backs of negatives, the project half of it (1 to 4 in the diagram above) can be removed if sheets produced for one project are later thought to be applicable to others. Some offices have chosen—particularly on small jobs—to leave out this half altogether and include any project division codes with the written title for the sheet, as has been done with the specimen documents in Part II.

PROJECT DIVISION BOX (project codes). See **38**.
1 Project code. Must be used on all sheets. May incorporate use of Table 1.

2 Blocks. Any major sections of building works or external works which need to be separately identified.

3 Levels: horizontal divisions of works (but not necessarily storeys) and Zones: vertical divisions of the works such as groups of rooms.

4 Rooms. Individual spaces of any size.

DRAWING NUMBER BOX (general codes)
5 This space is reserved for any code which the producing office wants to use but which otherwise has no place in the box. It might include Standard Method of Measurement codes or codes for 'repetition units' such as departments, house types or room types **40**.

Where the codes in this space may be used as part of the sheet code, to be quoted in correspondence etc, they should be written as bold as the codes in the next spaces 6, 7 and 8.

6 Element (CI/SfB Table 1) possibly preceded by Process type. Should be used on all sheets and will normally, with the codes that come after it, be given as the sheet code in all correspondence, lists of drawings and so on.

7 Construction form/Material/Activity/Property or Requirement (CI/SfB Tables 2, 3, 4). It is most unlikely that codes from many or all these tables would be used together on an individual sheet.

8 Identification code. This uniquely identifies each sheet from all others, when used in conjunction with codes in boxes 6 and 7 (or boxes 5, 6 and 7). It includes an amendment number (see below).

This description of the codes used together must seem rather daunting, and it is worth emphasising that many of them are already used in some shape or form on project drawings or schedules, and that only the general codes in the standard box (spaces 5, 6, 7 and 8) would be used to form the sheet code for most purposes. Codes from spaces 2 to 4 may occasionally need to be used as well, for location sheets. As an example, the sheet code for Services (layout) drawing 2 for room 5 in block 1 in a single storey building might be in the form: 1/5 (5–) 2 Services: Location. This is not an unusually long code, and every part of it is doing a necessary job.

SHEET TITLE

This should be placed as near the codes as possible, and particularly near those in spaces 5 to 8. The title word-order should reflect the order of the codes, and as far as is reasonable employ the words used with them at the head of the definitions in Part II of this manual. The last word in the title should usually be 'location', 'assembly' or 'component' or any other terms the office may use for a more detailed breakdown of Process type. The title for the sheet represented by the code in the example above might be:

Block 1: Room 5. Piped Services: Location.

SEARCH PATTERN

For users it may be helpful to indicate the codes of sheets likely to include related information, eg (27)-(2–)-(– –). The specimen documents in Part II show this.

● Second, other information, not needed to help retrieval:

PROJECT TITLE

Much less important, to the user outside the producing office, than the sheet code and title. It must be included but need not take up much space.

Consultants' codes for the project, for use inside their own office, can be included with project title.

PRODUCING ORGANISATION

Name, address and telephone number of the architect and, where relevant, the consultant. This information, although essential, does not normally help users to retrieve a particular sheet, and should therefore be arranged to take up very little space.

SCALE, DATE, DRAUGHTSMAN, TRACER, CHECKER

Space, however little, should always be found for the first two of these.

Key diagram

A plan or axonometric, showing the whole or part of the site areas and the main blocks to small scale, coded with the appropriate Project division codes can be associated with the title box and is useful as an aid to retrieval on large projects which necessitate splitting plans between sheets. If copy negative techniques are used it should go on the base negative (see below). The part of the project with which a particular sheet is concerned can be blacked in on the copy of the diagram on that sheet.

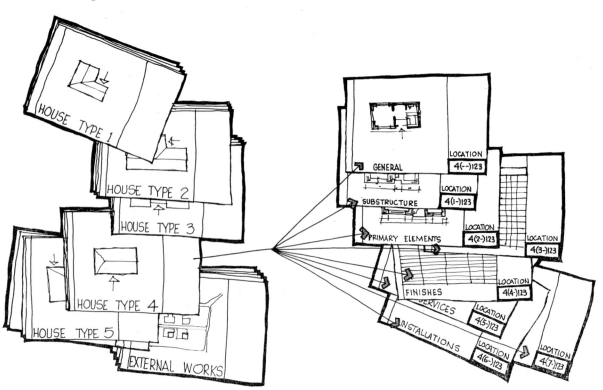

40 *House type sets of sheets*

A: Structural opening
altered from 800 to
900 mm

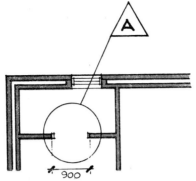

41 *Indication of amendment*

The key diagram should define boundaries for areas of the project which can be shown the right way round, at the scales selected, on the sheet sizes selected for the project, by all members of the design team. Boundaries, once defined, should be respected by all the team including consultants.

Amendments

Most sheets, however carefully prepared, are eventually amended in some way, although the number and extent of post-contract amendments to assembly and component details should be fewer where these details have been used on previous projects.

Four points need considering:

1 Whatever method is used for indicating amendments (some offices simply change the date), it must be clear to the recipient that the sheet is different from the similar document previously received, yet it must maintain its previous position in the sequence of sheets. To ensure that the sheet code is always quoted with the appropriate amendment it is suggested that the amendment letter or number may be known as a 'Mark' and that all sheets may be described at the time they are first issued (before amendment), as 'Mark a' eg: (5–) 33a.

2 A brief description of the amendment and the date on which it was made should be indicated on the sheet itself. A possible layout incorporating space for amendment with a distribution record is shown on the specimen documents in Part II of this manual.

3 The part of the detail or schedule which has been changed should be clearly indicated where possible. One way to do this is to circle the area in pencil on the back of the negative, and link this to a triangle or other device enclosing the mark or amendment symbol **41**.

4 A systematic search must be made by the person amending the sheet for any related information that may require amendment on other sheets. This will be helped by the search pattern produced by the proper use of Project division and Table 1 element codes. For example, if amendment is required to a sheet coded

1/5	(53)
Project division;	Element:
block 1 room 5	Services, water

then the search pattern indicates that all sheets with Table 1 codes of (53), (5–) or (– –), or project division codes 1/5 or 1 should also be checked for possible amendment.

But this is only an aid. It does not guard against the case of the amendment to the door swing on (3–) *Doors: Location* which affects the light switch on (6–) *Electrical installation: Location*. The system is no substitute for thought.

The use of copy negative techniques (see below) facilitates the production of negatives for specific purposes. But it will not normally be practicable to make amendments to the background information on copy negatives except where this has a direct bearing on the subject of the drawing, and this should be made clear to users.

4.29 Copy negatives

Copy negative printing techniques guarantee accuracy and save much drawing time where a number of drawings need to contain a good deal of common information. Location drawings frequently fall into this category since external and internal walls and general building carcass form a basis on which further detail can be added for many purposes. A quick turnround on printing of copy negatives is important; ideally a printing machine should be available within the office.

Information is added to a base negative which is used to produce copy negatives at different stages of its development **42**. Only the additional information required for a specific purpose (eg services layouts) is then added to each copy negative, as necessary. Flow charts and checklists are needed for each project so that information will appear on certain drawings as required. An acceptable balance will be found by experiment, and will depend on factors such as the construction method used, the sequence in which information is to be passed for taking off, and the number and types of consultants. Consultants should be asked to say what information they need on copy negatives sent to them for completion.

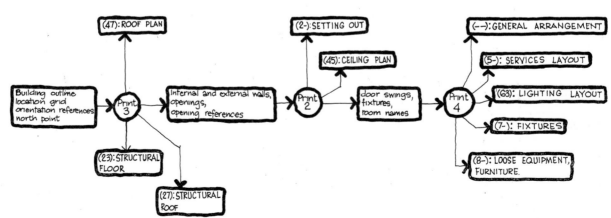

42 *Flow chart for drawings production*

4.3 Item type coding

Item types are types of specification items, describing assembly construction requirements as well as materials, products, and components.

Item type codes are codes built up from CI/SfB Tables 1, 2 and 3, which link specification notes (annotation) on drawings and schedules with the full quality and quantity descriptions given in the specification and/or the bill of quantities. The aim of item type coding is the production of fully cross referenced drawings, specification and bill.

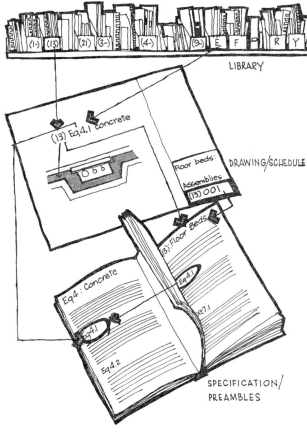

43 *Complete cross reference between drawings and specification using item type codes*

This section, which should be read in conjunction with the specimen documents in Part II, discusses the use of these codes on drawings and schedules. Methods of building up codes are described in detail in Section 5.

Introducing item type coding to the office

Some offices, varying from the very largest using computers to produce bills of quantities, to the very smallest producing bills of quantities manually, have introduced item type coding at the same time as sheet structuring. Others, more cautiously, or without benefit of enthusiastic co-operation from QSS, have used SfB-based methods for sheet structuring (see para 4.2) for as many as four or five years, claiming advantages from doing so, without using item type coding at all.

Clearly, item type codes and annotation cannot usefully be put on drawings to link to the specification and bill of quantities in the way shown above **43**, until the specification or the bill is arranged using CI/SfB-based codes and headings.

And the bill of quantities cannot be prepared until a coded specification (or notes for it) are available for the project. So the first step in introducing item type coding is the preparation of a specification coded and arranged by CI/SfB, as described in Section 5.

Use of item type coding and annotation on drawn and scheduled information

Some typical item type codes and annotations are given below. In each case the code and annotation, as written in the left hand column, should appear either on a sheet having the same Table 1 code as the annotation, or on a sheet carrying one of the two 'summary codes' on the right. These are the codes which fall in each case within the Table 1 search pattern (see para 3.3). For example, (13) Eq4.01 should appear on either a sheet coded (13), or on one coded (1–), or on one coded (– –).

(13) Eq4.01 concrete slab	(1–), (– –)
(23) Hi2.05 timber joists	(2–), (– –)
(27) Hi2.05 timber joists	(2–), (– –)
(43) Tn6.03 pvc tiles	(4–), (– –)
(56) Yh2.01 boiler and pipework	(5–), (– –)

Looked at the other way round, a sheet coded (– –) may have on it an annotation carrying any Table 1 code; a sheet coded (1–) may only have on it annotations coded (11), (12), (13), (16), (17); a sheet coded (13) can only have on it annotations coded (13).

Drawings: To save repeating the same codes (eg Fg2.01) in many different places on a location drawing, the codes and accompanying annotation may be shown at the side of the sheet as a 'mini-spec'. An example of this is:

(21)		External wall
	Ff4.01	Lightweight blocks
	Fg2.01	Facing bricks

The mini-spec on each sheet can be typed on a strip of tracing paper and overlaid on the sheet during printing and can include notes on symbols, hatching and so on to relate individual item type codes on the mini-spec to the drawn information. This will reduce the need to show codes on the drawn part of the sheet. It will, of course, include only types of items which fall within the search pattern for that sheet.

This useful technique has obvious advantages but care needs to be taken:

1 that the mini-spec covers all items shown on the drawn information;
2 that the mini-spec and the sheet are always amended together;
3 that the amount of space available for the mini-spec does not encourage people to fill out the annotation to such an extent that users feel that they need not refer to the full specification.

Schedules: The use of item type codes on schedules will have little effect on their present appearance. Precise cross reference will be given to a specification or measured item. As has been said, codes and annotation will be of the form: '(31) Ro1.03 $\frac{1}{4}$in plate' instead of simply '$\frac{1}{4}$in plate'. In the latter case the user has to set about finding the quality description of $\frac{1}{4}$in plate glass in the specification or preambles, and the description of the quantity of it required for windows, in the bill. On the other hand (31) Ro1.03 leads straight to the appropriate clauses in both documents.

Code lengths on drawings and schedules can be reduced in various ways:

1 The example above refers to the quality of glass to be provided in a particular window. If the schedule which includes this item covers (32) internal doors as well as (31) windows, the schedule itself will be coded (3–) and every item on it will be coded (31) or (32). It can however be divided into two sections, one for all (31) items, the other for all (32) items.

All the individual Table 1 codes can then be left off so that the item type codes may be written in the form 'Ro1.03 ¼in plate' instead of '(31) Ro1.03 ¼in plate' provided that a boldly written note makes it clear that the element number should be given where necessary in spoken or written reference to the item. Another way to achieve the same result would be to divide the schedule on to two separate sheets, one coded (31), the other (32).

2 The code length can be still further reduced if the head of each column displays the part of the code which is common to all items in the column.

Glass
Ro1
03 ¼" plate
05 24 oz sheet
03 ¼" plate

Evidently these techniques, which save space and time and make coding much less formidable, are best introduced slowly since they leave it to users to add together the various parts of each code. Experienced users will not find this at all difficult.

3 Item type codes and the annotations which accompany them can be brought together on a very simple form of assembly schedule (no reference to location) in commonly occurring groups, each of which can then be given a short ad hoc identification code like 01, 02, and so on, following the appropriate Table 1 code.

(42)	WALL FINISHES
(42) 01	Fg2.02 Fairfaced brick work in stretcher bond Vv6.05 Three-coat emulsion paint
(42) 02	Pq4.01 Plaster ½" finished thickness Vv6.06 Two-coat emulsion paint

These ad hoc codes are known as *overcodes*. The particular overcodes shown above can be used, instead of the item type codes which they cover, on location drawings or schedules coded (42) showing wall finishes for particular rooms; or on location schedules coded (4–) showing floor, wall and ceiling finishes; or on general

arrangement drawings coded (– –). In the example below, wall A in room 2/1 is to be finished to specification (42)02 (ie plaster as bill and specification item Pr4.4110 and two coats emulsion as Vv6.6212).

	(42) INTERNAL WALL FINISHES				(43) FLOOR	(45) CEILING		KEY: WALL FINISHES	
	WALL A	WALL B	WALL C	WALL D			(42) 01	Fairfaced brickwork 3 coat emulsion	Fg2.2446 Vv6.7212
							(42) 02	Plaster ½" thick 2 coat emulsion	Pr4.4110 Vv6.6212
								KEY: FLOOR FINISHES	
1/1 Utility	01	01	01	01	01	01	(43)01	½" Fibreglass quilt ¾" sand cement screed Wire mesh reinforcement Softwood skirting ⅛" Thermoplastic tiles	Kml.1002 Pq4.1112 Jh2.2012 Hi2.4226 Tn6.0024
1/2 Garage	01	01	01	01	–	01			
2/1 Kitchen	02	02	02	02	01	02	(43)02	1" t & g boarding 3 x ¾" softwood	Hi2.2671 Hi2.4226
2/2 Dining	01	02	02	02	02	02			
								KEY: CEILING FINISHES	
							(45)01	Light caulking coat 'Artex'	Pq4.2210 Vv9.5101
							(45)02	⅜" plain plasterboard 2 coat emulsion	Rf7.3612 Vv6.6212

The use of overcodes in this way helps to establish consistent office practice in specifying and reduces the number and length of codes on location drawings and schedules. The price paid for it is that reference can no longer be made direct from the location sheet to the bill or specification: the assembly schedule has to be consulted first. In some cases however, it may be possible to arrange for assembly overcodes like those above to be given on the location schedule itself, as shown in the illustration above.

Section 5: Specification information

This section is concerned with the application of the principles set out in Section 2 Basic principles (using some of the facets described in Section 3 Facets in use) to specification information. It leads to the use of item type coding on drawings and schedules as explained in the last section, to link the annotation on them with full specification information, whether this is in a separate document or is in the form of preambles to a bill of quantities. It assumes some knowledge of the methods of organising drawn and scheduled information set out in the last section. Examples of specimen documents are given later, in Part II of this manual.

5.1 Introduction

5.2 Specification structuring and coding

5.1 Introduction

Function of specification information

Specification information fully describes the *quality* of work required as distinct from measured information which describes the *quantity* of work. It does this either:

1 By describing the type and quality of all materials, etc needed, as well as the way in which they are to be brought together.
2 By describing the required qualities of the finished result without tying the manufacturer or contractor to specific methods of achieving it.

The first of these methods leads to traditional materials and workmanship specifications in which the workmanship clauses specify building construction or 'work' (assembly information); and the materials clauses specify basic resources (commodities)* before assembly.

The second type is the performance specification—or the performance clause embedded in an otherwise traditional specification—which relies for its successful use on the development of effective means of verifying or testing that the required performance has been achieved by the contractor or manufacturer.

CI/SfB based methods can be used for the arrangement and cross-referencing of performance specifications and traditional materials and workmanship specifications, and for any combination of the two.

Introducing CI/SfB *based methods*

Offices who have used sheet structuring for some time as described in Section 4 should not find it difficult to use CI/SfB item-type coding as a means of cross referencing from drawings and schedules to specifications and bills of quantities, but it is desirable (as already explained—see para 4.3(to prepare a coded specification *before* either putting codes

* See glossary, appendix C

on drawings and schedules or taking off measured information for the bill of quantities for a particular project.

It is fairly unlikely that the fees earned on a single small project will absorb the whole cost of preparing such a specification in the first place. The amount of work involved depends very much on the scope and complexity of the construction methods used in the office as well as on the adequacy of existing available specifications which can serve as a 'quarry' for clauses, the nature of the coding methods employed, and the skill of the people involved. It seems probable that in many offices specification writing will be best done by senior and experienced staff, when time permits. It may therefore be advisable to allow a relatively generous period for preparation of the bulk of the specification as a *specification library*, even if with a particular project in mind.

This manual is being published about two years before the National Building Specification. Offices who master coding without difficulty (like the office which was using CI/SfB for all project information, including bills of quantities, only three months after first hearing of it) can expect a reasonable return in this time from the work involved in setting up a specification library. It is impossible to say now what coding methods will be used in the NBS. It seems probable, however, that offices will derive useful experience from setting up their library at this stage, whatever codes may be used in the NBS.

Once the bulk of the specification library has been prepared it can be used as the basis for coded project specifications. These will provide the basis for coding and annotating project drawings and schedules, so that fully coded project drawings, schedules and specifications (or at least coded specification notes) can be available to the QS before 'taking off' the bill of quantities for any particular project.

5.2 Specification structuring and coding

Search Pattern and cross referencing

Specification items provide—or should provide—full and detailed answers to specific questions which arise from examination of the drawings or the quantities. For example, an assembly drawing may show timber studding in a partition, and details of the quality of timber will be required by the contractor, so that the right type can be ordered. Using a traditionally organised specification, probably in the form of preambles to the bill of quantities, information on quality is found by examining and comparing the abbreviated uncoded description on the drawing with the full description in the specification. If the drawing defines the timber merely as '3in × 2in sw studding' and the preambles include three specifications for soft wood, the process of finding out which one applies can be time consuming and tiresome, and often produces no definite result.

A direct and specific coded cross-reference from drawings to full specification items is clearly needed. But the use of trade (SMM) codes as a means of achieving this is difficult, partly because adequate knowledge of 'who does what' is not possessed by many producers of information, and partly because trade definitions are often tenuous and unstable, with fine distinctions between one category and another varying according to locality and circumstances.

The following headings are fairly typical of those in traditional specifications:

Excavation and earthwork   Engineering installations
Piling   Electrical installations
Concrete work   Floor, wall and ceiling finishes
Brick work and block work   Glazing
Asphalt work   Painting and decorating
Roofing   Drainage
Carpentry and joinery   Etc

Some of the headings refer to assemblies defined by *functional element* (ie part) using terms such as those found in CI/sfB Table 1, for example roof (roofing), installations, finishes. Others appear to refer to assemblies defined by *material* or by other characteristics such as *form*, as with classes found in sfB Table 2 using terms such as brickwork and block-work. Separated out into their separate categories the above headings group as follows:

By functional element: By construction form or
                                   material:
Piling
Roofing   Concrete work
Engineering installations   Asphalt work
Electrical installations   Brickwork and blockwork
Floor, wall and ceiling   Carpentry and joinery
finishes   Glazing
Drainage   Painting

Each of these lists is clearly not comprehensive (there are more elements than those listed), yet every project specification must be able to find a home for *any* relevant item. Since the framework provided by these and similar headings is so sparse and so muddled as to order, specification writers have to do the best they can, by following precedent as far as possible and by including items where it seems most sensible. Unfortunately several places usually seem equally sensible and as a result these traditional headings do not provide users with a competent search pattern.

CI/sfB Tables 1, 2 and 3 in effect fill out and rationalise the headings above to provide a home for every possible item, and provide users with a consistent and logical search pattern and cross-reference facility. It is also worth noting these further advantages:

1 The codes are brief and those in the two main tables (Tables 1 and 2) can be memorised without great effort.
2 Codes are similar to those used for office library and other source information.
3 All three tables code 'permanent' characteristics which are largely independent of changing situations or requirements, and thus define information items in ways likely to enable them to be re-used.

There are several ways of using CI/sfB codes for organising specification information but if the method described below is used, as it has been in the specimen documents in Part II, the cross-reference from drawings or schedules to full specification information in a project specification will be made as shown in **44**.

In the case of 'Hi2 Softwood sections' the specification clauses may of course take a page or more and will be similar to those given for softwood sections in a traditional specification. In the case of (31), the information provided will either:

1 Fully describe items (assemblies and commodities) which are to do with external openings and *no other element*

44 *Component drawing, specification and bq for softwood in windows*

2 Provide a performance specification for external openings assemblies and commodities (eg windows). In this case it will consist of clauses specifying requirements for standards of weather-proofing and other performance characteristics required, and tests for those characteristics.

Section (31) may also include coded cross-references and annotation for all the items in external openings—like Hi2 softwood sections—which are fully described elsewhere in the specification.

The specification library

The specification library may be based on existing specifications which the office has used and found satisfactory, and which need to be rearranged and coded. This is bound to be a 'scissors and paste' exercise. The temptation to use punched cards or other mechanical devices for sorting, and to do a very great deal of analysis, rewriting and sub-division of existing clauses should almost certainly be resisted. This is partly because the library is bound to improve as a result of using it as a basis for project specification, and there is no point in spending more time on it initially than is absolutely necessary; partly because an attempt to make a technical review of the clauses (their clarity, relevance to modern practice, etc) at the same time as rearranging them may only mean that neither job gets done properly; and partly because contractors receiving the rearranged specification will be reassured if they find that they are already familiar with individual clauses.

There are various ways in which the actual work of rearrangement can be done, but the best and simplest in many circumstances is probably to set up an A4 'subject sheet' for every heading given in *capital letters* in the typical specification outline which follows. Clauses from one or more existing specifications can then be cut out and clipped to the appropriate subject sheet. Where necessary, new subject sheets can be added for subheadings. It is probably as well to use only *one* specification as a quarry in the first place, because if two or more are merged, there is a risk that clauses will be incompatible. Once there seems reasonable certainty

45 *Specification library*

that all clauses dealing with the subject represented by the heading (see the definitions in Part II) have been extracted from the existing specification, the separate pieces of paper with the old clauses on them, and any new clauses which may be written to fill obvious gaps, can be arranged following the recommendations below, coded and stapled on to the subject sheet. Experience with CI/SfB specifications has shown that the framework provided by the system often reveals alarming areas of omission in the specification which is being replaced. The sheet can finally be typed, checked, and filed with other sheets, in the order given by the codes. When this work is complete for every subject in the outline the office will have a specification library such as the one shown in **45**, which can be updated and improved as time goes by, and will form a basis for individual project specifications.

Form and arrangement: The specification outline opposite demonstrates a possible arrangement both for the office specification library, and for a typical project specification. It makes use of CI/SfB Table 1, 2 and 3 codes included in the *Construction indexing manual* 1968*, but with some minor alterations and additions which are helpful (though not essential) for specification purposes. It is likely that both the *Construction indexing manual* and this manual will be revised and republished at the same time, more or less concurrently with the National Building Specification. All available experience with both manuals and with the work towards the National Building Specification will be taken into account and the republished versions will be complementary to one another. Until then, all variations from the code structure set out in the *Construction indexing manual* must be regarded as experimental. Offices using the specification outline will therefore need to decide, in respect of the few codes listed below which differ from the manual, whether to adopt them for project information purposes only, or adopt them for both project information and library

*See bibliography, appendix D

purposes; or whether to use present library codes for all project information purposes.

The new codes are as follows—see **46**:

A is used to provide a place right at the beginning of the specification for the sorts of prelimnairy clauses which occur at the beginning of traditional specifications. These are clauses which describe the conditions under which building work is to be done, rather than the work itself. They do not include any descriptions of *particular* works or assemblies or commodities or operations related to them.
B is used for demolitions, the 'de-construction' work of clearing the site to prepare for construction work and
C is used for earthworks, being 'construction' work on the material of which the site is made. Codes B and C are used by CBC* and they have a relationship with the appropriate sections of the Standard Method of Measurement.
D is the first code in the sequence which is used to classify clauses to do with work carried out using building materials (commodities), but it relates only to preliminary work, eg mixing of mortar, not to assemblies in their final position. Information on basic materials (materials of undefined form) and formless materials will be found in CI/SfB arranged libraries at Y, and offices who want to maintain maximum consistency between the office library and the specification library can, of course, use Y instead of D.
E is used to code clauses about assemblies made of cast materials of which the most obvious—though not the only—example is in-situ concrete.
F is used for brickwork and blockwork (ie brick and block assemblies), and from E to (86) every code and heading taken from Table 2 and 1 of the *Construction indexing manual*, classifies in-situ assemblies or 'constructions' defined first by form F to Y or otherwise by function (10) to (86).

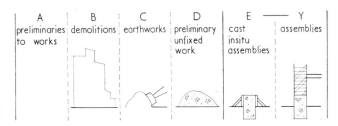

46 *Codes A to D are in operational sequence*

(61) is the only new code in Table 1, used here experimentally as a result of users' experience with the *Construction indexing manual*.

Lower case letters are from Table 3 in the manual except that *a* to *d* derive from (A) to (D) in Table 4. The *Construction indexing manual* should be consulted for further subdivision of codes where the outline does not provide enough detail. For convenience Part II of this manual includes detailed definitions for all the primary codes, from A to (86).

Content of clauses: If inconsistencies and overlaps between clauses are to be avoided in the specification, it is usually important to observe one basic rule in writing or editing.

*See glossary, appendix C

On facing page: typical specification outline.
Use of upper and lower case, and double and single
underlining, reflects hierarchy of headings. It is
recommended that these conventions be adhered to

A PRELIMINARIES

Aa Administration

Aa0 General*

Aa1 Communications*⌗
eg:
Name and address of project
Namesand addresses of employer, architect, quantity surveyor etc
Scope and description of the works and the site
Procedures
Classification and coding
Rules for measurement
List of documents available (drawings, bills of quantities)
Reference to and/or headings from conditions of contract,(including any
circumstances leading to special conditions of contract)

Aa2 Controls, constraints*
eg:
Compliance with building regulations
Compliance with controls and constraints for noise, flying operations, use of
explosions, safety health and welfare, advertising, security etc
Compliance with controls and constraints imposed by authorities, eg:
Statutory and local authorities, police
Compliance with constraints, on eg: free use of existing buildings

Aa3 Design
eg:
Shop drawings

Aa4 Finance, tender
eg:
Tendering procedure, errors and omissions, contractor's commitment
Variations, dayworks
Fluctuations
Final account
Security bond
Insurances

Aa5 Production
eg:
Programme, networks
Site organisation
Attendance on subcontractors
Conduct of site meetings
Overtime

Aa7 Quality
eg:
Full and adequate supervision to be provided
Samples to be submitted for approval
Testing equipment to be kept in good condition
Defective work

Aa8 Feedback

Aa9 Sundry administrative matters

Ab Aids, temporary works, plant

Ab0 General matters including definitions

Ab1 Aids for protecting, storing

Ab2 Aids for supporting

Ab3 Aids for handling

Ab4 Aids for making

Ab5 Aids for treating

Ab6 Aids for placing

Ab7 Aids for making good

Ab8 Aids for cleaning

Ab9 Sundry aids

Ac Labours

Ac0 General matters including definitions

Ac1 Labours for protecting, storing

Ac2 Labours for supporting

Ac3 Labours for handling

Ac4 Labours for making

Ac5 Labours for treating

Ac6 Labours for placing

Ac7 Labours for making good

Ac8 Labours for cleaning

Ac9 Sundry labours

Ad Operations (Labours aids)

Ad0 General matters including definitions

Ad1 Protection, storage

Ad2 Support

Ad3 Handling

Ad4 Making

Ad5 Treating

Ad6 Placing

Ad7 Making good
eg:
Damage caused by inadequate protection to be made good

Ad8 Cleaning

Ad9 Sundry operations

B DEMOLITIONS

C EARTHWORKS

D PRELIMINARY (UNFIXED) WORK, BASIC AND FORMLESS MATERIALS

De Natural stone

Df Formed (precast) concrete

Dg Clay

Dh Metal

Di Wood

Dj Natural fibres and chips, leather

Dm Mineral fibres

Dn Plastics

Dp Loose fill, aggregates

Dp1 Natural aggregates
Quality
Each type of natural aggregate shall be obtained from one approved   )
source capable of maintaining consistent supplies throughout the contract.)
Samples of the fine and coarse aggregate shall be submitted to the Architect)
for approval before delivery in bulk is made.   All natural aggregates shall)
be truly represented by the samples

Protection, storage
Natural aggregate shall be stored on clean hard surfaces so as to prevent all)
contamination and admixture with foreign materials and facilitate the drainage)
of water   )

Dp1.1 Fine natural aggregate (except sand)·
Fine natural aggregate shall be sharp and reasonably free from chalk, loam,   )
clay, organic matter or other deleterious substances and shall be a well graded)
mixture from 500 gauge downwards complying with the requirements of BS 882   )

Dp1.2 Sand:
Sand shall comply with BS 1200 and shall be clean, sharp, coarse grain river)
or pit sand, free from salt, loam, clay or other deleterious substances   )

Dq Cements, mortars etc

Dq2 Cements

Dq4 Mortars

Mixing
The materials for mortars shall be separately gauged and accurately   )
measured, by volume, in proper gauge boxes distinctly marked. The materials)
shall first be thoroughly ------   )

Dq4.1 Cement mortar:
Cement mortar shall be composed of one part of Dq2.1 cement and three parts   )
of Dp1.2 sand   )

Dq4.2 Coloured cement mortar:
Coloured cement mortar shall be composed of one part of Dq2.1 cement and three)
parts of Dq4.5 bricklaying mortar   )

Dq4.3 Composition mortar
Composition mortar shall be composed of one part of Dq2.1 cement and six parts)
of Dq4.5 bricklaying mortar   )

Dr Special mortars

Ds Bituminous materials

Dt Fixing and jointing agents

Du Protective materials, admixtures

Dv Materials for paints

Dw Other chemicals

E CAST INSITU ASSEMBLIES

F BRICK AND BLOCK ASSEMBLIES

---

* This heading differs from the Construction indexing manual

⌗ 'Information only' clauses setting up a communications framework for the project.
These may not be priced but should be read in conjunction with later clauses

eg:
Rubble work, masonry, brickwork, blockwork

Ff <u>Concrete blocks</u>

Ff2 <u>Dense concrete blocks</u>

<u>Design</u>
Concrete blockwork shall rise 4 courses to 900 mm including joints. 4 blocks)
laid end to end shall measure 1800 mm including joints)

<u>Commodities</u>
Concrete blocks shall comply with BS 2028.)
Ties type Xt7.3 shall be zinc coated mild steel 'butterfly ties' to BS 1243.)
Mortar shall be as specified below)

Ff2.1 Concrete blocks in Dq4.3 mortar:
Concrete blocks shall be size 440 mm x 215 mm x 100 mm and shall be)
obtained from -----)

Fg <u>Clay bricks and blocks</u>

Fg2 <u>Clay bricks</u>

<u>Design</u>
All materials and workmanship shall conform with the recommendations)
contained in British Standard Code of Practice CP121.101 'Brickwork'.)
Clay brickwork shall use 4 courses to 900 mm including joints. 4 bricks laid)
end to end including joints shall measure 900 mm)

<u>Protection</u>
Newly erected work shall be effectively protected against damage by heavy)
rain or frost and no bricklaying is to be carried out when the temperature is)
below 2°C.)

<u>Placing</u>
All bricks are to be well watered immediately before being laid and the top)
of brickwork shall also be well watered prior to the recommencement of work.)
All joints and cross joints in brickwork shall be well filled with mortar and)
all perpends, quoins and the like kept strictly true and square.)

<u>Making good</u>
All brickwork shall be left in perfect condition on completion of the work,)
entirely free from flaws, cracks, settlements, strains, damage or other)
defects.)

<u>Facework</u>
Facing brickwork to be built in stretcher bond.)
The price for facing brickwork shall include for carefully selecting, from)
the stack, bricks of true shape and even colour.)
Facing brickwork shall be carefully protected from any staining by mortar,)
ground or scaffold board splashings, rust stains or other causes of dis-)
colouration or disfigurement and all facings shall be carefully cleaned down)
on completion.)

<u>Commodities</u>
Clay bricks shall comply with BS 3921.)
Ties type Xt7.3 shall be zinc coated mild steel 'butterfly ties' to BS 1243.)
Mortar shall be as specified below)

Fg2.1 Facing bricks in Dq4.4 mortar:
'-----' facing bricks to be obtained from '-----' in a single batch to offset)
possible variations in colour.)
A sample panel using Dq4.4 mortar is to be prepared for the architects')
approval.)

Fg2.2 Common bricks (not used for facework) in Dq4.1 mortar:
These bricks when laid below ground shall be recommended by the manufacturer)
for this purpose.)

Fg2.3 Common bricks (not used for facework) in Dq4.3 mortar:)

Fg2.4 Engineering bricks in Dq4.1 mortar:
Engineering bricks complying with BS 3921 Table 6 Class B and laid in Dq4.1)
mortar.)

G <u>LARGE UNIT ASSEMBLIES</u>
eg:
Lintels, large structural units

H <u>BAR, SECTION ASSEMBLIES</u>
eg:
Bar reinforcement sections

I <u>PIPE WORK ASSEMBLIES</u>

J <u>WIRE, MESH ASSEMBLIES</u>
eg:
Mesh reinforcement

K <u>QUILT ASSEMBLIES</u>
eg:
Quilt pipe insulation

L <u>FOIL ASSEMBLIES</u>
eg:
Felt

M <u>FOLDABLE SHEET ASSEMBLIES</u>
eg:
Flashings

N <u>OVERLAP TILE, SHEET ASSEMBLIES</u>
eg:
Corrugated sheeting

P <u>THICK COATING ASSEMBLIES</u>
eg:
Asphalting, plastering, rendering, screeding

R <u>RIGID SHEET ASSEMBLIES</u>
eg:
Flat sheet glazing; plasterboarding, building boards etc

S <u>TILE ASSEMBLIES</u>
except overlap tiles, see N

T <u>FLEXIBLE SHEET ASSEMBLIES</u>
eg:
Carpeting

U <u>FINISHING PAPERS, FABRIC ASSEMBLIES</u>
eg:
Papering, upholstery

V <u>THIN COATINGS</u>
eg:
Painting, bitumen silicones, polishes, rot preventatives etc

X <u>COMPONENT ASSEMBLIES</u>
eg:
Shop joinery

Y <u>ASSEMBLIES (CONSTRUCTIONS)</u>
eg:
Joinery

(1-) <u>SUBSTRUCTURE ASSEMBLIES</u>

(10) <u>SITE SUBSTRUCTURE</u>*

(11) <u>EXCAVATIONS</u>+

(13) <u>FLOOR BEDS</u>

(16) <u>FOUNDATIONS</u>

(17) <u>PILE FOUNDATIONS</u>

(2-) <u>PRIMARY ELEMENT ASSEMBLIES</u>

(20) <u>SITE PRIMARY ELEMENTS</u>ø
eg:
External works structures

(21) <u>EXTERNAL WALLS</u>

including work with:

Ff2.1	Concrete blocks (Dq4.3 mortar)	)
Fg2.1	Facing bricks (Dq4.4 mortar)	)
Fg2.2	Common bricks (Dq4.1 mortar)	)
Fg2.3	Common bricks (Dq4.3 mortar)	)
Fg2.4	Engineering bricks (Dq4.1 mortar)	)
Hh2.4	Mild steel angles	)
Hi1.1	Unwrot softwood sections	)
Hi2.1	Wrot softwood sections	)
Ln2.1	Damp proof courses	)

(22) <u>INTERNAL WALLS, PARTITIONS</u>

(23) <u>FLOORS</u>

(24) <u>STAIRS</u>

(27) <u>ROOFS</u>

(28) <u>FRAMES</u>

(3-) <u>SECONDARY ELEMENT ASSEMBLIES</u>

(30) <u>SITE SECONDARY ELEMENTS</u>•
eg:
Fences, gates and other ancillaries to external works structure

* Clauses for site substructure should be written at this point but may then be
coded (90.1) and filed at (90.1) if preferred.

+ (10) may be used for items which are covered by (11) in the Construction indexing
manual page 47.

• Clauses for site secondary elements should be written at this point but may then be
coded (90.3) and filed at (90.3) if preferred.

ø Clauses for site primary elements should be written at this point but may then be
coded (90.2) and filed at (90.2) if preferred.

(51)   EXTERNAL WALL OPENINGS

           including work with:

Gh2.1   Patent lintels   )

H12.1   Wrot softwood sections   )

H13.1   Hardwood sections   )

R14.1   Blockboard   )

Vv5.2   Paint   )

X   COMPONENTS

    Xi   Components, timber

X12   Softwood units   )

X12.20   Softwood units, side hung:

X12.21   Combined door and frame units to suit blockwork.   )
         Fixing   )
         Both jambs to be plugged, and screwed to blockwork -----)
         Commodities   )
         Door to be 1⅞" finished (47 mm) external quality solid core flush door   )
         giving 1 hour fire resistance, primed ------
X12.212 Overall size 900 mm x 1975 mm to suit 100 mm thick blockwork:)

X12.30   Softwood units, pivoting   )

X12.31   Horizontal pivot window and frame units to suit blockwork:)
         Fixing
         Window and frame units shall be built into Ff4 concrete blockwork inner   )
         leaf.   Full allowance shall be made for tolerances recommended by the   )
         manufacturer.   )
         The sash must be able to move freely through 180°.
         Commodities
         '------ horizontal pivot' window to be obtained from -----   )
X12.311 Overall size 600 mm x 600 mm to suit 100 mm thick blockwork.   )

Xy0.01   Windows *
         Purpose and use:)
         High rise housing.   )
         Dimensions:)
         -----------   )
         Air infiltration:)
         In accordance with ----- etc   )

(32)   INTERNAL WALL OPENINGS

(33)   FLOOR OPENINGS

(34)   BALUSTRADES

(35)   SUSPENDED CEILINGS

(37)   ROOF OPENINGS

(4-)   FINISHES ASSEMBLIES

(40)   SITE FINISHES ⨍

(41)   EXTERNAL WALL FINISHES

(42)   INTERNAL WALL FINISHES

(43)   FLOOR FINISHES

(44)   STAIR FINISHES

(45)   CEILING FINISHES

(47)   ROOF FINISHES

(5-)   SERVICES ASSEMBLIES
        (mainly piped and ducted)

(50)   SITE SERVICES ⨍
        eg:
        Drainage and other piped services below ground

(51)   REFUSE DISPOSAL

* Performance specification.

⨍ Clauses for site finishes should be written at this point but may then be coded (90.4) and filed at (90.4) if preferred.

⨍ Clauses for site services should be written at this point but may then be coded (90.5) and filed at (90.5) if preferred.

(52)   DRAINAGE

(53)   WATER

(54)   GAS, COMPRESSED AIR ETC

(55)   REFRIGERATION

(56)   SPACE HEATING

(57)   VENTILATION & AIR CONDITIONING

(6-)   INSTALLATIONS ASSEMBLIES
        (electrical and mechanical)

(60)   SITE INSTALLATIONS *

(61)   ELECTRICAL CENTRE

(62)   POWER

(63)   LIGHTING

(64)   COMMUNICATIONS

(66)   TRANSPORT

(68)   SECURITY

(7-)   FIXTURES ASSEMBLIES

(70)   SITE FIXTURES **

(71)   CIRCULATION FIXTURES

(72)   GENERAL ROOM FIXTURES
        (other than fixtures classified (73) to (76)

(73)   CULINARY FIXTURES

(74)   SANITARY FIXTURES

(75)   CLEANING FIXTURES

(76)   STORAGE FIXTURES

(8-)   LOOSE EQUIPMENT

(80)   SITE LOOSE EQUIPMENT ⧢

(81)   CIRCULATION LOOSE EQUIPMENT

(82)   GENERAL ROOM LOOSE EQUIPMENT

(83)   CULINARY LOOSE EQUIPMENT

(84)   SANITARY LOOSE EQUIPMENT

(85)   CLEANING LOOSE EQUIPMENT

(86)   STORAGE LOOSE EQUIPMENT

* Clauses for site installation should be written at this point but may then be coded (90.6) and filed at (90.6) if preferred.

** Clauses for site fixtures should be written at this point but may then be coded (90.7) and filed at (90.7) if preferred.

⧢ Clauses for site loose equipment should be written at this point but may then be coded (90.8) and filed at (90.8) if preferred.

That is, that the specification writer should begin at the beginning of the specification outline and work through to the end, *taking care that the wording of all clauses avoids reference to subjects not yet reached.*

For example, no clause coded A should include reference to subjects identified by B or later codes; within A, clauses coded Aa2 should not include specific references to any of the matters listed at Aa3.

This is not always an easy rule to follow. The word *wall* for instance, may creep into clauses describing brickwork at F, but should not be allowed to do so, because wall comes later in the outline at (21) and (22). Similarly, *slab* or *horizontal slab* can be used in clauses describing in-situ concrete assemblies at E q4, but *floor slab* cannot, because floor is an element with its own codes later in the outline, at (13) and (23). The Table 1 part of the specification will consist of clauses describing items for which only Table 1 names can be used, such as *window*; or performance requirements for these items.

The process of classification can be shown as below

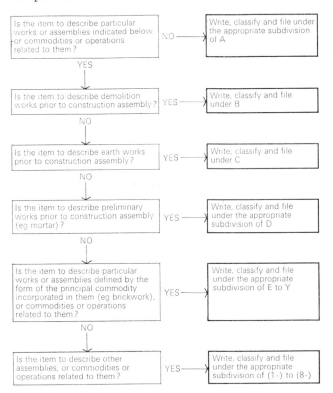

The effect of the above rule will be that clauses which include reference to several subjects in the specification outline will be given the code for whichever subject comes *last.* A clause about quality control *and* networks would be coded Aa7, not Aa5.

Examples: A number of sections in the preceding outline have had actual clauses included under them to show how the specification can be arranged in detail. These clauses, at Dp1, Dq4, F, (21) and (31) were taken from an existing office specification and the rearrangement took about an hour. Taking them in the order in which they were dealt with:

●Dp1 natural aggregates*:
The order in which subjects are listed in the outline, and thus are written about in the specification, reflects the order in which commodities are brought together in the building

*i.e: Preliminary work with natural aggregates.

process to form more and more complex materials, products, components, assemblies, elements, etc.

Natural aggregates are among the most simple, 'uncombined' materials to be specified, and will therefore be one of the first subjects to be tackled. The first point to note about the way the clauses are arranged is that all the clauses at Dp1 (a code with three symbols) may apply to both the clauses Dp1.1 and Dp1.2 (codes with four symbols). This keeps repetition of clauses or parts of clauses to a minimum. Second, the clauses for quality control and storage, although not actually coded, follow the order in which these subjects are given at A. General clauses for quality control (at Aa7) precede general clauses for storage aids (at Ab1) so quality control of natural aggregate precedes storage of natural aggregate.

The codes Dp1.1 and Dp1.2 are the item-type codes which will appear on project drawings (as appropriate) and will link them to the specification clauses in the project specification.

These item-type codes are distinguished from others in the specification library and the project specification by having an identification code after a point. In examples shown previously in the manual this 'point number', which may be of any type and length that seems suitable to the office, has been shown as '01' rather than—as here—simply '1' or '2'. Either method of coding may be used. Therefore it is essential to set up identification codes which will permit organized expansion of the office specification library and will distinguish clearly between one item and another.

Lastly, and most important, it should be noted that a clause such as 'Dp1.2 sand' will be taken to incorporate more general but possibly relevant information under previous codes with fewer symbols, ie to incorporate:
1 whatever is written at D preliminary (unfixed) work, basic and formless materials
2 whatever is written at Dp preliminary work loose fill, aggregates
3 whatever is written at Dp1 preliminary work, natural aggregates

But *not* to incorporate whatever is written at Dp1.1 or Dp1.3 or Dp1.4, etc.

●Dq4 mortars*
As in the case of natural aggregates the clause at Dq4 may apply to each of the three item-type codes for various types of mortar. Details of each type are given against its own item-type code and heading, eg 'Dq4.1 cement mortar', and the description is shortened in each case by the use of cross-references consisting of the appropriate item-type codes and headings for sand, cement, etc. It is important to identify all the variants by using different codes.

●Fg2 clay bricks†:
The general arrangement of clauses is the same as in the two previous examples. Any clause which applies to brick and block assemblies as a whole, whether they are of concrete blocks or clay bricks should be included at F to avoid the need for repeating it for Ff2, Fg2, etc. Similarly, clauses at Fg2 should generally apply to the clauses given item type codes at Fg2.1 onwards. But note that Fg2 includes special clauses for facework. These clauses will clearly not be taken to apply to the item type code and heading 'Fg2.2 common

*ie: Preliminary work with mortar
†ie: Brick and block assemblies of clay bricks (= brickwork)

bricks (not used for facework) in Dq4.1 mortar'. All the clauses about facework could have been included under Fg2.1 but might then have to be repeated under other item type codes, such as Fg2.4. There are four other points to be noted about this section. The first is that the clauses under Ff2 and Fg2 include specification for commodities which make up assemblies as well as for the assemblies themselves. In the case of assemblies of concrete blocks these material clauses cover blocks and accessories (ties). The requirement that blocks comply with BS2028 could equally well be given against the item-type code at Ff2.1, but might then need to be repeated against all the item-type codes if the clauses under them are for blocks complying with BS2028. There is no reason why descriptions of commodities should not be included against the three-digit codes but they should be given last, after all the clauses describing the assembly as a whole. The ties are included here since they are relevant to blockwork and briekwork and to no other kind of assembly. They are also listed in their own positions in the sequence, at Xt7.

Second, it will be seen that Fg2 makes reference to Dq4.1 which makes reference to Dp1.2. It is by means of this chain of cross references that the specifier is enabled to prepare thorough descriptions while being saved much unnecessary duplication of effort, and the user is taken quickly to the clauses he wants to find.

Third, this example highlights the need to use the first digit of the identification code as a classifier*, particularly in the specification library. The item type codes shown here for brickwork of common bricks are Fg2.2 and Fg2.3. If new codes are always added to the end, item-type codes for brickwork of common bricks, as distinct from brickwork of facings or engineering bricks, may occur at, say, Fg2.7, Fg2.15, Fg2.17, Fg2.35, etc, and it will become time consuming and difficult to find clauses relevant to brickwork of a particular type of brick. The arrangement of the specification library will be improved if the first digit of the identification code is used to classify the *type* of brick, so that clauses under Fg2 might for example be coded decimally:

All clauses to do with common bricks coded Fg2.1 etc, eg: Fg2.10, Fg2.11, Fg2.12.

All clauses to do with facing bricks other than engineering bricks coded Fg2.3 etc, eg: Fg2.30, Fg2.31, Fg2.32.

All clauses to do with engineering bricks coded Fg2.6 etc, eg: Fg2.60, Fg2.61, Fg2.62.

Any clauses unlikely to recur on future projects (not added to library included in project specifications only) can then be coded Fg2.9 etc, eg: Fg2.90, Fg2.91, Fg2.92.

Lastly, permutations such as 'common bricks in Dq4.4 mortar' and 'common bricks in Dq4.3 mortar' should probably be kept out of the office specification library as far as possible to avoid unnecessary bulk, unless they are wanted as a record of office practice. These permutations will need to be made in project specifications and bills of quantities. They are shown in the specification outline because it is used here to illustrate the form of specification library and project specification. The illustration **47** represents the process of assembling library information–as an alternative to using an existing specification–and writing specification clauses for Fg2.

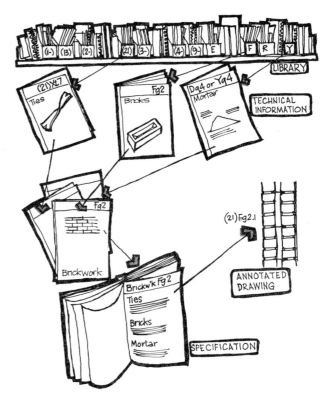

47 *Cross reference between library and specification*

●(21) External walls*
In this example the information given is entirely made up of cross references (item-type codes) for clauses which appeared in earlier sections of the specification. Together they add up to a complete specification record or index of clauses applying to external wall construction. They act as a quick finding device for a specifier who wants to see what alternative clauses are available, and they can be grouped together for this purpose according to type of external wall, using the codes in the *Construction indexing manual* (eg: (21.4) curtain walling). Notes can be added to show on what projects they have been used, so that previous experience can be consulted. Lastly, commonly occurring groups of them can be given overcodes as described in para **4.3**. Schedules of item type codes of this kind in project specifications provide qs and contractor—as well as architect—with a check index showing which specification items apply in which elements, and provide 'belt and braces' search facilities which may not, however, justify the time taken to produce them. Such schedules are referred to in para **4.3** as mini-spec schedules.

●(31) External wall openings†
In this case the information given may include descriptions for work with external door and window assemblies and components, as well as cross references such as those at (21). All special requirements which apply to work with external doors should be given as separate clauses under appropriate headings (eg: 'fixing' and 'protection'), just as in the case of preliminary work with natural aggregates and mortar, and work with bricks. Care must be taken to see that the same identification code is not given, in error, to two different clauses, one in the Table 2 part of the specification and one in the Table 1 part. There must be only *one* clause coded Xi2.2 whatever bracketed numbers

may be associated with it (a clause with this particular code will probably refer to general requirements for shop joinery using softwood). It will help to guard against accidental duplication if clauses written in full in the bracketed number half of the specification are given identification codes which look different from those in the first half. They can, for example, be given three digits instead of one, eg: Xi2.201. Also blocks of identification codes can be allocated to clauses for particular types of components, eg: Softwood units (side hung) Xi2.200 to Xi2.299. The last entry under (31) illustrates how performance specifications can be built into the sequence.

Project specifications
Compiling lists of item type codes Many decisions on specification relating to a particular project will be made before the production drawings and schedules are prepared or during their preparation and these are best recorded as a list of item-type codes for each element taken from or based on those in the office specification library. As the project develops the codes will be modified and added to where necessary, and the project specification itself will only need to be typed out in full when taking off begins. It may be possible to defer typing if the qs has a copy of the specification library and is thus able to interpret the codes.

Typing The typist will need to be provided with the library and the list of codes for the project arranged in the filing order indicated in the outline, ie with all codes without a bracketed number filing before all codes with a bracketed number, eg:

Aao.1
Aao.3
Aao.7
.
.
.
Abl.1
.
.
.
Dq4.1
Dq4.2
.
.
.
Fg2.1
.
.
.
Fg2.3
Xi2.5
(31) Xi2.12

She will then type all clauses relevant to the project. If she is given the item-type code **Fg2.1** Facing bricks, for example, she will need to type the heading and the whole of the clauses in the library at F, Fg and Fg2 (but not Ff, etc), and the whole of the clauses at Fg2.1 (but not those at Fg2.2, Fg2.3 or Fg2.4).

If the specification library codes are long, eg Xi2.211, but if only one or two clauses in the library apply on a particular project it is, as suggested earlier, possible to use special short codes in the project documents instead. In this case great care must be taken to guard against errors, and a record will need to be kept to show the connection between the codes used on the project and the library codes. It may usually be preferable to use library codes on projects.

Sortation It is possible to sort specification items by more than one facet if the content of each page of the specification (in the case of sortation carried out manually) or each item (in the case of sortation carried out by computer) is restricted to one code and heading from each facet.

For example, a manually sorted specification could be arranged by smm Work Sections at tender stage, and by ci/sfb Tables 1/2/3 for use during the running of the project if each page included information common to only one work section and one ci/sfb definition. However, it seems doubtful whether this is worthwhile because the specification is rarely the first point of reference when a search is being made for project information. All users will be able to find the correct clause quickly by means of the item type code on the drawings or in the bill of quantities. For this reason it is suggested that the specification should normally be typed as one continuous sequence of codes and headings, and should not be arranged for sortation.

Coding drawings When the item type codes for the project specification are finally settled, the drawings can be coded and annotated (see Section 4). Some codes in the specification, like (31) Xi2.211 above, will already include a Table 1 number as part of the code, and will be put on (31), (3–) or (– –) drawings as explained in Section 4.

Other codes—such as 'Fg2.2 common bricks'—will not be preceded in the specification by Table 1 number and these will need to have any relevant Table 1 numbers added to them when putting them on drawings or when coding items for elemental billing.

For example, if Fg2.2 Common bricks are used in brickwork in foundations, external walls and partitions, Fg2.2 will appear on the drawings as:

'(16)Fg2.2 common bricks' [on drawings coded (16), (1–) or (– –)]
'(21)Fg2.2 common bricks' [on drawings coded (21), (2–) or (– –)]
'(22)Fg2.2 common bricks' [on drawings coded (22), (2–) or (– –)]

It should be explained to users that a search for a clause in the project specification from an item-type code on a drawing or in the bill of quantities should always begin with the Table 2/3 code (eg Fg2), *not* the Table 1 code. The Table 1 code should be looked up if inadequate information or no information is found in the Table 2 part of the project specification.

Conclusion
The method of using item type coding set out in Sections 4, 5 – and 6 – as the link between drawings specification and bill of quantities, can be summarized briefly as follows:

In respect of each type of commodity, assembly, element, there will be
(*a*) A ci/sfb classification code accompanied by an identification code or codes
(*b*) Annotation
(*c*) A specification description, which may include cross references to other relevant descriptions
(*d*) Quantities
Of these, (*a*) and (*b*) appear on drawings, (*a*), (*b*) and (*c*) in specifications and (*a*), (*b*) and (*d*) as measured items in bills of quantities.

Section 6 Measured information

This section is concerned with the application of the principles set out in Section 2: Basic Principles (using some of the facets described in Section 3: Facets in use) to measured information.
It leads to the use, in bills of quantities, of the item type codes appearing on the drawings and in the specification, as a means of providing contractors with cross referenced information. It assumes knowledge of the methods of organising specification information set out in the last section, and availability of CI/SfB arranged drawings and specification.
Examples of typical documents are given in Part II of this manual.

6.1 Introduction

6.2 Bills of quantities structuring and coding

6.1 Introduction

Whereas many of the applications of CI/sfB methods described in the manual are within the normal professional competence of most architects, the manipulation of measured information is not usually undertaken by them. For this reason, this section makes no pretence to being a manual of quantity surveying methods and it is assumed that sympathetic quantity surveyors will develop their own techniques for using the system. The section aims:

1 To give enough general background information on the arrangement of measured information to enable architects to discuss the subject with their quantity surveying colleagues in relation to other applications of the system.
2 To acquaint qss with the methods adopted so far by qss using CI/sfB. Manual methods at present appear to offer significant advantages over computer methods (described in the next section) for many projects.

Function of measured information

Bills of quantities or quantities in other forms (eg on drawings) provide full descriptions of works and of the quantities of resources, both labour and material, required to enable work to be carried out.

Their prime function is to enable work to be priced, but they have potentially a much wider range of uses, which were identified by a committee of the Royal Institution of Chartered Surveyors in 1966 as:

(*a*) cost planning
(*b*) tender evaluation
(*c*) financial forecasts and control
(*d*) standard pricing
(*e*) materials ordering
(*f*) labour and plant allocation
(*g*) bonusing
(*h*) network analysis
(*i*) construction analysis

Bill production

The traditional processes for producing bills of quantities manually are generally as follows, although there are some regional variations (in Scotland and Northern England, for example, quantities are normally taken off by trades, although this practice may be changing now).

Taking off Quantities are 'taken off' by direct measurement from the drawings. The dimensions are recorded at this stage on dimension or 'dim' sheets, together with an abbreviated description.

If the London method is used the order of taking off is commonly by a series of basic 'elements'—eg foundations, structure, finishings, windows, doors, services and so on.

These are similar to CI/sfB Table 1 Elements. They are said, by qss with experience of taking off from Table 1 structured drawings, to be convenient for this purpose.

This procedure does not follow a trade or SMM work section sequence. Brickwork, for example, is measured over all openings in the basic elements listed above. Adjustments for openings are taken in the element which generates them: for example, when a door is measured a corresponding deduction is made for the quantity of wall it displaces.

Abstracting This is the 'shuffle' in 'cut and shuffle', and can be made easier by CI/sfB coding. Similar items within the separate elements—both original items and those created by the process of adjustment—are brought together and processed to give the final quantities for each description (ie for each unit of the finished bill of quantities). In the case of bills of quantities arranged according to CI/sfB each Table 2/3 heading within a Table 1 heading will normally define a unit of the finished bill of quantities (see Section 5).

Billing The total quantities are typed with full descriptions in the accepted sequence to form the finished bill of quantities.

It is necessary, before starting the taking off, to decide on the bill arrangements or types likely to be required. The manner in which the information is processed at the taking off and abstracting stages determines the layout and form of the bill. The stage requiring most expertise is the taking off. It sets the pattern for all subsequent stages and contains almost all information necessary for their execution, thereby making abstracting and billing little more than mechanical processes.

Types of bill

A summary of bill types at present in use is broadly as follows:

Work section This is the traditional bill of quantities (see **48**), the principle of division being the work section, such as Excavation, Concrete work, etc. This is basically a trade division. SMM work section arrangement is widely used at present for tendering. It is based on the Standard Method of Measurement*, agreed jointly by the Royal Institution of Chartered Surveyors and the National Federation of Building Trades Employers. This type of bill can be further

---

* SMM's primary purpose is to provide a series of rules as a basis for the consistent measurement of building works, not to provide a standard format for bills of quantities

```
SECTION : CARPENTRY                    £  s  d

STRUCTURAL TIMBERS

SOFTWOOD VACUUM PRESSURE IM-
PREGNATED WITH 'TANALITH C'

SOLE PLATES ( 1½" x 4" )       10 Cu.ft.


LABOURS AND SUNDRIES

IN SOFTWOOD

WROUGHT FACES                 160 Sq.ft.

SINKINGS FOR BOLT HEADS OR NUTS  90   NO

HOLES FOR ¼" DIAMETER BOLTS
THROUGH 1½"                      90   NO
```

48 *Work section order* (SMM) *bill page*

```
                              MANUFACTURED GOODS

                          Unit - Rate - Labour - Materials
JOINTERS SHOP                              £  s  d   £  s  d
404 DOOR FRAMES (Operation No.12)

Wrought softwood frames (see
drawing No. 14).

  Frame type II to suit door   )
  size 2'0"x6'6" in 2"x3¼"      ) 18 No.      - - -
  with ½"x1" splayed top        )
    (Door No.9)                 )

  Ditto as last but door size   )
  2'6"x6'6"                      ) 54 No.      - - -
    (Doors No.4,5 & 6)          )

  Ditto do but door size        )
  2'9"x6'6"                      ) 18 No.      - - -
    (Door No.3)                 )

  Frame type 1, 8'-0" high over )
  -all,to suit door size        )
  2'6"x6'6" with fanlight over  ) 18 No.      - - -
  in 2"x3¼" with ½"x1" splayed  )
  top.                          )
    (Door No.7)                 )
```

49 *Operational bill page*

divided into elements or parts, eg outer walls in super-structure, inner walls in superstructure.

Elemental bill This is divided primarily by elements or parts such as walls, floors, roofs and so on. The division within each individual element is usually by work section, but sometimes by sub-element. This arrangement is claimed to be helpful to contractor and architect in post-tender work. Breaking the bill down into recognisable building parts makes it easier to relate the quantities in it to the actual parts of the building. The arrangement is useful for interim valuations and for cost analysis of tenders. The elemental bill has been found to relate fairly well to the contractor's breakdown of the work into 'workpieces' on site.

The Operational approach* is reflected in the following two types of bill, in which attention is focused on production for feedback of costs, and pre-tender and post-tender management. Each type requires a substantially complete set of drawings and each attempts to give more information than conventional bills. Both types include reference to location as a secondary facet.

Bill of quantities (operational format): This type of bill (introduced originally as the activity bill) seeks to present the erection of the building in operational terms, as dictated by the design, without considering constraints imposed by the contractor's organisation. It uses this as the main principle of division. A precedence diagram is first drawn up which shows the relationship of site activities in the erection of the building and their relationship to factory-made components. Quantities are then allocated to each activity shown. This bill uses the SMM as far as possible within activities, and items are of finished work including both labour and materials, thus following conventional methods.

Supporters of this type of bill claim that it gives a clearer picture of the building in terms of the contractor's resources and that it is a good management tool at post-tender stage. Varieties of this bill have been developed as transitional documents only, forming stepping stones to the truly operational bill.

Operational bill: This follows a similar arrangement to the activity bill but does not use the standard methods of measuring building and civil engineering works. Materials are expressed in dimensions suitable for ordering direct from the bill, and are not collated into total quantities as in the trade bill. Joists, for example, would be given as 6 No 7in × 2in × 11ft long and not 6 c.f. **49** gives an example of an operational bill item, showing material measured separately from labour. This bill, in which labour is priced on a duration basis, aims at more realistic estimating methods by consideration of the production process, and interdependence of gangs of men.

Location bill This is divided primarily according to the location of the work in the building. The latter is first analysed by location areas, and as quantities are taken off they are allocated to their appropriate location.

Measurement may be by the standard methods, but present developments tend to use variations which call for a more detailed subdivision of labour and materials. Within locations, quantities may be subdivided into 'units of work' (assemblies) sometimes called features or sub-elements. These units of work can be abstracted from the

* See BRS Digest 97 (second series), CI/SfB (A4)

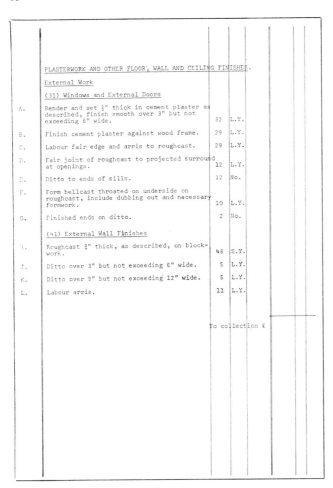

50 *Work section order* (SMM) *bill page with Table 1 codes added*

51 *Bq arranged primarily by* CI/SfB *Table 1, incorporating Table 2/3 item type codes for cross reference to specification and drawings. Note that this example uses codes* Yq4, Yt4 *rather than* Dq4, Dt4 *in order to link with library information. Gleeds, chartered quantity surveyors, Newcastle upon Tyne*

bill and used to build up activities in a planning network or sequence diagram.

Introducing CI/SfB *based methods*

CI/SfB can be introduced in one move, or gradually to other types of bill. For example:

1 Table 1 codes can be added to a bill of quantities which is otherwise arranged in SMM or some other order. Some bill items may need division. The result will be a fixed arrangement bill if produced manually. Typing will be continuous and it will be impossible to sort pages into a different order.

In this case (31) in the bill will tell the user that the information referred to in the bill description may be shown on a drawing or drawings coded (31), (3–) or (– –). See **50**. There will be no cross reference from drawings to bill.

2 An elemental bill of quantities can be produced arranged primarily using CI/sfB Table 1. This will have the advantages and disadvantages of other elemental bills—with the important difference that the content of bill section (31) will identify with drawings and schedules series (31), (3–), (– –). Code (31) will provide a broad cross reference. Again, this will be a fixed arrangement bill. See **51**.

3 The bill can be arranged according to CI/sfB Table 1 and Table 2/3 headings to provide direct and precise cross

reference to and from the specification, drawings and schedules, as described below.

6.2 Bills of quantities structuring and coding

Search pattern and cross referencing

The essential features which distinguish bills of quantities using CI/sfB Table 1, Table 2 and Table 3 codes are that they are arranged (like a library) using a classification system for easy retrieval, and that they can be linked by similar arrangement or by coding—or both—to all other project information. The importance of adequate cross referencing was recognised in the BRS/MPBW *Study of coding and data co-ordination for the construction industry* (see para 2.1), and its usefulness on site has been noted by many contractors. Methods of cross reference using item type coding have already been described in Section 4 and Section 5.

CI/sfB codes can be incorporated in any of the bills above, as already explained, but much of the ease and value of cross referencing will be lost unless the items in the bill are arranged in the linear sequence provided by the codes, so that they can be found quickly and easily from the item type codes given on drawings and schedules. For example, full measured information on work with softwood sections used in staircases will be found quickly in the bill from the code (24) Hi2 on the drawings only if the bill is arranged

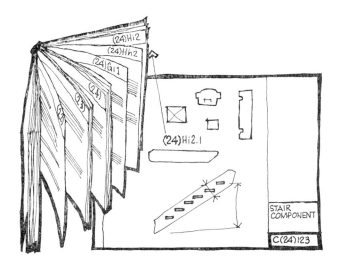

52 *Bq arranged primarily by Table 1, showing cross reference between bill and drawings*

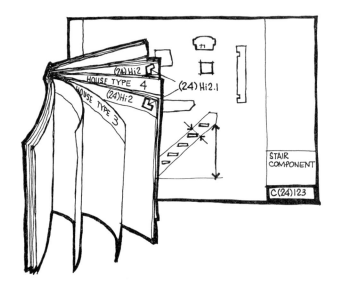

53 *Bq arranged primarily by house types (ie functional division), showing cross reference between bill and drawings*

so that items coded (24) follow those coded (23); and/or items coded H follow items coded G; see **52**.

Consistent use of the linear sequence from one project to another will ensure that the codes soon mean something to the user, to whom they serve as a quick finding device. This use of the linear sequence does not mean that the rules for measurement are affected, or that labour and materials must be or must not be shown separately.

Neither does it mean that the Fletcher Moore standard phraseology cannot be used for the detailed arrangement of bills of quantities (see below).

Facets in use

Process type (see Section 3, para 3.1) Bills of quantities, however arranged, describe work with components, products and materials in different locations. Commodity information may take the form of a schedule of components, products and materials at the back of the bill. Or, in

operational bills, a 'production bill' will be included for work which may be done off site.

Project division (see Section 3, para 3.2) Most bills of quantities are divided into separate sections for external works and building works in any case. The works may be further separated into bills for individual blocks. Project division cannot be said to affect the order between individual items unless individual zones or rooms are identified and coded, or co-ordinate references are given for each description.

CI/sfB *Table* 1 (see Section 3, para 3.3 and Section 4, para 4.23) Table 1 in conjunction with Project division will almost inevitably be one of the facets used for bills of quantities using CI/sfB (see **54**).

Bills of quantities arranged primarily according to Table 1 are particularly useful for production control on site where supported by Table 1—arranged specification and drawings. Some contractors' estimators also appear satisfied with them for pricing.

CI/sfB *Table* 2/3 (see Section 3, para 3.4) Bills of quantities have also been arranged primarily by Table 2/3, to bring together (for example) all work with E (cast in-situ) concrete; no matter which element it may be in. But the main use of Table 2/3 is to provide cross reference between bills of quantities, specification and drawings. See **55**.

SMM Useful for tendering purposes.

Item	FLOOR FINISHES: INTERNAL WROT SOFTWOOD			Qty.	Unit	Rate	£	s	d
	Block 1	Block 2	Block 3				(43)Hi2.02		
1	⅞" Tongued and grooved boarding.		308	308	S.F.				
2	Raking cutting.		4	4	L.F.				
3	⅞" x 4" Skirting. 126	161	436	723	L.F.				
4	Extra short length. 2	2	4	8	No.				
5	Protection								
	Allow for protecting the work in this section.					Item			
	TOTAL TO COLLECTION						£		
	T:13:01								

54 *Bq arranged primarily by Table 1, subdivided by Project division. Turner & Townsend, chartered quantity surveyors, Durham*

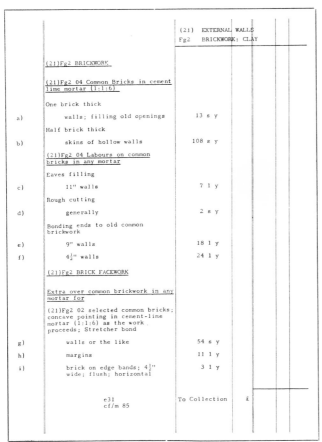

		(21) EXTERNAL WALLS Fg2 BRICKWORK: CLAY			
	(21)Fg2 BRICKWORK				
	(21)Fg2 04 Common Bricks in cement lime mortar (1:1:6)				
	One brick thick				
a)	walls; filling old openings	13 s y			
	Half brick thick				
b)	skins of hollow walls	108 s y			
	(21)Fg2 04 Labours on common bricks in any mortar				
	Eaves filling				
c)	11" walls	7 1 y			
	Rough cutting				
d)	generally	2 s y			
	Bonding ends to old common brickwork				
e)	9" walls	18 1 y			
f)	4½" walls	24 1 y			
	(21)Fg2 BRICK FACEWORK				
	Extra over common brickwork in any mortar for				
	(21)Fg2 02 selected common bricks; concave pointing in cement-lime mortar (1:1:6) as the work proceeds; Stretcher bond				
g)	walls or the like	54 s y			
h)	margins	11 1 y			
i)	brick on edge bands; 4½" wide; flush; horizontal	3 1 y			
	e31 cf/m 85	To Collection £			

55 *A page from bq coded by* CI/SfB *Tables 1 and 2/3. The Fletcher Moore Standard Phraseology for bills of quantities was used for the detailed arrangement of measured items. Manual sorting from Table 2/3 or* SMM *order to Table 1 order for cost analysis of tender took about three hours. Roger Thorpe & Associates, chartered architects, Sheffield*

Sortations

The need for sortations to suit different users at different times and thus to provide different 'ways in' to project information has already been discussed. Bills of quantities can be sorted rather more easily than drawings, but unless computers are used it will be possible to sort a particular bill by any facet only so long as each bill page contains no more than one class from that facet. In practice, it is doubtful whether the bill of quantities for a project can reasonably be sorted manually by more than two

sortations in detail (but see below). This is not because of the work involved in sorting but because the amount of information on each individual page, if more than two sortations are required, may become very small and the number of pages very large and inconvenient to handle.

Paper is not expensive and the amount of typing involved if several sortations are required is not significantly greater than for a fixed arrangement bill, except that a separate set of collection pages will be required for each sortation which requires pricing. On the other hand, printing costs based on the number of plates or stencils will increase.

The example bill page **55** illustrates the principle of limiting information on each page so that pages can be sorted in varying ways, like a pack of cards. In this particular case the limitation is that each page includes information about only one process type (Assembly, not coded); one project division (Block, not coded); one Table 1 element (External walls, coded (21)); and one Table 2/3 construction form (Clay brickwork, coded Fg2).

The bill pages can be sorted in detail in three ways. Either all pages on external walls coded (21) can be brought together and sub-arranged by Table 2/3, or all pages on brickwork coded Fg2 can be brought together and sub-arranged by Table 1. Also, any page that is a common denominator of one Table 1 class and one Table 2/3 class can normally be allocated to an appropriate work section of the SMM, and will not overlap with another work section.

It follows from this that pages defined by both Table 1 and Table 2/3 can normally, without any further subdivision of items on to separate pages, be collated into SMM *work section order as well, for pricing purposes. This additional sortation is a very important bonus given by use of* CI/SfB, *since it provides a link with present procedures for obtaining quotations.*

To avoid errors in collating and ensure that sortations are complete a sequential page number can be included for each sortation on each page, using codes as shown in **55** or eg 1 for Table 1; 2 for Table 2/3; 3 for SMM (if an SMM sortation is required).

SMM work section codes need not be put on individual pages, since they may cause confusion on site during later stages when the bill is available in CI/SfB sortations. If they are included, merely to help the collation of pages, they should be kept well away from the SfB code. The pages can be

56 *Bq pages coded by Table 1, Table 2/3 and collated by* SMM, *subarranged by Table 2/3, then by Table 1*

collated behind work section dividers for the SMM sortation, as shown in **56**.

A typical arrangement for bills arranged by Table 1 might be:

Contents of Bill 1	Contents of Bill 2
Specification items: Prelims and preambles	External works
Measured items: Building works	(10)
(10)	.
.	.
.	.
.	.
.	.
.	(30)
(86)	

†Excavations and work in connection with services which straddles 'Building works' and 'External works' can be split or included in a 'General works' section of measured items, coming before Building works. Alternatively, 'External works' can be taken to include site works under the building.
*Some offices may prefer to use (90.1) instead of (10),(90.2) instead of (20) etc.

Item.	INTERNAL WALL FINISHES: TWO COAT BELLROCK PLASTER WORK.						(42)Pr2.01			
	Block 1	Block 2	Block 3	C.A.	Qty.	Unit	Rate	£	s	d
1	¾" Thick on block walls.									
	311	21	142		474	S.Y.				
2	Ditto, exceeding 3" not exceeding 6" wide.									
	124	7	56		187	L.Y.				
3	¾" Thick on concrete column exceeding 6" not exceeding 9" wide.									
	51	-	34		85	L.Y.				
4	Fair joint to flush fair edge of tiles.									
	-	-	12		12	L.Y.				
5	Ditto, to flush or projecting surround to openings.									
	78	3	54		135	L.Y.				
6	Make good wall plaster around small pipe.									
	8	2	5	(53)	15	No.				.
7	Ditto, large pipe.									
	-	-	4	(52)	4	No.				
8	Ditto, extract fan, size 10½" diameter.									
	-	2	-	(57)	2	No.				
9	Ditto, metal grille, size 12" x 9".									
	3	1	2	(56)	6	No.				
	Protection									
10	Allow for protecting the work in this section.						Item			
	TOTAL TO COLLECTION						£			
	T:13:01									

Labour only items can, where necessary, be coded in the body of the bill using Table 4 codes for preliminaries, eg: Brick and blockwork: protection Fd1, or Brickwork, clay bricks: protection Fg2(d1).

Use of Table 1 sortations for cost analysis Priced bills of quantities coded by Table 1 (either in Table 1 or SMM sortation) can be used to help provide CI/SfB elemental cost analyses. Prime cost items should be coded by Table 1 and included with the appropriate sections of the bill; and Table 1 sortation collection sheets will need to be prepared. The page totals priced by the contractor can then be copied on to the collections and general summary of the Table 1 sortation.

Building work items such as making good wall finish around services each relate to two headings and two codes in Table 1. In the example shown below the code for wall finishes will be used on schedules and in the bill (see Section 2 para 2.2) rather than the codes for services ((52), (53), (56), (57)). But for cost analysis purposes the extra cost of these items is normally regarded as part of the cost of particular services. This can be made clear in the coding of the measured item in the bill by using a separate CA (cost analysis) column for 'office use only'; see **57**. Alternatively, these codes may be shown on taking off sheets only.

Conclusion

Bills of quantities arranged using CI/SfB can provide cross reference to and from the drawings and specification, and will have a search pattern which will lead users quickly to the information they want. The arrangement of measured items will largely coincide with contractors' work packages.

The rules of the Standard Method of Measurement can be applied and the Fletcher Moore Standard Phraseology for Bills of Quantities can be used for bill production. Labour and materials can be shown separately, or in combination.

57 *For cost analysis purposes, the prices shown for items 6, 7, 8 and 9 will be allocated as follows:*
Item 6 to (53) *water supply*
Item 7 to (52) *drainage*
Item 8 to (57) *ventilation*
Item 9 to (56) *space heating*
Turner & Townsend, chartered quantity surveyors, Durham

Section 7: Computer methods

This section briefly describes the use of the computer for data co-ordination. Understanding of it is not necessary to use of the manual as a whole. As an example of the way that SfB can be used with computers, detailed reference is made to the application of SfB known as CBC (Co-ordinated Building Communications).

7.1 Introduction
7.2 CBC system
7.3 CBC applications

7.1 Introduction

Little or no reference is made elsewhere in this manual to computer processing, and practical experience of using CI/SfB-based methods of data co-ordination in offices shows that the system can be used to integrate information to a large extent *without* using the computer.

There is no doubt, however, that computers can provide an effective and economical means of supplying information and improving project co-ordination and management, and the purpose of this Section is to give some guidance on ways in which they may be applied. It should be read *after*— not before—Sections 1 to 6.

Function of computers

Computers store, calculate, sort and retrieve information. The storage and retrieval functions are a necessary adjunct of the other two functions and may not directly affect most people who use project information because the man on site —the eventual user of drawings, specifications and bills of quantities—is unlikely, at least in the foreseeable future, to have a terminal giving him direct access to the information held in the machine. He will continue to need to be supplied with information written or printed, manually or by computer, on pieces of paper.

The ability of the computer to sort information is probably far more significant in building communications than the speed at which it can make calculations, although once information has been converted into a form which can be accepted by the machine, it usually makes good economic sense for it to do whatever calculations may be needed at the same time as sorting information.

Computers using graphic display terminals (cathode ray tube and 'light pen') or other special devices can manipulate drawn as well as written information, but the capital and operating cost of these machines seems likely to keep them out of reach of all but the largest organisations in the foreseeable future.

High-speed sorting of information by computer makes it technically possible for the architect, quantity surveyor or contractor each to obtain schedules or bills of quantities arranged in the order which is most useful to him at each stage of the job, provided that the required arrangements were all foreseen so that the information was appropriately coded and processed before being fed into the machine. This suggests that much of the old controversy about the rival merits of sortations for elemental, trade or operational purposes is—or should eventually become—unnecessary, because each sortation can be provided when required.

Despite these advantages, the advance of computers in the construction industry has so far been slow. This is partly because most organisations in the industry are relatively small units with little time, money or enthusiasm available for making experimental use of new methods or machines; partly because of lack of expertise in arranging information manually, let alone in forms suitable for computer processing; partly because there is no recognised and established industry-wide data co-ordination system; and most of all because the organisation which benefits most from computer operation is often not the organisation which bears the cost of producing information. If architects pay to use computers to produce extensive schedules of materials, components and fittings, qss and contractors benefit; and if qss make it possible to produce various sortations of bills of quantities, contractors benefit most. Except where contracts are negotiated it is difficult or impossible for architects and qss to ensure that they will be repaid the cost of producing information in a form suitable for manipulation by computer.

It follows that the organisations most able to take advantage of computers are at present large contracting firms with their own design divisions, dealing directly with clients, or large client organisations such as local authorities which are able to use computers for many other purposes as well.

The only way open to relatively small design and quantity surveying offices wanting to use computers (in order to provide their clients with a better professional service) is to make use of ready-prepared computer programs* and ready-prepared computer equipment through computer bureaux and data processing agencies of various kinds. Design organisations using data co-ordination can find their way to use of computers in this way if they are prepared to extend rather than restrict their direct responsibilities, particularly if they find—as organisations using sfb-based methods have found—that development work in this general direction can be financed at each stage from the savings made possible at previous stages by the use of data co-ordination.

CI/SfB *and computers*

CI/SfB can be used with computers. The codes and many of the techniques described in this manual provide an effective way in to computer operation, and there is no doubt that offices having a good working knowledge of CI/SfB-based methods will find the eventual introduction of computers far less risky or onerous than will offices without any grounding in data co-ordination.

CI/SfB is already in use with computers for various purposes, but the most comprehensive suite of computer programs so far available using sfb coding is that developed by the Danish-based organisation CBC Ltd, which has grown from an office of three people (two architects and one computer specialist) in Copenhagen in 1964, into a large organisation with its own computer and offices in several countries.

*Instructions to the computer on how to manipulate data for various purposes

The following section describes CBC coding methods and their application in some detail, simply as an example of how SfB may be used with computers; it is based largely on information supplied by courtesy of CBC[1], and the *Architects' Journal*[2]. The codes used are nearly identical with CI/SfB codes.

7.2 CBC System†

CBC is an integrated project management system for building and civil engineering works, and the computer programs that have been developed make provision for co-ordinated communication between the parties within the building team. The system was developed in Denmark, and since 1963 it has been used for the management of projects of many kinds: housing, schools, hospitals, office buildings, shopping centres etc.

CBC has been used for the following purposes:

● Organisation of the building team for co-ordinated communication at all stages of planning and production

● Preparation of the brief, and organisation of the design process, by means of coded identification and electronic data processing of design decisions

● Preparation of estimates and cost plans in different sortations by means of computers

● Organisation of resource* catalogues by means of computers for the preparation of specifications without quantities

● Organisation of drawings, coding of drawn information, and preparation of drawing lists by means of computers

● Preparation of bills of quantities by computer for all trades in a number of formats and sortations, including operational and activity bills††

● Pricing of bills of quantities in a number of sortations

● Preparation of cost analyses, cost statistics and so on by computer on the basis of priced bills of quantities

● Preparation of production documents such as purchase lists, room specifications, activity valuation lists and so on by means of computers

● Preparation of progress charts (such as networks, line of balance charts and so on) with integration between activities and items in the bill of quantities. Computer print-outs of activity lists, follow-up schedules and so on

● Cost control at all stages of planning and production by means of computer-programmed accounting systems. If necessary, integration with progress charts can be provided.

● Preparation of final accounts, cost statistics etc on the basis of actual costs.

1 Introduction to the CBC system, second edition, CBC publication No 18, 1969

2 CBC Progress: the full use of CBC, with computers, *Architects' Journal Information Library*, 7.2.68

* See glossary appendix C

† Paras 7.2 and 7.3 are by Professor Bjorn Bindslev, and some of the methods advocated, and terms used (eg 'constructions' for 'assemblies') are at variance with those in the rest of the manual.

†† See Section 6, para 6.1

Coding

CBC codes include a general code and a number of specific codes; eg:

General code   Specific codes
(21)FG2.1234   0000 00 00 00 000 000

The general code identifies each particular item, while the specific code locates each item within the project.

The *general code* is divided into a classification part and an identification part*.

                              (21) FG2   1234

Classification part ————————————┘   │
Identification part ———————————————————————┘

The classification part is based on SfB facets (Tables) 1 and 2/3 and describes the nature of the item, while the identification part (which is also called the fourth facet or the catalogue number) identifies each item within its class.

The classification part consists of three facets. One classifies resources, another classifies constructions (assemblies) and a third classifies building elements (parts), as follows:

                                        (21)   F   G2

First facet: Building elements (parts)—┘   │   │
Second facet: Constructions (assemblies)————————┘   │
Third facet: Resources——————————————————————————————————┘

The third facet classifies all *costs* relating to the project, while the first and second facets signify '*cost bearers*'.

The general code may therefore be illustrated thus:

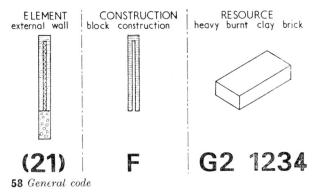

| ELEMENT external wall | CONSTRUCTION block construction | RESOURCE heavy burnt clay brick |

(21) F G2 1234

58 *General code*

The *specific codes* are very important and should be used from an early stage in the design process. The following is a typical combination:

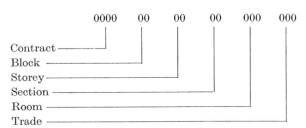

          0000 00 00 00 000 000

Contract ——┘   │   │   │   │   │
Block ——————————┘   │   │   │   │
Storey ——————————————┘   │   │   │
Section ——————————————————┘   │   │
Room ——————————————————————————┘   │
Trade ——————————————————————————————┘

Specific codes can also be used for the identification of client (where a job is financed by two or more clients), job-stage, road-section, 'feature' and so on. The codes can be extended during the job and may altogether include up to thirty-three alpha-numeric characters.

*See glossary appendix C; also Section 2, para 2.3

The faceted* construction of the coding system makes it possible for the computer to sort any list of coded items in a catalogue, specification, bill of quantities etc. The number of possible sortations on the basis of the four facets of the general code is twenty-four (ten facets would allow 3 628 800 potential sortations).

Sortations are named according to the sequence in which facets are sorted. For example, sortation 1234 consists of items sorted primarily on the first facet, secondarily on the second facet, and so on.

The codes used by CBC, being based on SfB, are almost identical with those used elsewhere in this manual. The notes which follow briefly describe them and the way they are used in conjunction with each other.

RESOURCES (THIRD FACET)†

The third facet of CBC is a list of resources, similar to, but wider in scope than CI/SfB Table 3: materials. Resources include all production factors, ie administration, plant, and labour as well as materials (commodities).

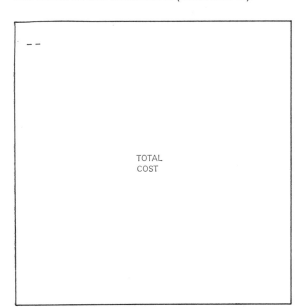

Total cost is represented in the diagram above coded '– –' (dash dash). The diagram below divides total cost between administration work and building work.

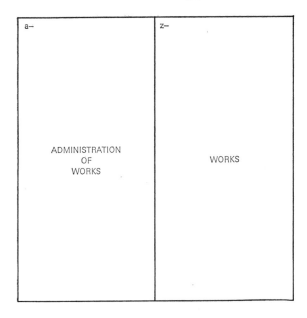

Administration costs are signified by the symbol a– or A–‡ and costs relating to building work by the symbol Z–. The latter can be divided as shown below into D– Operations and Y– Commodities.

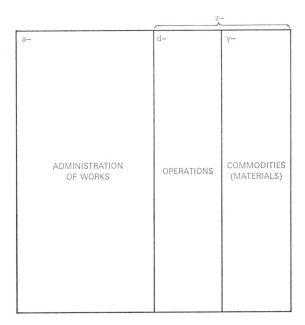

In other words, a 'work-item' is a collection of operations and commodities, considered as an entity. In a bill of quantities a work-item describes commodities and operations carried out with those commodities. Cost of operations, signified by D–, can in turn be divided as shown below, into B– Aids for labour (plant), and C– labour.

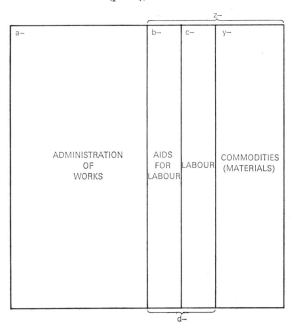

In other words, an 'operation' is a collection of plant and labour items considered as an entity. The operation 'fixing by means of a hammer' includes the tool itself and movement of the tool by means of the hand.

*See Glossary appendix C and Section 2, para 2.2

† This facet includes (in addition to a, b, c, d, y, z and –), all the classes in CI/SfB Table 3 (Materials)

‡Capital letters are used here because only capital letters are used on the computer

Finally, the total cost of commodities signified by the symbol Y– can be divided into a number of types, signified primarily by symbols E– to X– from the materials table of sfB.

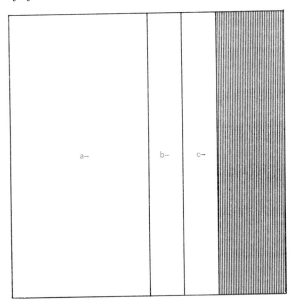

The codes described above are used to manipulate texts on magnetic tape or disc. These texts constitute the basis for the creation of combined headings in bills of quantities.

The third facet provides cost estimates grouped as follows:

Code	Resource		
a–	Administration (overheads)		£XX
b–	Plant	£XX	
c–	Labour	£XX	
d–	Operations	£XX	
y–	Commodities (materials)	£XX	
z–	Works		£XX
– –	Total		£XX

This can be shown thus:

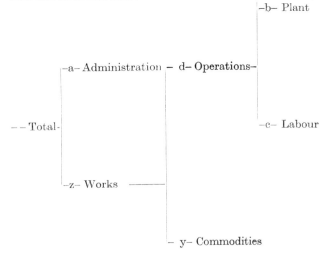

CONSTRUCTIONS* (SECOND FACET)

The second facet of the CBC system is a list of constructions similar to CI/sfB Table 2: Construction form. Constructions are collections of resources, ie sets of administration, plant, labour and commodities items, considered as entities. A 'block construction', for example, consists of resources such as blocks, labour with blocks etc.

*The equivalent CI/sfB term, used throughout this manual except in Section 7, is 'assemblies'

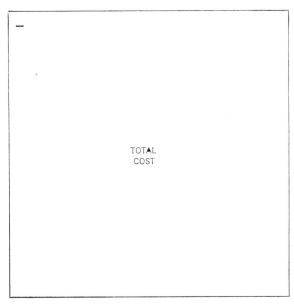

Total cost is signified in the diagram above by the summary code '–' (dash). The diagram below divides total cost between costs of production, and costs which do not belong to production, ie indirect costs.

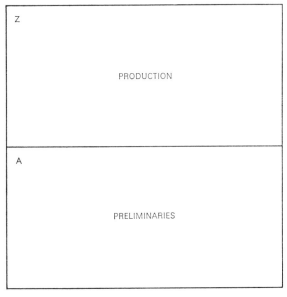

All indirect costs are denoted by the symbol A and all production costs (direct costs) by the symbol Z. Production costs can be divided into D preliminary works and Y constructions:

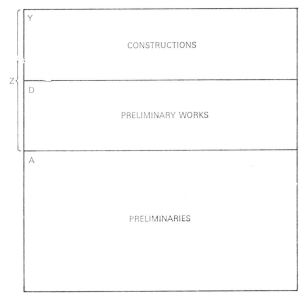

Preliminary works costs can be divided into B demolitions and C earthworks:

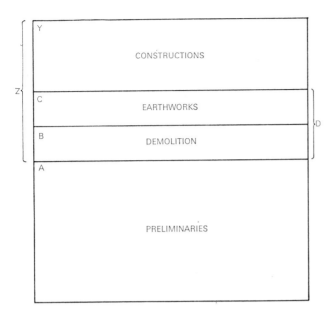

Finally, the total construction costs denoted by the symbol Y can be divided into a number of types of constructions, signified by symbols E to X from the Construction form Table of sfв.

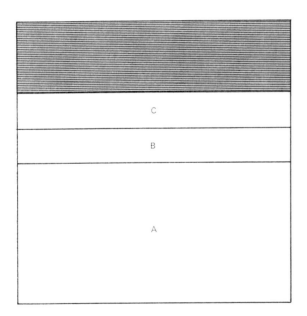

The codes described above are used to manipulate texts on magnetic tape or disc to create combined headings in bqs.

Constructions are classified on the basis of the form of the main material entering as an essential resource. For example, a 'cast in situ construction' denoted by the symbol E, is characterised by having a main material which is of fluid form when it is placed in position. Associated with this are certain 'secondary constituents', such as binders, plasticisers etc.

If block construction (ie construction work in which blocks

are dominant) is signified by the symbol 'F', from the second facet*, the total cost will be distributed as follows; using the second and third facets together:

Fa–	Block constructions: Administration		£XX
Fb–	Block constructions: Aids for labour	£XX	
Fc–	Block constructions: Labour	£XX	
Fd–	Block constructions: Operations	£XX	
Fy–	Block constructions: Materials	£XX	
Fz–	Block constructions: Works		£XX
F– –	Block constructions: Total		£XX

In this cost estimate 'F' is the 'cost bearer'.

If the construction to be coded and costed cannot be identified as one of the types represented by capital letters E to V it will be coded as follows:

Ya–	Constructions: Administration		£XX
Yb–	Constructions: Aids for labour	£XX	
Yc–	Constructions: Labour	£XX	
Yd–	Constructions: Operations	£XX	
Yy–	Constructions: Materials	£XX	
Yz–	Constructions: Works		£XX
Y– –	Constructions: Total		£XX

BUILDING ELEMENTS (FIRST FACET)

The first facet of cвc is a list of building elements (or parts), similar to cɪ/sfв Table 1. 'Building parts' are sets of Constructions (assemblies).

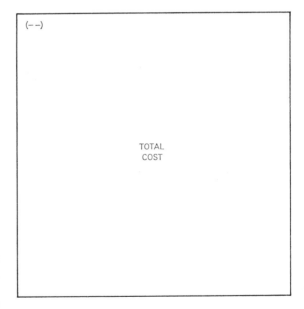

Total cost is signified in the diagram above by the summary code (– –) brackets dash dash. The next diagram divides total costs into costs that belong to building and costs that belong to site. All site costs are signified by the symbol (–0) and all building costs by the symbol (–9).

*This facet includes all the classes in cɪ/sfв Table 2 (Construction form) plus A Preliminaries, в Demolitions, c Earthworks, ᴅ Preliminary works, z Production and – Total

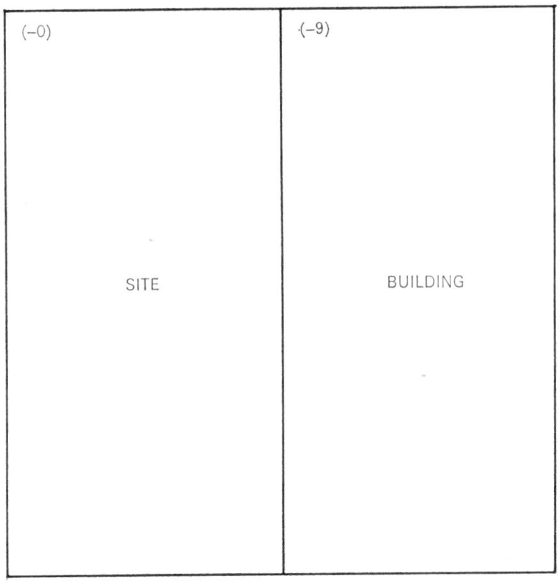

The total cost can also be divided into costs of production and general costs.

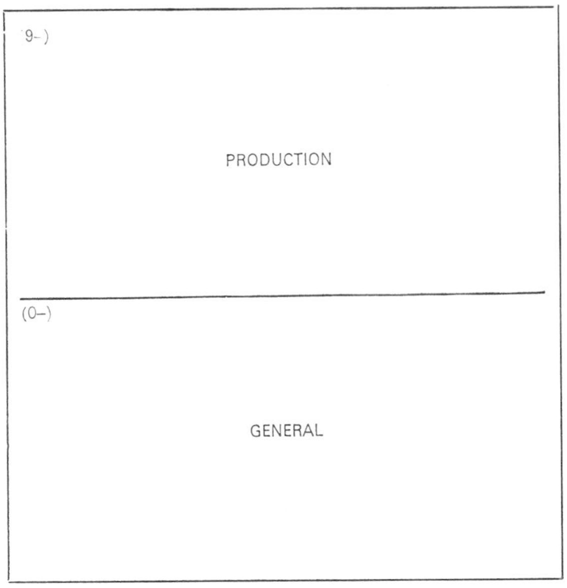

In this way all general costs (indirect costs) are signified by the symbol (0–) and all production costs (direct costs) by (9–).

Thus total costs can be divided as follows:

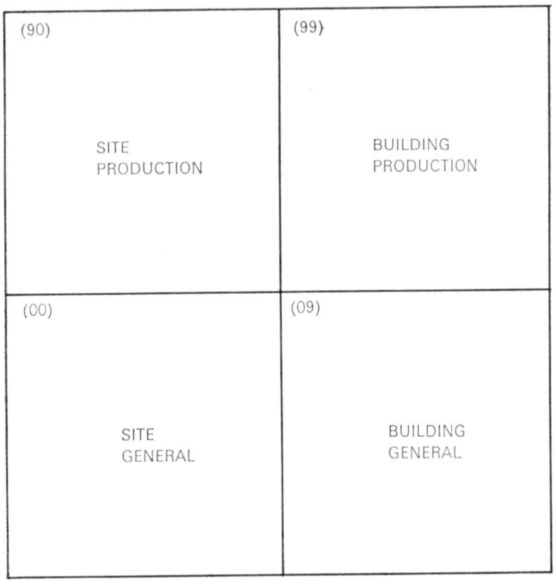

Each quarter can be further divided as follows:

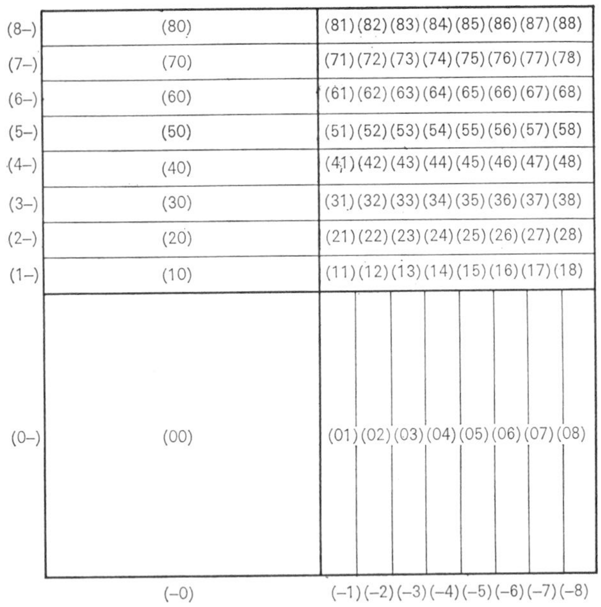

In this way total direct building costs, symbolised by (99) can be divided into 64 building parts, signified by symbols from (11) to (88).

Direct site costs, symbolised by (90), can be divided into eight site parts, signified by symbols from (10) to (80).

Total indirect building costs, symbolised by (09), are divided into eight indirect building parts from (01) to (08).

The codes described above are used to manipulate texts on magnetic taps or disk to create combined headings in bills of quantities.

If external walls are signified by the symbol (21) from the first facet,* the total cost will be distributed as follows, using the first, second and third facets together:

(21) Ya–	External walls: Constructions: Administration	£XX
(21) Yb–	External walls: Constructions: Aids for labour	£XX
(21) Yc–	External walls: Constructions: Labour	£XX
(21) Yd–	External walls: Constructions: Operations	£XX
(21) Yy–	External walls: Constructions: Materials	£XX
(21) Yz–	External walls: Constructions: Work	£XX
(21) Y– –	External walls: Constructions: Total	£XX

If these costs do not apply to any particular building part but to (say) several quite different building parts, they can be coded as follows:

*This facet includes all the classes in CI/SfB Table 1 (Elements) except (28), plus (00), (09), (0–), (90), (99), (9–) and (– –)

(99) Ya–	Building production: Constructions: Administration	£XX
(99) Yb–	Building production: Constructions: Aids for labour	£XX
(99) Yc–	Building production: Constructions: Labour	£XX
(99) Yd–	Building production: Constructions: Operations	£XX
(99) Yy–	Building production: Constructions: Materials	£XX
(99) Yz–	Building production: Constructions: Work	£XX
(99) Y– –	Building production: Constructions: Total	£XX

Specific codes

The specific codes (see the section on coding at the beginning of para 7.2) are used for the location of activities in the particular project. They divide the project into units or 'cells', to permit the preparation of time and progress schedules.

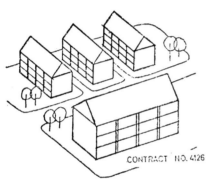

59 *Project code*

The project code is used for the identification of all activities and costs relating to a particular project. It normally consists of four digits which can be alphanumeric (or, of course, entirely numeric). An additional code may be used for the classification of *types* of projects eg housing, hospitals and so on and cɪ/sfʙ Table 0 may be used for this purpose.

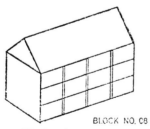

60 *Block code*

The block code is used for the identification of all activities and costs relating to individual blocks (including external works) within the project. The block code normally consists of two digits, which can be alpha-numeric.

61 *storey code*

The storey code is particularly important for network planning and is used for the location of all activities. It normally consists of two digits which can be alphanumeric.

Block codes and storey codes normally give a sufficient breakdown to permit identification of the cells in which activities should be located. In the computer print-out of activity bills sortation is normally on block and storey codes within each trade.

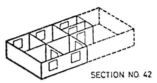

62 *Zone code*

On some projects, however, it may be necessary to divide storeys into zones and if this is the case a zone code of two or three digits is normally used. Again, the code can be alphanumeric.

63 *Room code*

It is traditional practice to number each room within the storey or section, but in cʙc the room code is used for data processing. It normally consists of three digits and is used particularly for the computer print-out of 'room specifications'.

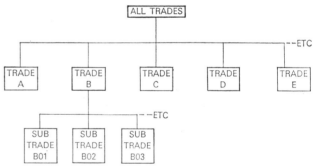

64 *Trade code*

If the project is divided into trades each trade should be identified by a code in order to locate all activities and costs associated with it. The trade code normally consists of two or three digits.

7.3 Applications

The stages in producing cʙc documentation can be described as follows:

1 In advance of all projects:
(*a*) Develop or make arrangements to use *computer programs*
(*b*) Develop or buy *catalogue(s)*
(*c*) Produce as many structured *drawings* as possible, for future re-use.

2 For a particular project:
(*a*) Produce structured drawings for the project, and reuse those already produced
(*b*) Code drawings using material schedules in the catalogue
(*c*) 'Take off' coded drawings, using labour schedules in the catalogue
(*d*) Produce *bill of quantities* on the computer.

7.31 Computer programs

The program diagram for preparation of bills of quantities shown below gives some idea of the work carried out by the computer. The names OVEOPD and so on in the boxes refer to CBC programs.

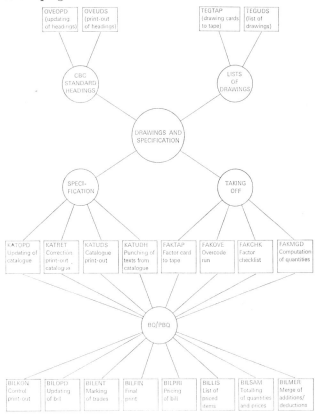

7.32 Catalogues

The catalogue, which is essential to the use of CBC, was originally developed in 1964 during the first three or four CBC projects. Since then, six different but related types of catalogues have been developed.

1 Catalogues of resources, containing eg:

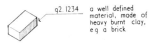

q2.1234 a well defined material, made of heavy burnt clay, eg a brick

2 Catalogues of constructions (assemblies), containing eg:

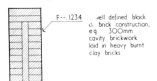

F--.1234 well defined block or brick construction, eq 300mm cavity brickwork laid in heavy burnt clay bricks

3 Catalogues of resources in relation to constructions, containing eg:

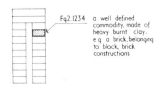

Fq2.1234 a well defined commodity, made of heavy burnt clay, eg a brick, belonging to block, brick constructions

4 Catalogues of building or site elements, containing eg:

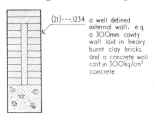

(21)---.1234 a well defined external wall, eg a 300mm cavity wall laid in heavy burnt clay bricks, and a concrete wall cast in 300kg/cm² concrete

5 Catalogues of constructions in relation to elements, containing eg:

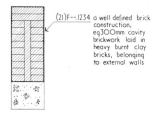

(21)F--.1234 a well defined brick construction, eq 300mm cavity brickwork laid in heavy burnt clay bricks, belonging to external walls

6 Catalogues of resources in relation to constructions in relation to elements, containing eg:

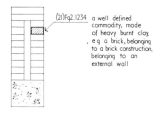

(21)Fq2.1234 a well defined commodity, made of heavy burnt clay, eg a brick, belonging to a brick construction, belonging to an external wall

Texts for some typical items printed out by the computer from the catalogues are shown below:

Within class a: Administration
(21)FA5.9001*   TIME AND PROGRESS SCHEDULES FOR THE) EXECUTION OF BRICKWORK IN EXTERNAL) WALLS SHALL BE PREPARED BY THE CON-) TRACTOR AND APPROVED BY THE ARCHITECT.)

Within class b: Aids for labour
(21)FB6.9001   SCAFFOLDING USED FOR THE ERECTION OF) FACING BRICK-WORK SHALL BE ERECTED) COMPLETELY FREE STANDING FROM THE) WALL.

Within class c: Labour
(21)FC1.9001   FACED WORK SHALL BE KEPT PERFECTLY) CLEAN AT ALL TIMES. SCAFFOLD BOARDS) NEXT TO THE BRICK FACES MUST BE TURNED) BACK AT NIGHTS OR DURING HEAVY RAIN) RUBBING TO REMOVE STAINS WILL NOT BE) PERMITTED.   )

Within class d: Labour including aids
(21)FD1.9001   BRICKS SHALL BE PROPERLY STACKED ON) LEVEL AND HARD STANDING AND BE) ADEQUATELY PROTECTED FROM INCLEMENT) WEATHER.   )

Within class y: Materials
(21)FG2.9001   COMMON BRICKS REFERRED TO AS TYPE 'A') SHALL BE ENGINEERING OR COMMON BRICKS) WITH A MINIMUM CRUSHING STRENGTH OF) 5000 LBS.SQ.IN.   )

Within class z: Works
(21)FZ9.9001   SUPPLY AND BUILD 4½IN. BRICKWORK) FACINGS TYPE 4, EXPOSED ON ONE FACE) ONLY IN CAVITY WALLING.   )

Note that none of the items above includes reference to geographical location. Location is not described in the text of the items but only below them by means of the specific codes, as follows:

(43)SC6.2015   PLACING OF 10 × 10 IN. FLOOR TILES IN) CEMENT AND SAND (1:3).   ) BLOCK 01, STOREY 04, ROOM 038 BLOCK 01, STOREY 04, ROOM 039 BLOCK 02, STOREY 03, ROOM 120

*The number 9001 identifies this particular clause. It has no special significance

7.33 Drawings

The principles involved in arranging drawn information using CBC are very like those of CI/sfB which were described in section 4.

The only important point of difference is the use of the summary structure shown below. Drawings containing only information on external walls would be coded (21). If a drawing illustrates a relationship between the external wall (21) *and* the roof (27) it is given a summary code (29).

(10) SITE SUBSTRUCTURE	(20) SITE PRIMARY ELEMENTS	(30) SITE SEC ELEMENTS	(40) SITE FINISHES	(90) SITE SUMMARY
	(21) EXTERNAL WALLS			
	(22) INTERNAL WALLS			
	(23) FLOORS			
	(24) STAIRS			
	(25) VACANT			
	(26) VACANT			
	(27) ROOFS			
	(28) FRAME			
(19) BUILDING SUBSTRUCTURE SUMMARY	(29) BUILDING PRIMARY ELEMENTS SUMMARY	(39) BUILDING SECONDARY ELEMENTS SUMMARY	(49) BUILDING FINISHES SUMMARY	(99) BUILDING SUMMARY

If it also contains information from any other of the main groups, for example (39), it is coded (99)*.

Drawings are prepared so that all the information within one main group ie (19) or (29) is completed at one time.

Not only does this make it possible to plan the production of drawings but it also enables the qs to work in parallel with the architect, knowing that as he receives each main group of drawings no further information is outstanding within that group.

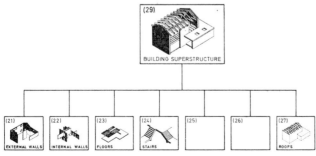

65 *Main group* (29) *Primary Elements*

Coding on drawings CBC catalogues should—as far as possible—be available, or should be prepared, during drawing production stage if item type coding is to be used on drawings to establish cross reference to bills of quantities, ordering schedules and so on.

Coding *on* drawings takes place before coding *of* drawings ie before numbering of the drawings in the title box. Contents of drawings decide the code in the title.

Coding 1st stage: All commodities shown on drawings should be coded on the basis of the CBC central catalogue. Coding for the identification of labour and operations is seldom necessary. In some circumstances, however, plant (aids, tools, machines) may need to be identified by codes.

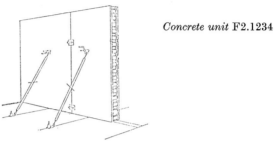

Concrete unit F2.1234

As an example, a required concrete unit coded F2.1234 may be found in the central resource catalogue with the following description:

F2.1234 Concrete unit, quality XYZ, dimension A × B × C

2nd stage: In the final bill of quantities items like the one above will be given the full code, using the 2nd facet and 1st facets. It may be helpful if the item is identified in the same way as the drawing.

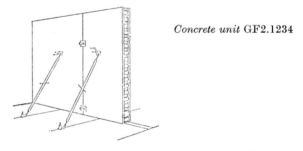

Concrete unit GF2.1234

The code GF2.1234 signifies that the commodity is part of the construction G.

3rd stage: Full cross reference can only be achieved by the addition of the 1st facet symbol, thus:

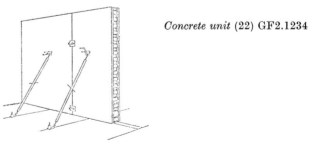

Concrete unit (22) GF2.1234

The full code (22) GF2.1234 signifies that the commodity is relevant to the construction G, and to the Building Part or Element (22), ie internal walls or partitions.

Cross references may also be given to other drawings.

Lists of drawings can be prepared for large projects by computer, using the same programs as for printouts of bills of quantities. They can be inserted in the bill or printed out separately.

* The method generally followed using CI/sfB would use (2-) to summarize (21) and (27); see Section 4 para 4.2

Drawing lists can be sorted like bills of quantities and presented according to blocks, storeys, departments, rooms, trades and so on.

7.34 Bills of quantities

A detailed CBC bill of quantities is effectively a list of activity-allocated resources quantified for a specific project. The priced bill of quantities represents a detailed cost estimate.

Traditionally, a bill of quantities is prepared partly as a basis for competitive tendering and partly to arrive at unit prices for the different work items in case of variations during production. The bill also constitutes a basis for site management and cost control during the building process.

Using computer techniques, each item may be allocated to building block, storey, section or room, and this makes it possible to prepare block specifications, storey specifications, room specifications and so on. Printouts can be made for drawing lists, purchase lists, activity lists etc on the basis of original tape files. It is possible to rationalise quantity surveying work and re-use measurements at all stages of the planning and building process. Quantities and prices can be summarised and regrouped by sortation on the general and specific codes of the system.

The bill of quantities is also considered an essential pre-requisite for the preparation of detailed time and progress schedules, because it represents the basic list of resources for the project.

Measurement according to the CBC system is done by means of the CBC codes which identify all text items and factors on the tape or disc belonging to each project. It is thus possible to have immediate access to all data in the form of bills, specifications, drawing lists, activity lists for all stages of planning or production.

Taking off The present factor (dimension) sheet is shown in **66**. Takers-off have been able to reduce the number of errors (errors in coding and transferring codes causes trouble with most computer systems), as they have grown more familiar with the system and by making increased use of overcodes.

An overcode is the bill of quantities equivalent of a standard drawing. Just as the construction details 'held' on a standard drawing can be tested and become more certain of success as time passes, the undercodes held by an over-code can be confirmed in accuracy. A bill produced by a relatively small number of overcodes is a bill of guaranteed accuracy if each overcode has been used on previous occasions.

Taking off is largely an arithmetical process, although calling for considerable skill and care. It is, however, in many cases, duplication of work which has already been carried out but is in a different form. An illustration of this is a BS bar bending schedule. This contains all the information necessary to produce the bill of quantities.

Control printout Is the last chance of correcting errors. It is not printed on bill paper and would not make a satisfactory document for work on site but it is produced by the computer like the bill itself. It includes quantities for each storey and each block, and the total for all blocks is produced for each item. Unit rates can be used in it as a cost check.

Bill sortation Two sample pages from a trade order labour material bill suitable for tendering are shown in **67, 68**. The top page shows labour items and the bottom page material items. The primary division is into trades followed by 3-2-4-1 sortation.

The examples were processed before CBC Ltd adopted the detailed coding principles set out in this section, but nevertheless illustrate these points:

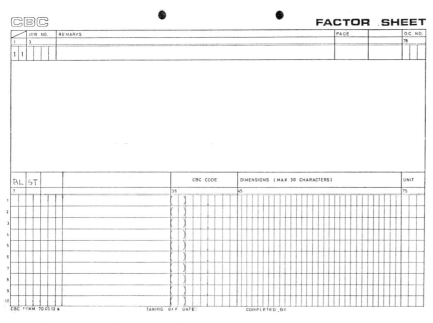

66 CBC *Factor sheet. Other* CBC *proformas include text sheets, text selection sheets, drawing registers, overcode sheets, trade code allocation sheets, price factor sheets, pricing sheets. Completion of the factor sheet is the first step in translating information on drawings into a form suitable for computer processing*

```
CONTRACT: CENTRAL HOSPITAL IN X-TOWN        8401  PAGE  54
          BRICKWORK                         G15   16.03.66
                                    QUANTITY UNIT RATE  L  S  D

          FOUNDATIONS: BRICKLAYING - (L)
          ------------------------------
(18) FC6.2001  COMMON BRICKWORK: HALF BRICK )
               WALL                         )

               BLOCK 01,                       380    YS
               BLOCK 02,                       300    YS
                                    TOTAL      680    YS

          EXTERNAL WALLS: BRICKLAYING - (L)
          ---------------------------------
(21) FC6.2002  COMMON BRICKWORK: HALF BRICK )
               SKIN OF HOLLOW WALL          )

               BLOCK 01, STOREY 02,             10    YS
               BLOCK 01, STOREY 03,             10    YS
               BLOCK 01, STOREY 04,             10    YS
               BLOCK 02, STOREY 01,            120    YS
               BLOCK 02, STOREY 02,            130    YS
                                    TOTAL      280    YS

          FOUNDATIONS: BRICKLAYING - (L)
          ------------------------------
(18) FC6.2001  COMMON BRICKWORK: ONE BRICK  )
               WALL                         )

               BLOCK 01,                        80    YS

          EXTERNAL WALLS: BRICKLAYING - (L)
          ---------------------------------
(21) FC6.2011  COMMON BRICKWORK: ONE BRICK  )
               WALL                         )

               BLOCK 01, STOREY 01,            240    YS
               BLOCK 02, STOREY 01.            120    YS
                                    TOTAL      360    YS

          FOUNDATIONS: BRICKLAYING - (L)
          ------------------------------
(18) FC6.2021  COMMON BRICKWORK: ONE AND A  )
               HALF BRICK WALL              )

               BLOCK 01,                        80    YS

          EXTERNAL WALLS: BRICKLAYING - (L)
          ---------------------------------
(21) FC6.2102  FACING BRICKWORK: HALF BRICK )
               SKIN OF HOLLOW WALL          )

               BLOCK 01, STOREY 02,             10    YS
               BLOCK 01, STOREY 03,             10    YS
               BLOCK 01, STOREY 04,             10    YS
               BLOCK 02, STOREY 01,            120    YS
               BLOCK 02, STOREY 02,            130    YS
                                    TOTAL      280    YS

          TO COLLECTION
```

```
CONTRACT: CENTRAL HOSPITAL IN X-TOWN        8401   PAGE 57
          BRICKWORK                         G15    16.03.66

                                    QUANTITY UNIT RATE   L  S  D

          CLAY BRICKS - (M).
          - - - - - - - -
(9-) FG2.1000  COMMON: TYPE *A*          )   40.1   THS

(9-) FG2.2001  FACING: P.C. 300 SHILLINGS)
               PER 1000.                 )   80.1   THS

          STEEL PRODUCTS - (M).
          - - - - - - - - - -
(9-) XH2.2500  GALVANISED WALL TIES TYPE )
               *A*: 6 IN. LONG.          )   480    YS

          MORTAR - (M).
          - - - - - -
(9-) YQ4.1001  CEMENT MORTAR TYPE *C*:  IN)
               HALF BRICK WALL.          ) 2170    YS

(9-) YQ4.1002  CEMENT MORTAR TYPE *C*: IN )
               ONE BRICK WALL.           )  760    YS

(9-) YQ4.1003  CEMENT MORTAR TYPE *C*: IN )
               ONE AND A HALF BRICK WALL. )  270    YS












          TO COLLECTION                                2
```

67, 68 *Trade order bills. Sortation in this example is primarily by trade (shown by G15 = brickwork at the top of each page). Individual items on the top page are arranged first by type of labour operation (C6 = laying)*

1 Each labour item has against it both the total quantity and the subdivision of the total quantity into individual blocks and storeys (see eg (21) FC6.2002). This enables the estimator to evaluate how the brickwork is distributed. He can either reflect this in his rate for the total quantity or by the way he prices individual storey quantities.

2 The labour items illustrated here are in the sequence of wall thicknesses within one type of brickwork. Similarly the same items of walling in different elements appear consecutively (see eg FC6.2011).

3 Each separate material in the tender bill is expressed as a total quantity for the whole project.

4 Where an identical material occurs in different elements the total quantity is summarised for quotation or ordering purposes under (9–), since location of materials is not relevant for estimator at tender stage (eg (9–) FG 2.1000).

5 The (9–) material summary should make it possible to establish direct identity between the manufacturers' code and the drawing or bill code. 'Single purpose' products such as windows and rooflights belong exclusively to one element, wheras 'general products' like bricks and pipes can be used in many elements. The manufacturer of general products is not concerned where they are to be used on site when dealing with quotations and invoices, and identification by the 2nd, 3rd and 4th facets, with the 1st facet summary position, enables him to ignore this, since the element location is not given. In present day practice the value of an element identification at the time of delivery is confined to such items as reinforcement, but industrialisation will tend to increase the value of block storey and element locations to identify the exact position of the product on site. CBC sets up a framework to enable this sort of integration to be achieved.

6 Materials quantities are generally given net and any conversion factors from the labour unit of billing are given in the preamble to the relevant material. The contractor can then add for waste or other allowances.

7 The suffix (M) appears at the end of each material item to avoid any possible confusion with labour items.

Two sample pages of the same basic bill information in a different sortation are shown overleaf **69, 70**.

The primary division in this case is block followed by 1:3:2:4 sortation. This is useful for site working and design costs analysis. In this case each labour and material item gives the total quantity for each element within the block subdivided into the total for each storey. Introduction of these additional codes for storeys, sections and rooms has greatly extended the number and usefulness of the bill sortations available.

Storey, department or room codes need not be used throughout the bill. It is, for example, possible to identify a specific part of a block or storey by using the department code only for that particular part. Similarly room identification can be used, for example, for (31) External openings and (43) Floor finishes.

while those on the bottom page are arranged first by type of material (G2 = clay, H2 = steel, Q4 = cement mortar). The secondary arrangement in each case is by the type (form) of assembly or product (F = brick) form

```
        CONTRACT: CENTRAL HOSPITAL IN X-TOWN        8401   PAGE  23
                  EXTERNAL WALLS                           BLOCK 01
                                                   (21)   16.09.66
                                      QUANTITY UNIT RATE

            EXTERNAL WALLS: CLAY BRICKS - (M)
            - - - - - - - - - - - - - - - - - -
(21) FG2.1000 COMMON: TYPE *A*              )
                STOREY 01,              23.0   THS
                STOREY 02,               0.5   THS
                STOREY 03,               0.5   THS
                STOREY 04,               0.5   THS
                              TOTAL     24.5   THS
(21) FG2.2001 FACING: P.C. 300 SHILLINGS  )
              PER 1000.                    )
                STOREY 02,               0.5   THS
                STOREY 03,               0.5   THS
                STOREY 04,               0.5   THS
                              TOTAL      1.5   THS
            EXTERNAL WALLS: STEEL PRODUCTS - (M)
            - - - - - - - - - - - - - - - - - - -
(21) XH2.2400 GALVANISED WALL TIES: TYPE  )
              *A*: 6 IN. LONG.             )
                STOREY 02,                10   YS
                STOREY 03,                10   YS
                STOREY 04,                10   YS
                              TOTAL       30   YS
            EXTERNAL WALLS: MORTAR - (M).
            - - - - - - - - - - - - - - -
(21) YQ4.1001 CEMENT MORTAR TYPE *C* IN   )
              HALF BRICK WALL.             )
                STOREY 02,                20   YS
                STOREY 03,                20   YS
                STOREY 04,                20   YS
                              TOTAL       60   YS
(21) YQ4.1002 CEMENT MORTAR TYPE *C* IN   )
              ONE BRICK WALL.              )
                STOREY 01,               240   YS


                TO COLLECTION
```

69

```
        CONTRACT: CENTRAL HOSPITAL IN X-TOWN        8401   PAGE  20
                  EXTERNAL WALLS                           BLOCK 01
                                                  (21)    16.09.66
                                      QUANTITY UNIT RATE  L  S  D

            EXTERNAL WALLS: BRICKLAYING - (L)
            - - - - - - - - - - - - - - - - -
(21) FC6.2002 COMMON BRICKWORK: HALF BRICK)
              SKIN OF HOLLOW WALL.         )
                STOREY 02,                10   YS
                STOREY 03,                10   YS
                STOREY 04,                10   YS
                              TOTAL       30   YS
(21) FC6.2011 COMMON BRICKWORK: ONE BRICK )
              WALL.                        )
                STOREY 01,               240   YS
(21) FC6.2102 FACING BRICKWORK: HALF BRICK)
              SKIN OF HOLLOW WALL.         )
                STOREY 02,                10   YS
                STOREY 03,                10   YS
                STOREY 04,                10   YS
                              TOTAL       30   YS
```

70

69, 70 *Above: block order bill. Sortation in this example is*
Block *(shown by 01 at top of each page)*/Element/
Labour: Material/Form/Catalogue number

Contractors apparently need at least two other sortations
(in addition to the tender sortation) of part or all of the bill.
For work planning, cost control and bonusing the choice
of primary sortations appears at the moment to be either
block: storey: trade, or block: trade: storey, followed by
1:2:3:4 if element is considered the most valuable, or 3:2:4:1
if labour and material is more appropriate.

CBC can produce any sortation. It may be that no generally
accepted sortations will emerge and that choice will depend
on the particular contractor's organisation.

7.35 Schedules

Another application of CBC is the production by computer
of schedules for large projects.

The alternative sortations available make it possible to
discover without difficulty the location(s) of a particular
item of equipment on a plan; or the numbers of that item
required for particular storeys etc; or the items of equipment
required in a particular room.

7.36 Programming

Programming using CBC is done on the basis of the finished
bills of quantities, which are sorted according to the subdivision of the project into activity types identified by
use of 1st and 2nd facets.

The resulting computer printout constitutes a basis for
drawing up network diagrams describing the sequence of
activities, and lines of balance which describe the cyclic
progress of the activities within individual cells of the
project.

During production the progress of each activity is controlled
and reports prepared to decide deviations and tendencies
in relation to the programme.

Activity bills can be prepared at tender stage and constitute
the basis for contractors' estimates. Tendering information
of this kind can be particularly important where contracts
are according to fixed time and costs.

The computer programs are set up to co-ordinate cost
planning with progress planning and ensure that efficient
and accurate cost control can be carried out during site
production.

Final accounts can be prepared quickly and feedback
of the data constitutes the basis for computer printouts
of cost analyses and production statistics for use in future
jobs.

Classification of activities Every activity is classified by means
of the 1st and 2nd facets of the general code. For example:

(21)– – – signifies the class (type) for all external walls,
ie the activity type: 'erection of external walls'
(21)F– – signifies the class (type) for all brick constructions
belonging to external walls, ie the activity type: 'erection
of external brick walls'

The dash symbols in the codes above indicates that all
required resources are taken to be included in the activity
types. This permits the preparation of lists of standard
activity types, eg:

(21)A– –	External walls: Prefabrication
(21)B– –	External walls: Demolition
(21)D– –	External walls: Preliminary works
(21)E– –	External walls: Concrete construction
(21)F– –	External walls: Brick construction
(21)Y– –	External walls: Constructions
(21)Z– –	External walls: Production
(21)– – –	External walls: Total

Resource content of activities The resource content of each
activity is estimated by means of the factor (dimension)

sheet using standard catalogues for resources based on the 3rd facet.

All activities are geographically located in block, storey, zone, room and so on. Normally definition by block and storey codes is sufficient.

Printout of resource content for each activity takes place through sorting on block, storey, activity type. After that an 'activity valuation list' is printed out providing all necessary information for deciding the duration and man-power to be allocated to each activity.

Sequence of activities The sequence of activity types can be determined before work on site starts by means of a network or 'precedence diagram'.

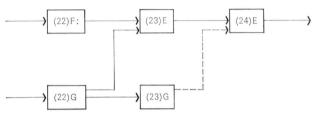

71 *Precedence diagram*

The example shows:

1 that the activity types (22)F and (22)G (at the same geographical location) shall precede activity type (23)E. Translated this means that 'erection of block or brick internal walls' and 'erection of large unit internal walls' shall precede 'construction of in situ concrete floors'.

2 that the activity type (22)G shall precede the activity type (23)G, ie 'erection of large unit internal walls' shall precede 'erection of large unit structural floors'.

3 that the activity types (23)E and (23)G shall precede the activity type (24)E, ie: 'construction of in situ floors' and 'erection of large unit floors' shall precede construction of in situ stairs'.

4 that the activity types (23)E and (23)G may take place simultaneously.

CBC plan CBC are developing a technique and a suite of programs, known collectively as CBC plan which uses precedence diagrams and aims to assist the management of large scale multi-activity building projects which entail a cycle of activity through several job sections. It normally requires as a starting point, a detailed, accurate and coded bill of quantities.

7.37 Cost control

The following codes will normally be used in CBC cost accounting:

1 Block code	eg:	08
2 Storey code	eg:	04
3 Trade code	eg:	E06
4 Firm code	eg:	0063
5 Process code	eg:	(42)Sc6.8213
6 Voucher code	eg:	17036806

The priced bill of quantities is continuously updated during the building period, but payments on account are not generally based on valuation of each bill item. Instead an activity bill is prepared in which sets of bill items are summarised to correspond with activities in the time and progress schedule (network, precedence diagram or the like). This activity bill together with the network constitutes the basis for valuations of executed work.

The accounting procedure can be briefly described as follows:

1 The priced bill of quantities is resorted and an accounts tape with activities is priced according to the contract.

2 Information about the financial basis of fluctuations is transferred to the tape.

3 Information about variation orders is continuously received during the construction period.

4 The accounts tape is updated with variation data immediately before the print out of the activity list.

5 The activity list is printed out with a blank column for valuation purposes.

6 The activity list is filled in with valuations for each activity.

7 An accounts statement is printed out showing the exact amount to be paid to the contractor.

8 The certificate is issued.

9 The accounts tape is updated ready for future print outs of activity lists for next valuation.

In this brief survey of CBC cost control principles no mention has been made of the integration between the budget tape and the accounts tape nor has it been possible to go into details as regards computer routines for book-keeping, check mechanisms, vouchers, invoices, etc.

Other applications of data co-ordination

Section 8: Cost planning information

This section briefly introduces the application of CI/SfB based methods to cost planning and describes the relationship between CI/SfB Table I and the 'Standard Form of Cost Analysis' as agreed and used by the Building Cost Information Service of the Royal Institution of Chartered Surveyors and government departments

8.1 Introduction
8.2 Cost breakdown
8.3 External works

8.1 Introduction

Cost planning aims to provide a series of target cost estimates for individual project divisions or elements of building works and external works, built up from available cost information about already-completed projects of a similar type. Once such cost estimates are available for relatively small parts of a project, tentative design decisions can be costed and matched against the target estimates. By this means a picture of likely total cost can be built up at a very early stage in the design process, when many design options are still available to the designer.

There are three basic activities in cost planning:

1 Establishing a total cost estimate for the project, based on cost information available about similar types of projects of a similar quality

2 Breaking down the total cost estimate into smaller parts, also on the basis of knowledge of previously constructed projects (not necessarily of the same building type), in order to prepare a cost plan giving a well balanced distribution of available finance

3 Checking design decisions against the cost plan.

8.2 Cost breakdown

The second of the three activities listed above corresponds directly with the need to provide a breakdown for drawings or bills of quantities, and there are clear advantages to be got from a coded cross reference facility between the cost plan and all other information sources. CI/SfB Table 1 provides a framework for an elemental breakdown of cost information which permits this direct cross reference.

It also facilitates the production of cost analyses from the collection pages of CI/SfB arranged bills of quantities (see Section 6).

CI/SfB is not used in the 'Standard form of Cost Analysis'.* Element definitions which are very similar to CI/SfB Table 1 are listed in a different order and identified by a unique code. Different cost summaries are thus provided.

*Standard form of cost analysis. Principles, instructions and definitions, available from the Building Cost Information Service of the Royal Institution of Chartered Surveyors, price 20s.

MPLE - COST PLAN					(99) BUIDING COST	
SfB	ELEMENT	SPECIFICATION	ELEMENT 535 m^2	ELEMENT PER m^2	TOTAL 535 m^2	TOTAL PER m^2
			£	£	£	£
		b/f			12,112	22.64
)	EXTERNAL OPENINGS	Windows:- Standard size, standard section glavanised metal windows in softwood subframe with hardwood sub-cill, Glazing	2,930	5.48		
)	INTERNAL OPENINGS	Internal Doors:- 'Durador' type: softwood frames, architraves etc; ironmongery	767	1.43		
)	SECONDARY ELEMENTS SUMMARY				3,697	6.91
)	EXTERNAL FINISHES	External decoration: three coat oil paint	137	0.26		
)	INTERNAL FINISHES	Wall finishes:- ½" two coat plaster to Church and link. Sandlimes to Hall measured with (21)	1,231	2.30		
		Decoration:- Two coats emulsion paint to walls. Three coats oil paint to woodwork and metalwork.				
)	FLOOR FINISHES	1½" Thick finished floor thickness overall Granwood to Church and Hall. Quarry Tiles to link. Softwood skirtings.	1,536	2.87		
)	CEILING FINISHES	Church and Hall:- ½" Insulation board between boxed out beams; ⅜" plywood boxings to beams. Link:- ½" Insulation board.	1,744	3.26		
)	ROOF	16 m.m. Formica chipboard prefinished with Nuralite	3,250	6.07		
)	FINISHES SUMMARY				7,898	14.76
01		c/f			£23,707	44.31

72 *Cost analysis using Table 1.*
Turner & Townsend, Chartered Quantity Surveyors, Durham

Because of these differences architects, quantity surveyors and others using CI/SfB based methods of data co-ordination who want to make use of SFCA data will need to translate from SFCA to CI/SfB. If cost plans are produced using the SFCA 'amplified analysis' this translation can be made without difficulty. SFCA records will also make it possible in future to translate data on their form of 'brief analysis' into CI/SfB terms. Translation inevitably takes time, but the CI/SfB Table 1 definitions in Part II of this manual will help designers and quantity surveyors to see how SFCA elements relate to CI/SfB elements.

Cost planners may want to use CI/SfB as a format for cost plans in order to avoid the need for translation. In this case the SFCA format can readily be adapted to CI/SfB using the definitions, codes and order of elements given in Part II of this manual. This can be done without affecting the principles or instructions for the SFCA format except in so far as these are affected by changes in the definitions or grouping of elements.

8.3 External works

Part II of this manual uses CI/SfB Table 1 codes (10), (20) to (80) for site,* but on many projects only a relatively small area of external works (ie site works not under the building) will be associated with a particular building. In addition, external works cannot be accurately cost planned in relation to building, since the ratio of external works area to building works area is largely fortuitous and unique to each site.

For these reasons the use of the eight subdivisions provided by the codes above may provide too fine a degree of breakdown, and it is therefore recommended that the total cost of external works and the expression of this cost in terms of gross floor area should usually be given as one figure at Project Division code 9 or 90 External Works. Table 1 codes (10), (20) etc will, however, be useful for cost planning purposes on civil engineering works or on building projects in which external works assume greater cost significance.

*Some offices may prefer to use (90.1) instead of (10): (90.2) instead of (20); and so on.

Section 9: Briefing information

This section outlines methods of using CI/SfB for collecting briefing information in a form which makes it available for room layout and design at Plan of Work stages A to D, and for element design at Plan of Work stage E

9.1 Introduction
9.2 Brief collection
9.3 Brief analysis

9.1 Introduction

The brief contains basically two types of information. The first defines the client's requirements (what he wants or needs) and the second, the constraints upon a design solution (factors which tend to prevent him having what he wants or needs). During the design process these requirements and restraints are matched against the evolving solution, and the briefing information should be organised so that this matching process is made as simple as possible.

Matching requires that the two objects being matched are expressed in the same way. In practical terms this means that the requirements should be classified using the same concepts and codes as those used to classify the solutions. The four tables of CI/SfB can be used for this purpose.

Information for the brief is usually received from a number of sources, in random order and in various forms. For example, information concerning a heating system may be received from the client, the heating engineer, the local authority, and the office library; it can be communicated by letter, through minutes of design team meetings, by word of mouth, by drawing or by telephone. These scattered items of information must be brought together so that they can be matched against proposed methods of heating the building and this can be achieved by classifying information as it is received.

The concepts which are used to classify it vary. During the early stages of design only the activities and requirements of the potential user may be known and the spaces may not be determined. For example, a client may require a place to perform the activities of cooking, washing and storing, and the 'kitchen' may be defined as a space which will satisfy the requirement for these activities. The requirements of the kitchen itself as a functional space can then be determined. As the design develops further the kitchen may be fixed locationally in a certain block and on a certain floor. The concept of building part or element may be used throughout the whole process. Information can thus be organised in different forms which will be useful at different stages in the job. The main levels or groupings are:

1 User requirements: (CI/SfB Table 4 provides the beginnings of a classification of user requirements and activities)

2 Rooms or spaces (by primary function): (CI/SfB Table 0 class 9 provides an outline classification)

3 Building element (part) and product: (CI/SfB Tables 1 and 2/3).

The organisation of the brief can therefore make use of all the tables of CI/SfB where necessary and these will often be used together as in library practice set out in the *Construction indexing manual.*

9.2 Brief collection

Relevant information received into the office and produced by the office is collected, abstracted, and presented in a useful form. This is achieved by classifying it using exactly the same techniques as used in the library. Two alternative methods can be used to collect the information.

1 *Collection, photocopying and classification of briefing correspondence and other relevant information for the project under* CI/SfB *headings:*

The content of letters sent out from the office can be controlled and restricted to one Table 1 element or other CI/SfB heading, so that they can be filed immediately according to content. If two elements (or two of any other classification category) are to be described, eg floor and roof construction, then either a summary code (eg (2–)) should be used, or two separate letters written or two copies filed. In this case the copies can be coded (23) and (27) as appropriate. Incoming mail, messages etc can be copied (a copy for each CI/SfB subject dealt with) and the copies can be filed under the appropriate codes.

The resulting file or files will then form the brief for the project. This method leads to a large volume of photocopying work and paper (see also Section 10).

2 *Abstracting from briefing correspondence onto* A4 *size sheets with* CI/SfB *headings, kept together as a briefing file:*

A loose leaf briefing file or 'index' can be provided for the project and filed at a3 (see section 10). Each time a CI/SfB subject is mentioned in any letter or other communication a separate entry should then be made in the briefing file.

For example, if a letter is received from the client containing relevant information on space heating requirements, floor finishes and internal wall treatments, brief entries about each of these matters can be made in the briefing file under Table 1 elements (56), (43) and (42) respectively, each entry being cross referenced by file number and date to the letter giving the full information. The letter itself can then be filed at a1 (see section 10) with all other letters to and from the client.

At early stages in the design process entries in the briefing file may be made one after the other without regard to subject, **73**.

Later on, when the design starts to take a definite form, it will be more convenient to allocate a separate sheet to each CI/SfB subject, and give project division codes as well **74**.

If further information is received on a subject which has already been allocated a page it is simply added to the end of it. If information is received dealing with two concepts, eg kitchen ventilation, an entry can be made on the sheets for both 93 *kitchen* and (57) *ventilation,* or the normal rules for library classification and filing can be applied, as set out in the *Construction indexing manual,* pp 15 to 20.

*See bibliography appendix D

DEPARTMENT OF ARCHITECTURE
HERIOT-WATT UNIVERSITY.

15 November 1973.

Multi-Discipline Team (Architect). David Cochrane.

Purpose of Seminar	- To hear an architectural viewpoint of the workings, problems and methods of a multi-discipline team recently set up.
Introduction	- Personal.
The need for such an office	- 1. Client demand. 2. Integrated service.
The Structure of the Team	- Allocation of Staff. 1. Architecture. 2. Structure. 3. Mechanical. 4. Electrical. 5. Q.S.
The Accommodation of the Team	- 1. Room allocation. 2. Communication.
The Plan of Attack for a Job	- The main purpose of a plan is to provide a framework for control of the project. It sets out to identify work stages by describing events, procedures, and activity in each. It contains the substance of each work stage as the design evolves from the most general to the most exact...
A. - Inception	- To set up the organisation for the project and decide the basic requirements.
B. - Feasibility	- To provide an appraisal for a decision to proceed or otherwise, checking functional/technical/financial aspects.
C. - Outline Proposals	- To determine general approach to design.
D. - Scheme Design	- To determine particular proposals for design.
E. - Detail Design	- To determine exact design of all components.
F. - Production information	- To prepare complete information for construction.

G. – Bills of Quantities   – To complete all documentation for tenders
                                 and the contract.

H. – Tender action   – To select the contractor(s) for the project.

Main Communication
_____

– 1. The aim is to communicate in order that
       something from two dimensions is constructed
       in three dimensions.

– 2. The correlation of information and integration
       of communication in a multi-discipline team is
       critical.

– 3. The **Flow** of information and drawings produced.

Problems & Lessons
_____

– 1. Good communication.

– 2. Advance information.

– 3. Brain-storming sessions.

– 4. Co-ordinator required.

– 5. Role of –   Architect.
            –   Structure.
            –   Mechanical.
            –   Electrical.
            –   Quantity Surveying.
            –   Draughtsmanhip.

Discussion
_____

Some points might be...

1. Who should be the co-ordinator of the team – should it be an Architect or Engineer or perhaps someone outwith all disciplines?

2. Are schematic or line diagrams normally produced by Services Consultants enough, or do Architects and other members of the Design Team require – pipework, conduit and ducting layouts.

3. Does a reasonably highly serviced building justify the appointment of an assistant specifically responsible for the integration of services design?   If so, should he be an Architect, Services Engineer, etc?

4. Should the Services Engineer automatically be expected to produce co-ordination drawings.

5. Is it possible that the present method of each discipline producing drawings is wrong and a new drawing system should be evolved?

6. If the end result is to produce a better quality of design in buildings – how can the present designer 'the Architect' – explain to the other disciplines what the term means?

DC:JM
14 November 1973

The Design Process   An Analytical and Systematic Approach

EXPLANATORY INTRODUCTION

There are those of us who believe design to be an intuitive and
creative act, and, those again, who believe it to be the result of
a thorough, logical analysis.   Surely, as long as the end in view
is an "architecture", and this is used in its broadest sense, it is
apparent that it will always be necessary to have a fusion of the
two - a means of resolving the benefits of designing by logical analysis
with the often conflicting ideas thrown up in creative, intuitive thought.
With the complexity of modern architecture, it is necessary to develop
a disciplined, systematic approach to the design process if one is to be
reasonably assured of a balanced solution.

It seems that the Design Process readily divides itself into
broadly, three separate, yet related parts, viz:

1.   The Analysis which is the all-in, exhaustive probing of the
     problem, as a result of which the problem becomes clarified:

2.   The Exploration, where the factual data accumulated in the
     Analysis is studied for its design potential and given three
     dimensional form: and -

3.   The Synthesis, which is the putting together of design ideas
     to form a balanced solution, as a result of the Exploration
     studies, based on decisions made on the Analysis.   As a "system"
     can be applied in approaching the Analysis, the Exploration and
     the Synthesis parts of the problem, this allows the subject to
     be taught and, therefore, more readily understood.   The analytical
     study of these "systems" in the approach to Design constitute the
     main theme of the teaching of the Third Year.

ANALYSIS

The first part of the design process is the analysis of the design problem. This means a full understanding of all architectural, physical and organisational issues relevant to the problem, and their inter-relationships.

The analysis forms the complete brief for the project, and is usually carried out in the following sequence:

1. Study all the activities to be carried out in and around the project, and decide what resources are needed to carry them out.

2. Analyse the information you have prepared, and decide whether or not the project is physically (and financially) feasible.

3. Consider the analysis very carefully and thoroughly. State clearly the main problems to be solved and the criteria which determine whether your solution is acceptable or not.

The techniques used in the analysis of a design problem vary from simple checklists to computer programmes, but their purpose is always to collect, store and manipulate all relevant design information in the most economical and efficient way. Obviously, large projects need more complex design techniques and management than small ones and it is important to choose the right methods for the project you are designing.

The final part of the design process is the synthesis of the design: it requires that both your judicial and creative facilities are used to create one design synthesis which optimises the feasible solutions derived from the analysis and the subsequent exploratory studies.

A competent designer can produce a mechanical solution by going methodically through the analysis process, but good architecture transcends the methodical solution and can only be achieved by the exercise of the designer's controlled creative skill in the systematic synthesis of the project.

EXPLORATION

The thorough analysis of a problem leads directly to a period of
exploratory study where the factual data gained in the Analysis is
given meaning by interpretation into architectural terms.   If
considered in part, and in detachment from the complexity of the
total problem, and illustrated diagrammatically, then opposing forms
for each major activity can be evaluated.   One, thereby, readily
acquires a certain conviction of direction and, at the same time,
becomes au fait with the architectural potential of the brief.
It must be appreciated that these"exploratory studies" do not in
themselves achieve balanced solutions to the problem, which comes
later in the forming of a synthesis.   The value of this exhaustive
and creative period of "exploration" is in free-ing one from slavishly
"accepted" forms, and it is here that original thought can be rewarding
and, perhaps, this can be more readily understood by the following
example:-
e.g. In consideration of the brief for a School of Architecture, it
is noted that an area for students leisure activities, of the type
usually provided for in a common room is required.   It may well be
that as a result of original "exploration" a considerable gain, out-
weighing any disadvantages, is seen to result from the breaking up
and linking of this area, as swellings off the concourse areas of the
School, in forming smaller scaled informal spaces.   It can be readily
understood, from this example that had this possibility not been probed
and comparatively evaluated during the exploratory periods, (before
synthesising a design), it is more than likely that all syntheses to the
problem would be based on an acceptance of a common room for this activity
and one's effort, in synthesis, would be limited to one of the integration
of this room within the total complex.

"Decisions" from these studies, which directly produce the basis of
the form of the architecture, are taken only after the completion of
this free-thinking period.

Note:- As the thought process during these studies is free-ranging, so too
should be the method of recording, which is to be carried out in
sketch diagram and note form on A3 sized note-books.

SYNTHESIS

Based on a design concept, the synthesis of a design, as a solution
to a brief, is the putting together of the parts, in a beautiful way,
to produce a balanced complex whole.   Certain design "issues" are
relevant in all design problems.   It is obvious that the relevant
"issues" will vary with the design problem.. (e.g. - there is no
issue of "circulation" or of "services" in the design of a piece of
furniture), but, in architecture, as distinct from, say, industrial
design, the following major "issues" always apply:-

1.   Circulation and spatial organisation.
2.   Structural organisation.
3.   Services organisation
4.   Three-dimensional massing.

It must be appreciated that each of these "issues", which integrate
to produce the form of the architecture must, firstly, be visually
stated and clarified in the design, according to the designer's chosen
way or "system" of forming.   Although the chosen "system" of form
will have infinite richness of variation, the form "theme" should remain
recognisably consistent throughout the design.   The visual clarification
and integration of these "systems" of form and the resultant articulation
to produce a unified whole, based on a design concept, is the essence
of an architecture.   The statement of these forms comes at the embryonic
stage of the design concept, and should be checked as consistent in
broad principle only.   Any attempt to consider aspects in detail,
at this stage, will prohibit the fluidity necessary at this formulative
design period, to allow a constant oscillation over the relevant
"issues"

Again, as in the "exploration", the discipline of detachment from the
complexity of the total problem will allow one to clarify, more readily,
the "system" evolving in the issues and this can be assisted by
illustration in colour, by overlay or detached diagram and - in the
case of three-dimensional massing - by rough model.   This will allow
the designer to satisfy himself of a reasoned consistency of treatment
and, thereby, eliminate "fault"- and this is our purpose - at this
early stage.   A "fault" built into a design, is much more difficult,
and sometimes impossible, to eradicate at a later stage.   It is necessary
to become "System-minded" and one must get into the way of rapidly
clarifying by overlay or detached diagram and by rough model.

It must be appreciated that the handling of form by the clarification and integration of these "issues" by visually consistent "systems" is a pre-requisite of all good design and, therefore, it is essential for designers to acquire the skill and an understanding of it.

October 1973   Andrew Jackson.

The Design Process   An Analytical and Systematic Approach

INTRODUCTORY STUDY:

See Explanatory Introduction with particular reference to the following "issues"

1. The "system of circulation and spatial organisation.

2. The "system" of structural organisation.

3. The "system" of services organisation.

4. The "system" of three-dimensional massing.

You are asked to select, carefully, a building of architectural quality, and to record, by sketch and overlay colour pattern to plan(s) and section and by explanatory concise notes, an analytical appraisal of the design, under "issues" 1,2,3, and 4 of the Explanatory Introduction attached.

(The approval and advice of the staff should be obtained for the selection, to ensure that the building has the necessary clarity of design to be rewarding in analytical study.)

NOTE: Care should be taken to select a design which is sufficiently interesting in the issues relative to the study, and this will be more readily understood after the illustrated introductory talk (see below).

It should be appreciated that this study is NOT intended to constitute a critical appraisal of the design for its purpose.

Any inconsistency in conforming to a "system" of forming should be noted (see illustrations).

PRESENTATION:

The work should be recorded on A2 sized sheets - to be meaningful, and, preferably, in free-hand, with concise explanatory notes - (the notes must be relative to the particular aspect of study, only)

The sheets should be so arranged that each sheet deals with one issue only.

TIME ALLOCATED:

11.00 hours Tuesday 2 October 1973 until
10.30 hours Tuesday 9 October 1073.

ILLUSTRATED TALK:

An illustrated talk will be given, as an introduction to the subject, in the Lecture Room at 14.30 hrs., Tuesday, 2 October 1973.

October 1973.

Of the two methods described above the second is almost certainly the most convenient for most offices. Its main advantages are:

1 Only relevant information is abstracted

2 The resulting file is fairly compact

3 New information can readily be inserted

4 Source documents from and to the client are kept together in the normal way (see Section 10).

9.3 Brief analysis

Room data sheets

It is usually necessary to abstract information methodically from the briefing file primarily in terms of potential spaces (for use during the early design stages of the project), and primarily in terms of Table 1 elements (in readiness for Plan of Work Stage E and onwards).

BRIEFING/ACTION RECORD (For use at planning stage)		JOB No.	, 0932
		BLOCK No.	02
		STOREY No.	ALL
(0–)991		DEPARTMENT	–
		ROOM No.	ALL

REF.	NOTE	( )	ACTION
Client letter 15.07.69	Cill height in office areas to be not less than 900 mm.	(31)	
"	Ceilings to be aconstically absorbent	(45)	
"	Low-maintenance wall finish preferred (consider vinyl fabric?)	(42)	
●			
Discussion with Building Insp. 23.08.69	Demountable partitions to corridors to be to Class O flame spread	(22) (42)	
"	PVC soil system will be acceptable	(52)	
Telephone from Client 27.09.69	Coloured eggshell wall tiles in toilets	(42)	
	Ceramic tile floors	(43)	
● "	Remote opening gear for top-hung vents is not desirable – transom height not to exceed 2,000	(31)	
"	Flexible lighting system essential (trunking?)	(63)	
M & E Consultant 28.09.69	Three-compartment skirting trunking will be required	(69)	
	100 mm. ceiling void will not be adequate for heating mains	(56)	

BRIEFING/ACTION RECORD (For use at detail design stage)		JOB No.	0932
			(42)

REF.	NOTE	CODE	
Client 27.09.69	Coloured eggshell wall tiles 152 x 152 x 6 fixed with CTA on plaster.	BLOCK	02
		STOREY	ALL
		DEPT	06
Action ✓		ROOM	19, 20
Client 15.07.69	Vinyl fabric on lightweight plaster.	BLOCK	02
		STOREY	ALL
		DEPT	04
Action ✓		ROOM	12
	Walls of escape stairs finished with cement glaze on fairface concrete.	BLOCK	02
		STOREY	ALL
		DEPT	02
Action /		ROOM	13, 15
	Walls of main stair in fairface brickwork (as for (41) external finishes) with recessed joints.	BLOCK	02
		STOREY	ALL
		DEPT	02
Action ✓		ROOM	14
Client 01.02.70	Walls of showroom to be left in keyed flettons for finishings by tenant.	BLOCK	02
		STOREY	02
		DEPT	03
Action ✓		ROOM	06

73 *Form for collecting briefing items in chronological order. Alun Jones, Ward & Partners, Chartered Architects, London. This practice uses CBC symbols such as (0–) on documentation*

74 *Separate form for each CI/SfB subject heading. Alun Jones, Ward & Partners, Chartered Architects, London*

In most building projects there will be some features (eg plaster wall finishes) which will be required in many rooms and spaces, and a useful time saving technique is therefore to analyse a 'typical' space using Table 1 as a check list and then record for other spaces only those characteristics which are to be different. Some Table 1 parts such as roof finishes and wall construction will be applicable to the project *as a whole* rather than to individual spaces and an additional section will therefore be required at the beginning of the room data sheets for 'the project in general'. See **75a** and **75b**.

Element data

Re-sorting the information contained on room data sheets into Table 1 elements is a secretarial activity and should not take much more time than that required for a normal retype. The typist is only required to work through the data sheets and abstract, say, all '(42)' information. The resulting information can be presented in scheduled or written form and will provide the basic information for detail design and production drawings at RIBA plan of work stages E and F. See **76**.

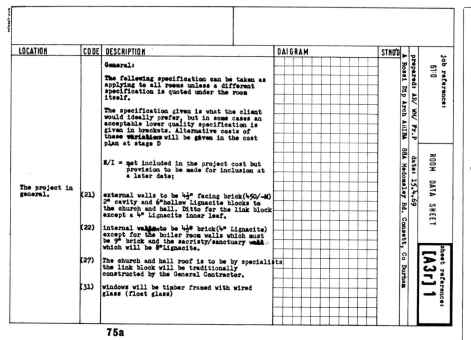

75a

75b

Fixing eyes for nets must be provided in the two side walls of the hall.

A seat must be provided in the repository.

A folding counter/shelf will be provided in the confessional to allow the priest to rest during long periods.

(73)   Culinary fixtures.

A 63" stainless steel sink unit is to be provided in the kitchen and a 42" unit in the sacristy (in working unit).

An urn for tea etc. is to be provided in the kitchen. This may be gas or electrically heated, whichever is the more convenient.

All fixtures will be build in.

(74)   Sanitary fixtures

These are as follows:

	Female WC	Male WC
low level Wc type.	2 no.	1 no.
6'0" urinal slab.		1 No.
Wash hand basins.	2 no. set in vanitory type top.	1 no.
Toilet roll holders.	2 no. type	1 no. type

(75)   Cleaning fixtures

Provision should be made for a suspended clothes drier – not included in contract.

76

75a, b *Briefing information arranged primarily by space location*
76 *Briefing information arranged primarily by element*

Section 10: Correspondence

This section briefly describes the application of CI/SfB based methods to the filing of project correspondence

10.1 Introduction
10.2 Project correspondence and related literature

10.1 Introduction

Cross reference to other sources which are themselves arranged by CI/SfB can only be achieved if correspondence is *classified* by CI/SfB subjects, and this is sometimes difficult to achieve, largely because of the difficulty of exercising control over the grouping of subjects in incoming mail.

Individual letters from clients and statutory organisations concerned with projects as a whole frequently deal with a wide variety of subjects, particularly at early stages in the design process. Many copies will need to be taken of such letters if they are to filed consistently by subject (see Section 9). Because of the expense and difficulty of doing this it seems probable that many offices either file all correspondence primarily by the names of organisations (ie by addressee or correspondent) with files arranged simply in alphabetical order, or else use a mixture of addressee and subject filing.

Offices have also used the stages of the RIBA plan of work to provide an overall arrangement for correspondence files, and some have used the chapter headings of the RIBA *Handbook of Architectural Practice and Management**.

This may be particularly suitable for correspondence which relates to the office as a whole rather than to individual projects. Alternatively, the lower case letters f, g etc at (A) in Table 4 of the *Construction indexing manual** may be used with minor modifications and additions.

10.2 Project correspondence and related literature

The project correspondence outline set out below must be regarded as experimental, since it has not been tested as a whole. It does, however, build on the experience of those using CI/SfB for correspondence filing.

First it accepts the distinction between (a) correspondents whose letters are so likely to deal with a wide variety of subjects that filing by subject becomes unreasonably expensive and time consuming, and (b) those whose specialist interests make filing by subject practicable. Letters type (a) can be indexed and used to build up the brief in the way described in Section 9 of this manual. The information they contain can then readily be found by using the brief itself as an index to them. These letters will all be filed at a1 or a2 as appropriate, in files (as many as are needed), carrying the name or function of the correspondent concerned.
All other letters or literature (eg architect's instructions, clerk of works' reports etc) will be kept in files (as many as are needed) carrying subject titles such as 'finance'. Headings from a3 onwards can be used for this purpose, subdivided where necessary using the codes in the *Construction indexing manual.**

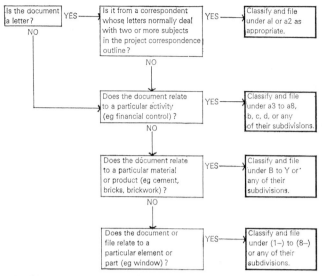

77 *Classifying correspondence*

When correspondence or literature type (b) is being drafted, it should, as far as is practicable and reasonable, be limited by subject in the same way as specification information (see Section 5). Following the principles set out in Section 5, correspondence or literature which is to be classified by subject should always—whenever there is an apparent choice of possible subject headings—be classified and filed according to the code and heading which appears *nearest to the end of the outline*. For example, a document dealing equally with cost and quality would be classified a7, not a4. This does not mean that pages which are best kept together must be dispersed. For example, all 'architect's instructions' will probably be best kept together in one file at a3 and subdivided either by date or by CI/SfB Table 1. If each instruction were to be treated as a separate document and filed according to the rule given in the last paragraph, all instructions would inevitably be scattered amongst many files. Those to do with primary elements would be filed at (2–), not a3, and those on piped services at (5–).

Project correspondence outline

a ADMINISTRATION

a0 GENERAL†
eg:
Agreements with clients and consultants, project procedures (eg: this Manual, job book), fees and all matters covered by the office administrative files so far as they apply to definitions of responsibility, allocation of tasks, etc for the project Form of contract, when available.

a1 GENERAL CORRESPONDENCE†‡
eg:
Design team correspondence and minutes of meetings with, for example:
Client and his advisers
Users
Consultants
Colleagues
Design team and/or building team
Correspondence with the general contractor.

---

* See bibliography, appendix D
† All files under these headings can be titled according to name (eg Water Board or XYZ Water Board) and *not* according to subject (eg water supply). Then files can be kept in alphabetical order
‡ This heading differs from the Construction indexing manual

a2 CONTROLS, CONSTRAINTS
Consents and approvals, correspondence and minutes of meetings with, for example:
Town planners
District surveyor, building inspector, fire officer
Adjoining owners
Water Board, Electricity Board, etc

a3 DESIGN
eg:
Activity data sheets, consolidated brief, reports, drawings issue and receipt registers
Instructions to the contractor.

a4 FINANCIAL CONTROL
eg:
Job costing
Cost plans, analyses
Tender documents
Valuations for certificates.

a5 PRODUCTION CONTROL
eg:
Programming, time sheets

a7 QUALITY CONTROL
eg:
Clerk of works reports

a8 FEEDBACK, APPRAISAL
eg:
Building owners maintenance manual

a9 SUNDRY ADMINISTRATIVE MATTERS

B
Y } ASSEMBLIES AND PRODUCTS†

(1–) SUBSTRUCTURE‡
Correspondence and quotations, etc

(2–) PRIMARY ELEMENTS‡
Correspondence and quotations, etc

(3–) SECONDARY ELEMENTS‡
Correspondence and quotations, etc

(4–) FINISHES‡
Correspondence and quotations, etc

(5–) SERVICES‡
Correspondence and quotations, etc

(6–) INSTALLATIONS‡
Correspondence and quotations, etc

(7–) FIXTURES‡
Correspondence and quotations, etc

(8–) LOOSE EQUIPMENT‡
Correspondence and quotations, etc

Section 11: Design details

This section briefly describes the application of CI/SfB based methods to the production of design details at or before RIBA plan of work stage E

11.1 Application of CI/SfB based methods

11.1 Application of CI/SfB based methods

The use and development of CI/SfB based methods of data co-ordination has centred on the arrangement of production information rather than design information.

Several factors contribute to this. In the case of production information logical and detailed arrangement of information is worthwhile and helpful, since the originator of documentation spends some time in producing each drawing, specification etc, which then has to be understood by people who may be unfamiliar with the project. He should and can afford to spend some time in thinking how best to present and arrange information both for his own future convenience and for the convenience of others. In the case of design information each document (sketch drawing etc) is produced relatively quickly and will be seen either by close colleagues who are thoroughly familiar with the project, or by clients and others whose contact with the building industry is transitory and who cannot be expected to use or understand building industry classification and coding.

Offices have found however, that there is a need at or before stage E of the RIBA plan of work for a broad breakdown of building works into elements which are helpful to designers.

The full range of specific codes and headings in CI/SfB Table 1 gives too detailed a breakdown to provide a framework for initial design and the table below shows a typical selection of codes and headings which some offices have found useful at stage E.

Typical selection of Table I codes and headings useful at stage E

(1–) Substructure	(2–) Superstructure	(5–) Services	(7–) Fittings
	(21) EXTERNAL WALLS including: completion, finishes		
	(22) INTERNAL WALLS including: completion, finishes		
	(23) FLOORS including: completion, finishes		
	(24) STAIRS including: completion, finishes		
	(27) ROOFS including: completion, finishes		
	(28) FRAME		

Used in this way, codes (21) to (27) aggregate secondary elements and applied finishes with primary elements to identify 'complete' elements in a way that is helpful to designers for initial design.

*This heading differs from the Construction indexing manual
†Subdivided as necessary using CI/SfB Table 2 and Table 3 codes and definitions in Part II of this Manual
‡Subdivided as necessary using CI/SfB Table 1 codes and definitions in Part II of this Manual

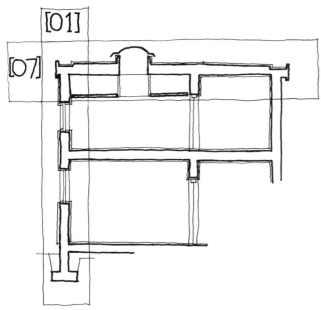

78 'Complete' elements

Section 12: Drawings programme

This section describes a method of programming drawings production based on CI/SfB drawing definitions

12.1 Introduction
12.2 Five steps
12.3 Conclusion

12.1 Introduction

Programming of drawings and schedules preparation and production can be carried out in five steps:

1 Estimate the number and content of drawings and schedules required

2 Estimate how much time each will take to complete

3 Predict a sequence

4 Define the resources available to carry out the work

5 Prepare a programme

On all but the smallest projects there will be more than one person or organisation responsible for drawings, and during the design stages (especially RIBA plan of work stages C, D and E) each will be dependent to some extent on the progress of others. The production of drawings is inevitably related to other activities such as meetings and report writing, and the programming of drawing production may effectively involve planning the design process as a whole.

The programming procedure suggested below can probably be applied most readily at Plan of work stages E and/or F but is also applicable to earlier stages.

12.2 Five steps

Step 1: Estimate the number and content of drawings to be produced

The number of location drawings (see para 4.25) produced will vary according to project size; the number of floor plans, for example, will usually increase as storeys or blocks are added. Assembly and component drawings, however, are unlikely to increase proportionately; the number of floor to wall conditions, for example, may remain more or less constant.

Location drawings

Use of the project division facet (see para 4.23) makes it easier to check systematically which areas of the building have to be drawn. Using the programming schedule (see **79**) the drawings required for the project in general are recorded first (layout plan, etc). Next, each block is considered separately. Each level, zone and room space is considered in turn, by working systematically through the Project division code structure. Drawings should be described in terms of levels, etc, *not* building elements: 'first floorplan', not 'first floor fixtures plan'.

There should be no confusion between the use of these Table 1 codes for design purposes at RIBA plan of work stage E and the use of the same codes for primary elements only at RIBA plan of work stage F, but in some cases offices have given 'complete' elements separately identifiable codes, using the free symbols in CI/SfB Table 1, as shown in the table below and in **78** above:

Codes in columns on left have been used by some offices to identify 'complete' elements at stage F

(01) External vertical envelope	= (21) External wall structure	+ (31) External wall openings and parts to fill them	+ (41) External wall finishes
(02) Internal vertical subdivisions	= (22) Internal wall structure	+ (32) Internal wall openings and parts to fill them	+ (42) Internal wall finishes
(03) Internal horizontal subdivisions	= (23) Floor structure	+ (33) Floor openings and parts to fill them	+ (43) Floor finishes
		+ (35) Suspended ceiling	+ (45) Ceiling finishes
(04) Vertical circulation	= (24) Stairs structure	+ (34) Balustrades	+ (44) Stair finishes
(07) External horizontal envelope	= (27) Roof structure	+ (37) Roof openings and parts to fill them	+ (47) Roof finishes
		+ (35) Suspended ceilings	+ (45) Ceiling finishes
(08) Frame	= (28) Frame		

Element (part) breakdown: Several drawings or schedules carrying Table 1 codes may be needed for each particular project division. In the example shown on the Programming schedule below for example, it is estimated that location drawings coded (– –), (2–), (23), (5–), (56), (6–), (63) and (8–) will be needed for 3/2 (block 3 level 2).

The degree of breakdown is a matter of experience and judgment (in some circumstances everything may be shown on sheets coded (– –)) and will depend on the way the office chooses to use CI/SfB, as well as on the circumstances of the particular project. On many projects, for example, separate fixtures drawings will not be needed, or some offices may prefer always to include fixtures information on a (– –) drawing. The codes along the top of the programming schedule show just one example of a possible breakdown.

79 *Form 1 Job Programming schedule (location drawings and schedules only). Location drawings and schedules likely to be required for the project should be listed on this sheet. The example shown lists drawings for the project in general and for blocks 3, 4 and 5*

80 *Form 2 Job Programming sheet. This example gives sketch information about each of the location drawings and schedules listed on form 1*

			JOB NO: / DATE PREPARED:						JOB PROGRAMMING SHEET	A5	sheet no.
TYPE / LOC	ELEMENT	SER. NO.	DRAWING TITLE / DESCRIPTION	MAN HOURS PLANNED	ACTUAL	TYPE/LOC	ELEMENT	SER NO	DRAWING TITLE / DESCRIPTION	MAN HOURS PLANNED	ACTUAL
			ASSEMBLY CONDITIONS						*COMPONENTS*		
A	(23)	200	Wall/floor junction: elev. A. blk 3	5		C	(23)	200-7	P.C. floor beams. 8N° sizes see dwg stage	5	
A	(23)	201	Wall / floor junction: elev. B level 4/1	5					E (2-) 209 for details		
A	(23)	202	" - " " " 4/2	5		C	(23)	208-19	PC cast floor slab to ducts. 12 No sizes		
A	(23)	203	Duct formed in suspended slab ⎱ Three No	3					see dwg E(23)207	6	
A	(23)	204	⎰ conduit runs for 4", 6"	3		C	(24)	200-1	P.C. stair 4/2/3 and 4/3/3	Standard dwg.	
A	(23)	205	and 12" slab	3		C	(24)	202-3	ditto 5/2/3 and 5/3/3	17	
A	(24)	200	Floor/stair junction 3/1/1	5		C	(27)	200-19	Roof beams to block 5 : 20 N° sizes	5	
A	(24)	201	Wall/stair junction 3/1/1	5		C	(3-)	200-14	G/f boot lintels : 15 sizes : see dwg E(3-)129	13	
A	(24)	202	" " " 3/2/1	3		C	(31)	200-3	Centre pivot windows to block 5 : 4 sizes	10	
A	(27)	200	Eaves detail: integral gutter at highest pnt.	2		C	(31)	204-5	Main exit door + frame	10	
A	(27)	201	ditto at lowest point	2		C	(31)	209-11	P.C. cills : 3 sizes	10	
A	(27)	202	Roof/wall detail elevation A. Block 4.	3		C	(32)	200-9	Internal doors : 10 sizes/types	10	
A	(27)	203	ditto elevation B+C Block 4 ⎱ 2N°	2		C	(32)	210-15	" " linings : 6 sizes	10	
A	(27)	204	⎰	2							

81 *Form 2 Job Programming sheet. Form 2 can also be used to list any assembly and component drawings which the sketches for location drawings show to be needed*

81

Forms of presentation: Next, it has to be decided how the information on each sheet should be presented, eg as plan section, elevation etc. Six forms of presentation have been defined and these are shown, with abbreviations, in the top left hand corner of the Programming schedule.

*Using the schedule:** If it is decided that a separate (1–) substructure drawing must be produced for a particular division of the project, the most appropriate form(s) of presentation (plan, section etc) is/are recorded in the (1–) column. In the example shown it was decided that a separate (1–) substructure location plan or section etc, was not required for the project as a whole because each separate block was to have its own substructure location plan, and because all sections through substructure were to be shown on assembly drawings. Each block, level and room is considered in this way.

Programming sheet (*Location sheets*), Next, a rough layout can be sketched on the Programming sheet for each drawing listed. Detail and drawing identification codes can be decided upon and shown on these rough layouts (see **80**).

Assembly and component drawings

Assembly and component drawings and schedules can be listed on another copy of the Programming sheet **81**. This is done by examining each entry on the Programming sheet showing location drawings (for example Block 3 level 2 first floor structure) and deciding what detailed assembly and component information is likely to be required in each case.

CI/SfB Table 1 should be used mentally as a check list. Sufficient information should be recorded on the Program-

ming sheet in each case to allow for easy identification later; information of this kind (essentially location information, see **81**) will not appear on the finished assembly or component drawings.

After CI/SfB has been used on several projects the word *Standard* is likely to be entered more frequently, and some drawing numbers will be those of already existing drawings.

Step 2: Estimate how much time each new or amended drawing or schedule will take to complete

An estimate of man hours required is entered against each entry in the appropriate column on the Programming sheets (**80** and **81**). To start with this can be little more than an experienced guess, but estimates will become more accurate on future projects if the actual time taken is recorded when each drawing is completed. Time taken should be recorded on time sheets to ensure accuracy, then summarised and shown on the programming sheets.

Step 3: Predict a sequence for drawings preparation

The procedure described below is only one of many which can be used. In more complex situations, or when more sophisticated routines (eg resource scheduling) are required, an alternative technique should be used.

A simple precedence diagram

First, each drawing or group of drawings which can be

*It may be helpful to have columns on the schedule for scale and sheet size

82 A6 *card used in building up a sequence of drawings*
83 *Use of cards in building up a sequence of drawings and other tasks which form part of the drawings programme*

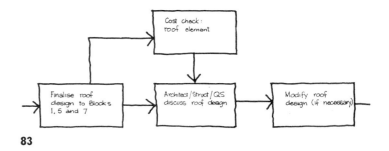

carried out as an uninterrupted sequence should be given a separate card (about A6 size) as shown in **82**.

When all the drawings listed on the Programming sheets are represented in this way the cards can be placed on a large piece of paper laid over a flat working top. Each card should then be considered in turn and the question asked 'What drawings must be complete before this drawing (or group of drawings) can be started?'

As cards are positioned in their correct relationship with other cards, depending on the reply to the question in each case, it may be necessary to include cards representing other tasks such as making cost checks, or team meetings. As new ones are placed, cards placed earlier will probably need to change position. First attempts will cover a lot of paper, but once all the cards are placed, it is usually possible to tighten up the arrangement and reduce the size of the diagram considerably.

When this has been done and all the cards are in their final position, lines can be drawn (see **83**) to show how they relate to one another. Each card (drawing) which is dependent on the completion of another should be connected to it and an arrowhead shown, pointing to the dependent drawing.

It is advisable to use a light pencil line for the connecting arrows so that they can easily be erased, because it is often necessary to adjust the position of some cards to allow for a more direct routing of the connecting lines.

First attempts at this technique may result in too many or too few cards and a rather untidy diagram. However, skill buickly develops.

Fairly sophisticated techniques of the network or sequence diagram type (see **84**) are required to predict a sequence for decision making and drawings preparation at Plan of work Stages C, D and E.

Production drawings at Stage F are a good deal easier to deal with. Simple bar (gantt) charts are usually adequate.

Step 4: Define the resources available to carry out the work

The number of staff working on a project will vary according to its type and the fee income as well as to the pattern of work adopted by the office. The length of time required to complete it will vary according to staff availability, and this must of course be decided before the drawings programme can be completed.

Step 5: Prepare a programme showing the estimated sequence start and finish of each task and the allocation of resources

A simple method of producing a programme is described below.

The drawings to be produced are listed in the lefthand column **85** in the order established at Step 3. The estimated total manhours necessary for completing each drawing is then entered in the second column. At the foot of the sheet the initials of those who will be working on the project can be listed, each person having a single horizontal line. Crossed rectangles can be used to show when each is available to work on the project.

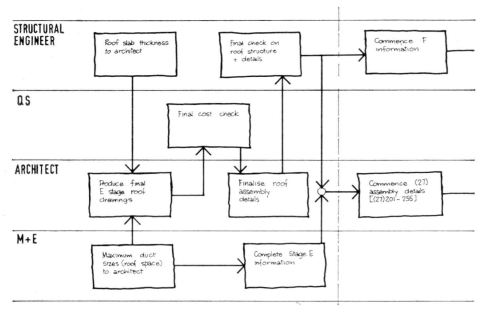

84 *Typical precedence diagram*

It will then be possible, by counting the number of crossed rectangles at the foot of any 'week' column, to see at a glance how many staff will be working on the project at any time. To complete the programme allocate a person to each drawing in turn, working from the top of the column. The number of drawings being prepared at any one time will correspond to the resources (number of persons) shown at the foot of the column. Taking the example shown in **85** there will be three drawings under preparation at any one time during week 4 (week ending 24 January).

The drawings will often fall into groups in which all are of one type. Where possible one person should carry out all drawings of a particular type. In some cases this may not be possible because of the sequence and it may be necessary, for example, to interrupt door scheduling in order to do a drawing which the engineer requires to complete other work.

12.3 Conclusion

The procedure suggested for drawings programming can be summarised as follows:

1 Estimate the content and number of location drawings and schedules to be produced, by examining each location in turn against the relevant Table 1 elements.

2 Make a rough sketch layout for each location drawing or schedule and allocate detail and sheet codes. Make an estimate of the time which will be spent on each drawing.

3 Analyse each location drawing for assembly conditions and components. As each potential drawing is recognised describe it briefly, allocate an identification code and estimate time required for completion. On completion of Step 3, all drawings necessary for the project should have been identified.

4 Using cards or some other suitable technique, define a sequence for carrying out the drawings.

5 List the drawing codes and durations in the order in which drawings are to be produced.

6 After all drawings are listed add the names of the people who will carry out the work. Indicate the periods during which each person will be available to work on the project.

7 Allocate people to drawings by entering initials in the bar which represents the particular drawing concerned.

8 If the resulting programme is too extended it must either be cut or resources must be added. A rough method of estimating resources is to add together all the estimated durations (entered against each drawing reference on the Programme sheets) and divide this by the intended project duration in weeks. This will show the average number of persons which must be available to work on the project in any one week. The results of these calculations should, of course, be checked against an analysis of the fee.

9 It is important to record the actual time spent on each drawing. If required this time can be abstracted to provide more accurate durations for future projects and allow for adjusting the programme as work proceeds.

The application of the procedure described above at Plan of work Stage E (detailed design) may be difficult, because of the large number of related activities many of which are not drawings, and are dependent on the performance of more than one person or organisation. The first attempt at introducing programming into the office should be for Stage F (production information) where the activities are relatively independent and where it may not be necessary to produce a sequence diagram at all.

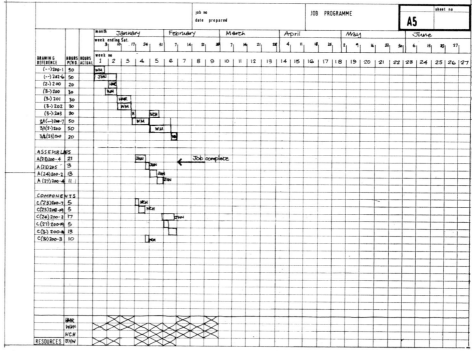

85 *Form 3. The Drawings Programme. The drawings will be listed in the order established at step 3*

Section 13: Feedback

This section describes the application of CI/SfB based methods to feedback and particularly to feedback of drawn information

13.1 Introduction
13.2 Systematic appraisal and feedback
13.3 Conclusion

13.1 Introduction

Appraisal of the drawings and specifications produced by offices in terms of the quality of the construction methods, finished buildings etc, which they describe, is one of the most important yet most neglected parts of architectural practice. It seems probable that relatively few offices manage to find the time and money to establish and record whether or not the detailed instructions implied by their drawings and specifications lead to trouble free and economical buildings produced by trouble free and economical methods.

Undoubtedly, one obstacle to appraisal and feedback of information is the lack of a generally accepted classification system for project information. If specifications are arranged one way, drawings another and the library a third, it is hardly surprising if information on the effect of design decisions is not collected systematically for feedback to designers as a means of improving performance on the next project.

Given the existence of a classification system (in this case CI/SfB) which can be used for the definition of contents and for the coding of drawings and specifications, it has to be decided:

1 Appraisal

Who will be responsible for appraising drawings and specifications for
(a) Work in progress
(b) Finished work
(c) Buildings in use for some time.

2. Feedback

Who will be responsible for feeding back the results of appraisal to designers and
How feedback will be ensured.

13.2 Systematic appraisal and feedback

Offices will vary considerably in the way they allocate responsibility for appraisal and feedback. For example:

Work in progress:

Continuous appraisal of the adequacy of drawings and specification for work in progress can be made by the project architect. All amendments made during construction work can be marked and explained in red on a record print of the drawing and/or a record copy of the specification.

Finished work:

Appraisal of the finished building can be made by a partner or chief officer, who will add to the record drawings or specification his comments on points which should be brought to the attention of those using these drawings or specification clauses in future.

Feedback:

At the end of the project a selection may be made by partner and project architect together, of component or assembly drawings which could usefully be added to the drawings library and of specification clauses which could usefully be added to the specification library.

The specification library was described in Section 5 and new clause may be typed on A4 sheets, to be filed at the appropriate point in it. This gives automatic feedback if all project specifications are prepared from the specification library.

Standard assembly and component drawings may be dealt with in various ways but two copies will usually be required of each drawing selected for the drawings library. One will be the record print already mentioned, which may have further information added to it, including cost factors (eg in the case of staircases, the cost per foot rise), and/or cross references to the priced bills of quantities for the project. The other will be a copy negative.

Both copies can be given a (library) code which may identify any special characteristics of the subject of the drawing which might lead to a need to find it for use on future work: see diagram.

The library code, like the project code, can be put on a self-adhesive sticker. The copy negative can then be stored in a plan chest or fire-proof cabinet, and the print can be folded to A4 size and stored in open-top library boxes in the library or drawing office, where it will be readily accessible

27·3	C	(32)	45		27	(32·4)	Xi4	(R)	123
Factory project Number 3	Component drawing	Doors	Identification number		Factory (CI/SfB Table 0)	Doors sliding (CI/SfB Table 1)	Timber, plywood (CI/SfB Table 2/3)	Fire stop (CI/SfB Table 4)	Identification number

PROJECT CODE LIBRARY CODE

to staff and provide a permanent reminder of the existence of standard or type drawings. Such prints will probably be kept in ci/sfB Table 1 order, and should be supported by an index or drawings register which will also give the original drawing number for the drawing. This may, of course, be supported by other indexes, as explained in *The organisation of information in the construction industry.*

Buildings in use:

A final appraisal should be made of the drawings and specification when the building has been in use for one or two years. This appraisal, which should probably not be made by either of the architects previously concerned and which should include an assessment of users reactions and the way that details have weathered, is almost certain to lead to limited further modification of the selected drawings and specification clauses.

13.3 Conclusion

The sort of procedure described above is not elaborate and can hardly be simplified if adequate feedback information is to be made available to the office. It can be made more certain and more sophisticated, particularly in larger offices able to retain their own libraries or technical information officer. A large office using ci/sfB based methods plans to introduce a formal feedback system, run by a staff member, with building industry technical qualifications. He will be responsible to a technical working party. The system is based on the use of four forms:

1 An information sheet which is prepared for each drawing or specification clause and gives its title, an abstract for it, cross references to codes of practice etc, brief notes on uses to which the detail may be put, notes of special considerations to be observed, notes of revisions.

2 A record sheet—one with each copy of the information sheet—which records the opinion of the technical working party on the drawing or clause and any action taken. It also shows on which projects the clause or drawing is being used.

3 A memorandum for each project which lists the standard drawings or specification clauses selected for use on it.

4 A feedback report to be completed to check the performance of specification clauses or details, or of any aspect of the building on which feedback is considered worthwhile.

Appendix A: Specimen list of Table 2/3 cross references

The cross references below have been used at the beginning of sections of specifications and bills of quantities organised according to ci/sfB Table 2. Not all will be relevant on all projects, and on others it may be necessary to add more. For example, the reference to J given under H SECTIONS, BARS should be deleted if mesh reinforcement is not used on a particular project or is included in the description of concrete at E. However, J should be added under F BRICKS, BLOCKS if mesh reinforcement is used in association with brickwork construction but coded separately.

E CAST IN SITU
See also   G : structural units
            H : bar reinforcement
            J : mesh reinforcement
            L : damp proof membranes

F BRICKS, BLOCKS
See also   G : lintels
            L : damp proof membranes

G STRUCTURAL UNITS
See also   H : sections
            R : rigid sheets

H SECTIONS, BARS
See also   G : structural units
            I : tubes, pipes
            J : mesh reinforcement

I TUBES, PIPES
See also   H : sections, bars

J WIRES, MESH
See also   E : cast in-situ concrete
            H : bar reinforcement

K QUILTS
See also   T : flexible sheets
            U : finishing papers, fabrics

L FOILS, PAPERS
See also   M : foldable sheet
            T : flexible sheets
            U : finishing papers, fabrics
and so on.

Appendix B: Work section headings and subheadings of the SMM*

A GENERAL RULES

B PRELIMINARIES
Preliminary particulars
Contract particulars
General matters
Temporary works
Works by public bodies
Works by nominated subcontractors
Goods and materials from nominated suppliers
Protecting, drying and cleaning the works
Contingencies

* Published by courtesy of the Standing Joint Committee for the Standard Method of Measurement of Building Works

C DEMOLITIONS AND ALTERATIONS
Generally to Section C
Demolitions
Alterations
Sundries
Protection

D EXCAVATION AND EARTHWORK
Generally to Section D
Site preparation
Excavation
Disposal of water
Planking and strutting
Hardcore filling

E PILING
Generally to Section E
Wood or concrete piles
Contractor-designed concrete piles
Steel sheet piling

F CONCRETE WORK
Generally to Section F
Plain concrete and reinforced concrete
Reinforcement
Formwork
Precast concrete units
Hollow block suspended construction
Sundries
Protection

G BRICKWORK AND BLOCKWORK
Generally to Section G
Brickwork
Brick facework
Brickwork built fair both sides or entirely of facing bricks
Brickwork in connection with boilers
Blockwork
Damp-proof courses
Sundries
Centering
Protection

H UNDERPINNING
Generally to Section H
Work in all trades

J RUBBLE WALLING
Generally to Section J
Stone rubble work
Sundries
Centering
Protection

K MASONRY
Generally to Section K
Natural stonework
Cast stonework
Clayware work
Sundries
Centering
Protection

L ASPHALT WORK
Generally to Section L
Mastic asphalt
Asphalt tiling
Protection

M ROOFING
Generally to Section M
Slate or tile roofing
Corrugated or troughed sheet roofing
Thatch roofing
Roof decking
Bitumen felt roofing
Sheet metal roofing
Sheet metal flashings and gutters
Protection

N CARPENTRY
Generally to Section N
Formwork and centering
Structual timbers
Boarding
Fillets, grounds, battens and bracketing
Sundries
Carpenter's metalwork

P JOINERY
Generally to Section P
Flooring
Eaves and verge boarding
Plywood linings and casings
Plain or panelled linings, casings and partitions
Doors, windows, skylights and lanterns
Frames, sills and kerbs
Fillets, glazing beads and grounds
Skirtings, architraves, picture rails and cornices
Shelves, table tops and seats
Sinks, draining boards and back boards
Fittings and fixtures
Staircases
Standard units
Sundries

Q STRUCTURAL STEEL WORK
Generally to Section Q
Girders
Columns and portal frames
Roof members, braces, struts and rails
Sundries

R METAL WORK
Generally to Section R
Work in plates, bars, sections and tubes
Work in sheet metal
Work in wire mesh or expanded metal
Composite units
Standard units
Sundries
Carpenter's metalwork
Protection

S PLUMBING AND ENGINEERING
Generally to Section S
Gutterwork
Pipework
Ductwork
Equipment
Appliances
Ancillaries
Thermal insulation
Sundries
Electrical work
Builder's work
Protection

T ELECTRICAL INSTALLATIONS
Generally to Section T
Equipment and control gear
Conduits and trunking
Cables and conductors
Fittings and accessories
Builder's work
Protection

U PLASTERWORK AND OTHER FLOOR, WALL AND
CEILING FINISHINGS
Generally to Section U
In-situ finishings
Tile, slab or block finishings
Plain sheet finishings
Beds and backings
Lathing and baseboarding
Suspended plain sheet linings with supporting fibrous
    plaster
Self-finished partitions
Protection

V GLAZING
Generally to Section V
Glass in openings
Leaded lights and copper lights in openings
Mirrors
Patent glazing
Domelights
Glass wall-linings
Glass blockwork
Protection

W PAINTING AND DECORATING
Generally to Section W
Painting and similar work
Polishing
Signwriting
Paperhanging
Protection

X DRAINAGE
Generally to Section X
Protection

Y FENCING
Generally to Section Y
Open-type fencing
Close-type fencing
Gates
Sundries

Appendix C: Glossary

Activity	A task, operation or process consuming time and possibly other resources
Annotation	The free translation of a code into plain language, used particularly on drawings and schedules for cross reference to specification information. *See also* 'Heading'
Assemblies (constructions)	One or more commodities brought together on site and fixed in position. *See also* 'Workpiece'
Assembly detail	Drawn details of an assembly
Bill of quantities	Document consisting mainly of measured information
Block*	A major division of the project, eg one building or part of a building. External works or parts of external works (see below) may also be regarded as 'blocks' of the project
Builder's work	Building work required for services or fixtures
Building elements or parts	Elements of CI/SfB Table 1 substructure or superstructure as distinct from services or fittings
Building work	The creation of assemblies on site, as distinct from manufacturing work which may be carried out off site
Building works	As distinct from 'External works'
Catalogue	A list of items with descriptive data, usually arranged so that a specific kind of information can be located readily. A bill of quantities is a form of catalogue
CBC	Co-ordinated Building Communications. A private commercial organisation with offices in Copenhagen and elsewhere, which has pioneered developments in integrated building documentation using the computer
CIB	International Council for Building Research, Studies and Documentation. The principal organisation concerned with international collaboration in the building field on technical matters
Citation order	The order in which the elements of a compound class (one reflecting two or more facets) and its codes are cited; eg (47) N Roof finishes—tiles or N (47) Tiles—Roof finishes. In computer working the order of elements in the code as printed out may not always reflect the citation order used in any particular sortation, eg: Tiles—Roof finishes may appear as (47) N
CI/SfB	The authoritative UK version of the international SfB classification system. The code handbook for CI/SfB is the *Construction indexing manual*.
Cited	*See* 'Citation order'
Class	A group of similar or related things, eg concepts, documents
Classification	A way of arranging information so that like concepts come together

Classification code (classifier)	One or more symbols used to represent a class to which a concept or group of concepts belongs. For example (21) is the CI/SfB code for a document or item dealing with External walls		specifically as a synonym for Part (CI/SfB Table 1)
		External works	All work outside the external face of the external wall of the building. *See also* 'Site (works)'
Code	One or more symbols or words, usually chosen to ensure economy and used to store, transmit or manipulate information and arrange it in a consistent order. For example 0 . . . 9 A . . . Z. *See also* 'Classification code,' 'Identification code'	Facet	A set of classes reflecting one principle of division: eg Blocks, sheets, tiles all indicate products ÷ form and so make up part of a Form facet
		Form	Geometric shape
Code, alpha-numeric	Code employing alphabetic and numeric symbols, eg A1, A2, etc	General arrangement drawing(s)*	Location drawing(s) showing the whole, or a very large part of a project, probably in plan, section and elevation. Primary function is to provide a map of the project, often by giving a location (Project division) code to every space which is described in more detail elsewhere in the Project information
Commodity	A general term covering products, components, materials. An article of trade		
Component	A manufactured article, finished and complete in itself, intended to be part of a complete building or structure, eg doors, doorsets, sink units		
		General information	*See* 'Project information'
Component detail	Drawn details of a component	Groups	*See* 'Main group'
Concept	Topic, idea	Heading	Brief formal statement of concept in plain language (ie not in code). For example 'External wall'
Contract	Legally binding agreement		
Construction form (CI/SfB Table 2/3)	Construction forms form, singly or in combination, the parts or elements in CI/SfB Table 1	Identification code (identifier)	One or more symbols used to identify a particular item of information, eg: 01 Number 1 02 Number 2 Usually the last part of a code so that no distinctions are made beyond it
Cross reference	A code, with or without a brief annotation, which refers or leads the inquirer to related information. This related information may or may not have the same code. If not, the word *see* is sometimes used in library practice, eg (22) *See also* (2–)		
		Index	A means of locating specific information
Data	Factual information	Information	Knowledge concerning some particular fact, subject or event in any communicable form. Information includes data
Data co-ordination	The organisation and control of data allowing the relating of data as and when required	Item*	Specification or measured item, usually found in a Specification or Bill of quantities. More generally, any separately recorded piece of information
Detail	Information in graphic form which may take up only part of a sheet		
Digit	A single character or symbol (a letter, number, dash etc) in a code	Item type code*	A code used to identify a type of specification or measured item rather than (say) a sheet or detail. For example, Fg2 01 = Bricks type 01, or Brickwork type 01
Document	Information carrier, consisting of one or more sheets or pages		
Drawing	Sheet or page consisting mainly of drawn information	Library	A collection or store of information. *See* 'Office library', 'Library of descriptions'
Drawn information	Information in graphic form	Library of descriptions	A library of descriptions of materials and work with materials from which specification and measured items can be partly derived
Element*	A part or member of a class, eg 'cost element' is an item belonging to the class of things having a cost. Used		
		Location	Geographical position

Main group*	Group of several classes together, as with the '(2–) group' in CI/SfB Table 1	**Resources (for construction)**	Labour, commodities, subcontractors, managers, services and capital at the disposal of the contractor for constructing the project
Manufacturing work	The creation of commodities		
		Scheduled information	Information in tabular form
Material*	1 Any substance arriving on site in an unprocessed state. 2 The material (often only the principal material) of which a product or component is made. For example, a window commonly referred to as 'aluminium' also includes glass	**Search pattern**	A means of leading the searcher to information required, particularly when this is scattered, eg information on External walls may be found at (21), (2–) or (– –). Good search patterns are those which seem natural to the user
Measured information	Information giving the quantities of materials and workmanship required	**Sequential number**	A number, usually the last part of a code, which represents an item in a series in order to identify it. Use 'Identification code' in preference
Mnemonic	Memory aiding		
Office library*	A collection of trade and technical information	**sfB**	These letters stand for *Samarbetskommitten för Byggnadsfrågor,* the name of a committee set up in Sweden in 1947 to consider methods of co-ordinating, more effectively, the building team's work. sfB may be translated as: 'The co-ordinating committee for the building industry'. The history of the sfB system—designed and developed by the committee and its secretary, L. M. Giertz—is given on p9 of the RIBA *Construction indexing manual*. The system is recognised and administered by CIB for use internationally for classifying technical information in the offices of building industry practitioners
Operation	A definable activity which can be completed using resources allocated to it without interruption from any other operation		
Overcode	A code used to identify any arbitrary aggregation of items		
Page	One side of a sheet of a document which may consist of one or more sheets		
Part (CI/sfB Table 1)*	Any item of any degree of magnitude which makes up building or site and which has constant functions, irrespective of building type		
Plain language	*See* 'Heading'	**Sheet**	Separately identified piece of paper used to convey drawn or text information, usually as a drawing or schedule
Product*	A commodity which has been processed but may require further working into shape for incorporation in building work (see 'Component'). Usually assembled in conjunction with others of its type. Examples are bricks, wallpaper	**Site (works)**	The part of the project that does not consist of building. Consists of External works + works in the ground under the building(s). *See also* 'External works'
Process	A sequence of changes undergone	**Sortation**	Arrangement of sheets, pages, cards or clauses and so on as one of several possible orders into which a file of items may be sorted
Project	Building project, including both site and buildings		
Project division	A division of a project into arbitrarily selected locations and named (for instance) External works. Also spaces defined by function	**SMM**	Standard Method of Measurement of building works. Rules for measurement published by the Royal Institution of Chartered Surveyors and the National Federation of Building Trades Employers
Project information (or documentation)	Information or documentation specific to the project (PD or Project documentation), as distinct from general information or documentation (GD or General documentation) from which project information may be derived	**Specification information**	Written description giving the quality of materials and workmanship required (materials and workmanship specification) or the performance required (performance specification)
		Specification	Document consisting mainly of Specification information

Symbol	That which by custom or convention represents something else
Table*	A list of classification codes and class headings covering one or more facets of CI/SfB
Unique reference	Use 'Identification code' instead
Workpiece (= work package)	A subdivision of a building convenient to a contractor for placing or in instructing operatives. Some workpieces will be related to jobs, eg scaffolding or demolition, that do not form parts of a finished building. *See also* 'Assemblies'

*This definition is special to this manual

Appendix D: Bibliography
For all users

ROYAL INSTITUTE OF BRITISH ARCHITECTS Construction indexing manual (editor A. Ray-Jones). London, 1968, RIBA [(Ahi)] 75s
The code handbook for CI/SfB, with an alphabetical index, a simple guide to classifying, filing and retrieving as well as a brief introduction and history. CI/SfB is a classification system for general (library) information and project information. The manual does not include any special guidance on the use of CI/SfB for these applications.

ROYAL INSTITUTE OF BRITISH ARCHITECTS The organisation of information in the construction industry. London, 1968, The Institute [(Ahi)] 20s o/p
In two parts: 1 general information on classification theory and the use of CI/SfB in libraries by J. Mills, RIBA consultant on SfB. Includes a chapter on post co-ordinate indexing. 2 project information by W. McCann. The use of CI/SfB and other SfB systems, with location and other codes, for arranging and cross-referencing project information. Part 2 is superseded by this manual.

ROYAL INSTITUTE OF BRITISH ARCHITECTS CI/SfB classified list of essential references. London, 1968, The Institute [(Agm)] 15s
A drawing-board-side guide to sources of information for designers; a buyer's guide for office managers and librarians and an example of CI/SfB for all users of the system, including those who are using it for project information.

ROYAL INSTITUTE OF BRITISH ARCHITECTS CI/SfB wall chart. London, 1969. The Institute [(Ahi)]
This chart, in A2 format, uses a type size which can be read across a drawing board. It consists of the main CI/SfB headings and can be used as a contents list for information arranged according to the system.

Guide to CI/SfB classification. AJ 1968, August 14, information sheet 1608, p321-326 [(Ahi)]
Describes CI/SfB in outline, class headings from all four tables, how to classify and how to file.

For those using CI/SfB for project information

ALLOTT, R. A. SfB contract documentation: a case study. RIBA *Journal*, 1969, January, p29-31 [(Ahi)]

WARD, W. R. V. Making a start on CBC drawings. RIBA *Journal*, 1969, January, p33-34 [(A3t) (Ahi)]
The pros and cons of SfB for project information.

ROYAL INSTITUTE OF BRITISH ARCHITECTS SfB for drawing numbering (SfB Agency UK Development Paper 2). London, 1967. The Institute [(A3t) (Ahi)]
This pamphlet describes the use of SfB for numbering drawings. Based on the CBC application, it is largely superseded by The organisation of information in the construction industry *and the* Construction indexing manual.

MCCANN, W. Drawings filing. RIBA *Journal*, 1967, November, p498-501 [(A3t) (Ahi)]
Methods of indexing and filing SfB numbered drawings, including the use of edge punched cards and feature cards.

MCCANN, W., H. M. R. RILEY and M. TALBOT Use of CI/SfB for project documentation. AJ, 1969, September 24, p763-778; October 8, p887-894, and 1970, February 11, p363-369 [(A1h)]
Using CI/SfB, without computers, for arranging drawings, specifications and bills of quantities. One of the authors is a qs. Though superseded by the Project information manual, *these articles provide useful background reading.*

For those using CI/SfB for office libraries

MCCANN, W. The construction index/SfB manual. 1 the new manual described; 2 how to modify your library. AJ, 1968, September 4, p441-449 [(Ahi)]
Superseded by the RIBA's Conversion kit for libraries.

ROYAL INSTITUTE OF BRITISH ARCHITECTS Conversion kit for libraries. London, 1969, The Institute. Price 60s [(Ahi)]
Includes CI/SfB Wall chart, self-adhesive stickers, labels for filing boxes, a conversion guide to the nearest CI/SfB equivalent to 1961 SfB UDC classifications, and instructions for converting libraries.

Background reading

How SfB works in Sweden. RIBA *Journal*, 1967, April, p166 [(Ahi)]
Brief history of SfB system. Illustrates the Swedish national standard specification of building work (ByggAMA), national price book and product data sheets.

QUANTRILL, M. Professional services in Scandinavia. RIBA *Journal*, 1967, December, p526-533 [(A1gm)]
Information services and the use of SfB.

SfB revised: the CI/SfB manual. RIBA *Journal*, 1968, August, p384-387 [(Ahi)]
Includes a description of the main changes made from 1961 SfB/UDC and deals briefly with the classifying process.

ROYAL INSTITUTE OF BRITISH ARCHITECTS Handbook of Architectural Practice and management. London, 1967, The Institute. £8 8s for 4 vols [(Aljw)]

BUILDING RESEARCH STATION AND MINISTRY OF PUBLIC BUILDING & WORKS A study of coding and data co-ordination for the construction industry. HMSO, £1 [(Ag)]

Part II: Handbook

Part II Handbook

A set of definitions and examples, showing how the principles set out in Part I of this manual can be applied in practice. Whereas Part I may be kept in the office library as a theoretical reference, once its contents have been mastered by those concerned, Part II is intended as a practical handbook for day-to-day use.

Near the end of this Part is a brief explanation, recapitulating the principles which were set out in detail in Part I, which may be consulted to refresh the memory of the user who has already read Part I, or be used by contractors who do not need the more detailed explanation.

Contents

1 Definitions
CI/sfB Table 1
CI/sfB Table 2
CI/sfB Table 3

2 Examples

3 Brief explanation of CI/SfB including matrices and an alphabetical index for Tables 1, 2 and 3.

4 Index to Tables 1 and 2/3

● The first section, DEFINITIONS, consists of a set of codes and definitions.

To assist progress towards the convergence of coding systems, the *Table 1 definitions* are aligned, as far as possible, with the definitions used in the *Principles, Instructions and Definitions of the Standard Form of Cost Analysis* (referred to on the following pages as SFCA), promulgated by the RICS Building Cost Information Service*. This has only been possible because of the close similarity which already existed between the headings and definitions in SFCA and those in CI/sfB Table 1, as set out in the *Construction Indexing Manual* (RIBA 1968) and *SfB for drawing numbering* (RIBA 1967). The separate set of notes provided for each element under the heading *Cost Planning* alters each definition in some respects for cost planning purposes only. Two slightly different definitions are thus provided for each element. The first (the definition in italics plus notes 1, 2 etc) keeps together, under the code, those parts which are *operationally* related to one another. The second (the definition in italics plus notes a, b, etc) keeps together, under the same code, those parts which are *functionally* related to one another. The effect of this for (27) Roof—as an example—is that the first (operational) definition excludes gable wall from *roof* since gable wall is operationally a wall. But the second (functional) definition includes gable wall as part of roof since it helps to form the roof space and needs to be included with *roof* if valid cost comparisions are to be made.

The Table 2 definitions are related throughout to the work sections of the Standard Method of Measurement, except where noted otherwise.

* References to SFCA amplified form of cost analysis are included with acknow-ledgments to BCIS; users should check them in detail against the Instructions and definitions of the Standard Form of Cost Analysis.

They will help users to decide which code to use for particular assemblies. For example, hollow block construction for horizontal slabs might be coded F (because it consists largely of blocks) or E (because it consists largely of in situ concrete). The definitions make clear that E is to be preferred, partly because hollow block construction is grouped in the Standard Method of Measurement with Concrete work, not Brickwork and Blockwork. The definitions also help users to decide on codes for commodities when coded separately from the assemblies of which they form a part. (See Section 5). For example, mortar as part of brickwork (assembly) is coded at F Brickwork; mortar as part of rigid tiles (assembly) is coded at S Rigid tiles. But mortar in general as a commodity is coded at D, as preliminary work with unfixed materials.

Table 3 codes and headings for materials are identical with those in the Construction indexing manual, and no definitions are given.

Users of the definitions will need to be familiar with the appropriate sections of Part I.

● These second section EXAMPLES explain one method of using these and other codes to cross reference drawings and other documents in accordance with the principles which were set out in Part I. It could be used as a model for internal office handbooks referring to the use of CI/sfB.

● The last section BRIEF EXPLANATION consists of a pamphlet, intended for contractors and other users of project information, giving a very brief summary and explanation of CI/sfB based methods. It includes matrics for Tables 1, 2 and 3, and an alphabetical index.

Part II, Section 1: Definitions

Table 1: elements

Definitions for purposes connected with project information, of CI/SfB Table 1: Elements (parts) as listed in RIBA Construction indexing manual 1968*. With additional code (61).

(--)
Project in general (Building and site)

Definition:
● *Any information item* (eg specification or measured item, detail, drawing, schedule, bill of quantities etc) *which includes elements from two or more of the main groups of Table 1*; as follows:

  (1—) Substructure
  (2—) Primary elements
  (3—) Secondary elements
  (4—) Finishes
  (5—) Services (mainly piped and ducted)
  (6—) Installations (mainly electrical and mechanical)
  (7—) Fixtures
  (8—) Loose equipment

Sheets and details

Location information:

All elements may be shown on sheets with this code just as on traditional small scale drawings, but detailed information should not normally be given where sheets coded by individual main group or specific codes are also provided. For example, if (2—) *Superstructure* drawings are prepared, setting-out dimensions should generally be shown on these and not on the (— —) drawings. (2—), (5—) and (6—) drawings will usually be necessary on all but the smallest projects.

General arrangement drawings coded (— —) may usefully include room names and numbers, wall opening numbers and door swings and any other information which is best shown in the context of the completed building.

Since this code comes at the beginning of the sequence of codes it may sometimes be omitted, and sheets identified with sequential numbers only, as in traditional practice.

Assembly information:

Used only where specification information on more than one main group is included on one sheet or detail.

* See bibliography (appendix D) in Part I of this manual.

Component information:

This code is most unlikely to be used for component information.

Items types, specification, bill of quantities

This code is very unlikely to be used as part of an item type code.

Cost planning

Definition as above. Represents the cost of elements from two or more (or all) main groups from Table 1 in any project division.

(1-)

Search Pattern
(1–)←→(– –)

Substructure (main group)

Definition:
● *All work below underside of screed or, where no screed exists, to underside of lowest floor finish*, including parts such as damp proof membrane together with relevant excavations and foundations.

Notes:
1 Stanchions and columns (with relevant casings) should be included with (28) Frame.
2 Includes floor finishes integral with floor construction
3 Includes retaining part of walls below ground level dpc.

Sheets and details

Used for sheets, details, etc covering two or more specific elements from (10) to (17).

Location information:

Sheets and details may include for example:
Setting out dimensions for substructure, and levels.
Outline of main structural walls over foundations.
Ducts formed in slab and other builder's work in connection with services (unless given separately and coded (13)).
Ducts preceding foundations.
Structural grids.

Piping embedded in substructure (details of pipe runs themselves should be given on the appropriate (5–) or (6–) sheets).

Assembly information:
May be used for sheets carrying details of two or more of elements (13), (16) or (17).

Component information:
Unlikely to be used to code component information.

Item types, specification, bill of quantities

This code is unlikely to be used as part of an item type code.

Cost planning

The summarized cost of (10) to (18). Definition as above except that the notes do not apply. Instead:
a Where lowest floor construction does not otherwise provide a platform the flooring surface shall be included with this element (eg if joisted floor, floor boarding would be included).
b Stanchions and columns (with relevant casings) shall be included with (28) Frame.
c Cost of piling and driving shall be shown separately stating system, number and average length of pile.
d Includes cost of the retaining part of walls below ground level damp proof course. This shall be stated separately for each form of construction.
Building works costs shall be shown separately from external works costs. Building costs may be shown separately from site costs, and coded (19).

Using SFCA the cost of substructure will be included at 1 *Substructure* except that land drainage and retaining walls in external works will be allocated to 6.A.2 *Surface treatment* and other site preparation in external works to 6.A.1 *Site preparation*.
The notes above will apply except that cost of frame, note b, will be included at 2.A *Frame* and note d will read as follows:
d The cost of external enclosing walls to basements shall be included at 2.E *External walls* and stated separately for each form of construction.

(10)

[or use (90.1)]
see p22

Search Pattern
(10)←→(1–)←→(– –)

Site substructure

Definition:
● *The equivalents below or external to the building, of (13) to (17), including site foundations, embankments (slopes), etc but excluding foundations to roads and other site finishes. Also including site preparation, clearance and demolitions, and land drainage but not services.*

Note: (11) Excavations may be used if necessary as a means of separating site preparation, clearance and demolitions, land drainage, etc from new work.

Sheets and details

Sheets with this code may be produced or information on site substructure given on (1–) or (– –) sheets.

Location information:
Setting out of site substructure, etc.

Assembly information:
Typical detail may show footings to site walls, etc.

Component information:
This code is seldom used for component information.

Item types, specification, bill of quantities

Used with Table 2/3 item type codes on sheets and details coded (10), (1–) or (– –) and in section (10) of the specification and bill of quantities.

Cost planning

Definition as above.
Any works coded (10) under the building will be included with Building works Substructure.
Any works coded (10) external to the building will be included with External Works.

Using SFCA the cost of site substructure will be included as follows:
Site preparation under building with 1 *Substructure*. Land drainage and retaining walls in external works with 6.A.2 *Surface Treatment*.
Other site preparation in external works with 6.A.1 *Site Preparation*.

(13)

Search Pattern
(13)←→(1–)←→(– –)

Floor beds

Definition:
● *Floor beds in direct contact with the ground up to underside of screed or, where no screed exists, to underside of lowest floor finish,* including relevant excavation, fill, damp proof membrane, insulation, reinforcement etc.

Notes:
1 Stanchions and columns (with relevant casings) should be included with (28) Frame.
2 Includes floor finishes integral with floor construction.

Sheets and details

Sheets with this code may be produced or information on floor beds given on (1–) or (– –) sheets.

Location information:

Setting out and located details for work bays, expansion joints, insulation ducting etc.

Assembly information:

Typical details may show construction within the slab such as forming ducts.

Component information:

Typical details may show pre-cast concrete duct covers and any other parts which may be made off site. Components which are fitted as part of the floor finishing operation such as mat well frames should be included with (43).

Item types, specification, bill of quantities

Used with Table 2/3 item type codes on sheets and details coded (13), (1–), (– –) and in section (13) of the specification and bill of quantities.

Cost planning

Definition as above. This cost may be included in (1–) *Substructure* or shown separately.

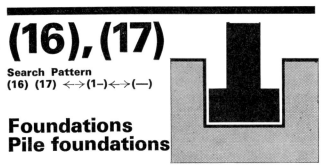

(16), (17)

Search Pattern
(16) (17) ←→(1–)←→(—)

Foundations
Pile foundations

Definition:
● *Foundations, footings, grillages; retaining walls as defined in element (1–) substructure Note 3; piers, abutments; coffer dams and caissons; tunnels and crawl ways*, including relevant excavation, fill, insulation, reinforcement, etc, up to and including damp proof membrane.
Sheet piles, displacement piles, etc.

Sheets and details

Sheets with these codes may be produced, or information on foundations and piles shown on (1–) or (– –) sheets.

Location information:

Setting out and located details for foundations, piles, etc.

Assembly information:

Typical details may show construction within foundations, such as reinforcement spacing, stepping and structural breaks.

Component information:

Most component sheets for in-situ foundation work will be bending schedules and bar bending diagrams. In precast concrete foundation work, the foundations themselves may be the subject of component details.

Item types, specification, bill of quantities

This code may be used with Table 2/3 item type codes on sheets and details coded (16) or (17) as appropriate, (1–), (– –), and in Sections (16) or (17) of the specification and bill of quantities.

Cost planning

Definition as above. This cost may be included in (1–) *Substructure* or shown separately.

(2-)

Search Pattern
(2–)←→(– –)

Superstructure
Primary elements
(main group)

Definition:
● *The carcass, building fabric, structure apart from substructure*, including secondary elements like windows, finishes, services and fittings only if these are integral in construction with the structure.

Sheets and details

This code is for sheets, details, etc, covering two or more specific elements from (20) to (28), but see *Assembly information* below.

Location information:

Layouts for roof, frame and possibly other primary elements may need to be shown and coded separately but otherwise sheets and details may include, for example:
Setting out dimensions.
Structural grid.
Room numbers.

Assembly information:

Typical details may show assembly conditions or junctions between external and internal walls, floors, stairs, roofs frames. These may be given the code of whichever primary element shown has the 'highest' code. For example, an assembly drawing showing the junction of (21) External Wall, (22) Internal Wall and (27) Roof may be coded (27) Roof.

Component information:

Unlikely to be used to code component information.

Item types, specification, bill of quantities

This code is unlikely to be used as part of an item type code.

Cost planning

The summarized cost of (20) to (28). Definition as above. Building works costs shall be shown separately from external works costs. Building costs may be shown separately from site costs, and coded (29).

Subscribers to SFCA can provide accumulated cost data for superstructure primary elements group although there is no SFCA code for it.

(20)

[or use (90.2)]

Search Pattern
(20)←→(2–)←→(– –)

Site superstructure primary elements

Definition:
● *The site equivalents of (21) to (28), including walls, fences (excluding gates and light fences), barriers; ramps, steps; shelter structures, pergolas; pools and fountains (excluding services and drainage), and sand pits.*

Sheets and details

Sheets with this code may be produced or information on site superstructure primary elements given on (2–) or (– –) sheets.

Location information:
Setting out and located details of walls, etc.

Assembly information:
Typical details may show junctions between site superstructure primary elements, etc.

Component information:
Typical details may show copings, and any other parts which may be made off site.

Item types, specification, bill of quantities

Used with Table 2/3 item type codes on sheets and details coded (20), (2–), (– –) and in section (20) of the specification and bill of quantities.

Cost planning

Definition as above. This cost will usually be included with External Works.

Using SFCA the cost of site superstructure primary elements will be included at 6.A.3 *Site enclosure and division.*

(21)

Search Pattern
(21)←→(2–)←→(– –)

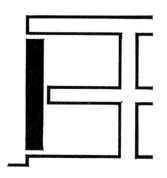

External walls

Definition:
● *External wall structure above ground level damp proof course* including air bricks, sill plates, bracings, barriers, copings, chimneys forming part of external wall, integral ducts, insulation, vertical tanking etc, but excluding eaves and verges, plates, and other parts of floor or roof structure.

Notes:
1 Includes secondary elements like balustrades, windows or window openings, finishes, services and fittings only if these are integral in construction with the external wall.
2 Includes only parts of external walls below ground level damp proof course which have no retaining function.
3 May include lintels unless these are treated as part of secondary elements.

Sheets and details

Sheets with this code may be produced or information on external walls structure given on (2–) or (– –) sheets.

Location information:
Setting out for external walls may usually be shown with internal walls, staircases etc on sheets coded (2–), but located details of external walls structure (eg in elevation) may be shown on location drawings with this code.

Assembly information:
Typical details may show construction within external wall rather than junctions with other parts.

Component information:
Typical details may show external wall structural units and any other parts which may be made off site.

Item types, specification, bq

This code may be used with Table 2/3 item type codes on sheets and details coded (21), (2–), (– –) and in section (21) of the specification and bill of quantities.

Cost planning

Definition as above except that the notes do not apply.
Instead:
a Excludes cost of applied finishes, and of external walls and chimneys above plate level (ie to roof space).
b The cost of structural walls which form an integral and important part of the loadbearing framework shall be shown separately.
c If walls are self finished on the internal face this shall be stated.
d Includes cost of parts of basement external walls below ground level damp proof course which have no retaining

function. These walls shall be shown separately and the quantity and cost given for each form of construction.

Using SFCA the cost of external walls structure will be included at 2.E *External walls.*
The notes above will apply except that notes a and d will read as follows:
a Includes cost of applied external finishes but excludes applied internal finishes, and external walls and chimneys above plate level (ie to roof space).
d External enclosing walling to basements (complete) shall be included but shown separately and the quantity and cost given for each form of construction.

(22)

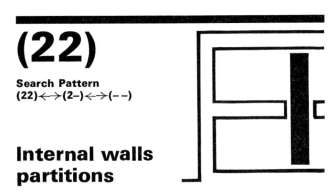

Internal walls partitions

Definition:
● *Internal walls structure above ground level damp proof course, and partitions or screens except where these have the character of doors,* including parts such as sill plates, bracing, barriers, chimneys forming part of internal walls, integral ducts, insulation, posts, heads and fire stops, but excluding plates and other parts of floor or roof structure.

Notes:
1 Includes secondary elements like balustrades, hatches and openings, finishes, services and fittings only if these are integral in construction with the internal wall structure.
2 May include lintels unless these are treated as part of secondary elements.

Sheets and details

Sheets with this code may be produced or information on internal walls structure given on (2–) or (– –) sheets.

Location information:
Setting out for internal walls may usually be shown with external walls, staircases etc, on sheets coded (2 –), but located details of internal walls structure (eg in elevation) may be shown on location drawings with this code.

Assembly information:
Typical details may show construction within internal walls and junctions with external walls.

Component information:
Typical details may show internal wall structural units and partitions and any other parts which may be made off site.

Item types, specification, bills of quantities

This code may be used with Table 2/3 item type codes on sheets and details coded (22), (2–), (– –) and in section (22) of the specification and bill of quantities.

Cost planning

Definition as above except that the notes do not apply. Instead:
a Excludes cost of applied finishes, and of internal walls and chimneys above plate level (ie in roof space).
b The cost of structural walls which form an integral and important part of the load bearing framework shall be shown separately.
c The cost of proprietary partitioning shall be shown separately stating if self-finished. Doors etc, provided therein together with ironmongery should be included stating the number of units installed.
d The cost of proprietary wc cubicles shall be shown separately stating the number provided.
e If design is cross-wall construction the specification shall be stated and the cost shown separately.

Using SFCA the cost of internal walls and partitions structure will be included at 2.G *Internal walls and partitions.*
The notes above will apply.

(23)

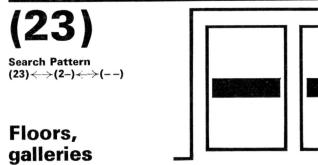

Floors, galleries

Definition:
● *Suspended floors structure, balconies, galleries and floor level staircase landings,* including parts such as integral ducts beams, bracing, decking, fire stops, joists, insulation, wall plates, reinforcement, structural screeds trimmers.

Notes:
1 Includes secondary elements like traps and openings, finishes, services and fittings only if these are integral in construction with the floor structure
2 Where floor construction does not otherwise provide a platform the flooring surface shall be included with this element (eg if joisted floor, floor boarding would be included here)
3 Excludes secondary floors such as continuous access floors, platforms, stages

Sheets and details

Sheets with this code may be produced or information on floor structure given on (2–) or (– –) sheets.

Location information:
Layout and located details for floor structure.

Assembly information:
Typical details may show construction within floors (for example the formation of integral openings and the assembly of units into a floor structure) and junctions with walls.

Component information:
Typical details may show floor decking units and any other parts which may be made off site.

Item types, specification, bill of quantities

This code may be used with Table 2/3 item type codes on sheets and details coded (23), (2–), (– –) and in section (23) of the specification and bill of quantities.

Cost planning

Definitions as above except that the notes do not apply.

Instead:
a Where floor construction does not otherwise provide a platform the flooring surface shall be included with this element, (eg if joisted floor, floor boarding would be included here)
b Beams which form an integral part of a floor slab shall be included with this element
c If the floor level staircase landings have to be included in this element this should be noted separately
d Access and private balconies are to be stated separately.
e Excludes the cost of secondary floors such as continuous access floors, platforms, stages.

Using SFCA the cost of floor structure will be included at 2.B *Upper floors*. The notes above will apply with the exception of note e. Continuous access and other secondary floors shall be included with this element.

(24)
Search Pattern
(24)←→(2–)←→(– –)

Stairs, ramps

Definition
● *Staircase structure, ramps, ladders, etc.* including strings, carriages, treads, risers, soffites, etc, and landings other than those at floor levels.

Notes:
1 Includes secondary elements like balustrades, finishes (eg in situ board finished concrete), services and fittings only if these are integral in construction with the stair structure.
2 Lift shaft structure may be given this code if shown separately from other parts.

Sheets and details

Sheets with this code may be produced or information on staircase structure, etc, given on (2–) or (– –) sheets.

Location information:
Setting out for stairs and ramps may usually be shown

with walls on superstructure setting out drawings coded (2–).

Assembly information:
Typical details may show stair or ramp construction and junctions with walls and floors.

Component information:
Typical details may show complete prefabricated staircases, ramp units and any other parts which may be made off site.

Item types, specification, bill of quantities

This code may be used with Table 2/3 item type codes on sheets and details coded (24), (2–), (– –) and in section (24) of the specification and bill of quantities.

Cost planning

Definition as above except that the notes do not apply.
Instead:
a The cost of external escape staircases shall be shown separately.
b If landings or any other part of the stair or ramps structure has had to be included in (28) *Frame* or (23) *Floors, galleries,* this should be stated.

Using SFCA, the cost of stair and ramp structure will be included at 2.D.1 *Stair structure.*
The notes above will apply except that note b will read as follows:
b If the staircase structure has had to be included in the elements 2.A *Frame* or 2.B *Upper floors* this should be stated.

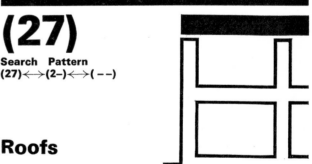

(27)
Search Pattern
(27)←→(2–)←→(– –)

Roofs

Definition
● *Roofs structure,* including parts such as eaves verges and fascias, plates joists purlins trimmers rafters integral ducts beams trusses bracing, barriers fire stops and integral insulation, decking reinforcement structural screeds, chimneys forming part of roof, parapets and integral gutters rainwater heads and roof outlets but not rainwater down pipes.

Notes:
1 Includes secondary elements like balustrades, rooflights rooflight openings, finishes, services and fittings only if these are integral in construction with the roof structure.
2 Where the roof construction does not otherwise provide a platform the roof surface shall be included with this

element (eg if joisted roof, roof boarding would be included here).

3 Roof top structures and housings (eg lift motor and plant rooms) should be included here or else divided into their constituent elements.

Sheets and details

Sheets with this code may be produced, or information on roof structure shown on (2–) or (– –) sheets.

Location information:
Layout and located details for roof structure.

Assembly information:
Typical details may show construction within roof (for example the formation of integral openings and the assembly of units into a roof structure) and junctions with walls, (floors), and staircases.

Component information:
Typical details may show roof trusses and any other units which may be made off site.

Item types, specification, bill of quantities

This code may be used with Table 2/3 item type codes on sheets and details coded (27), (2–), (– –) and in section (27) of the specification and bill of quantities.

Cost planning

Definition as above except that the notes do not apply. Instead:

a Where the roof construction does not otherwise provide a platform the roof surface shall be included with this element (eg if joisted roof, roof boarding would be included here).

b Beams which form an integral part of a roof shall be included with this element.

c Roof top structures and housings (eg lift motor and plant rooms) shall be broken down into the appropriate constituent elements.

d Includes cost of gable ends, internal walls and chimneys above plate level, parapet walls and balustrades.

e The cost of gutters where not integral with roof structure, rainwater heads and roof outlets, shall be shown separately.

Using SFCA the cost of roof structure will be included at 2.c.1 *Roof structure* and the notes above will apply.
The cost of gutters, rainwater heads and roof outlets (note e above) will be included at 2.c.3 *Roof drainage*.

(28)

Search Pattern
(28)←→(2–)←→(– –)

Frame

Definition:
● *Load bearing framework*, including columns and stanchions, beams and girders, bracing and ties, casings.

Notes:
1 Includes secondary elements, finishes, services and fittings only if these are integral in construction with the frame.

Sheets and details

Sheets with this code may be produced, or information on frame may be given on (2–) or (– –) sheets.

Location information:
Layout and located details for frame.

Assembly information:
Typical details may show construction within the frame, and junction of frame to all other elements.

Component information:
Frame components may be scheduled for cutting and drilling or shown on component drawings.

Item types, specification, bq

Used with Table 2/3 item type codes on sheets and details coded (28), (2–), (– –) and in Section (28) of the specification and bill of quantities.

Cost planning

Definition as above, with the following notes:

a Structural walls (and columns integral with them) which form an integral part of the loadbearing frame work shall be included either with (21) or (22).

b Beams which form an integral part of a floor or roof which cannot be segregated therefrom shall be included in the appropriate element.

c In unframed buildings roof and floor beams shall be included with (23) Floors, galleries or (27) Roofs.

d If (24) Stairs, ramps has had to be included in this element it should be noted separately.

Using SFCA element definitions and codes, the cost of frame will be included at 2.A *Frame*. The notes above will apply but for:

(21) External walls read 2.E *External Walls*.
(22) Internal walls read 2.G *Internal walls and partitions*.
(23) Floors, galleries read 2.B *Upper floors*.
(24) Stairs, ramps read 2.D.1 *Staircase structure*.
(27) Roofs read 2.c.1 *Roofs structure*.

(3-)

Search pattern (3–)←→(– –)

Superstructure secondary elements (main group)

Definition:

● *Completion on or within openings in the structure*, including parts required for completion. Includes services and fittings only if these are integral with secondary elements.

Sheets and details

Used for sheets, details etc covering two or more specific elements from (30) to (37).

Location information:

External and internal openings may often conveniently be shown together on drawings or schedules with this code. Schedules will link to general arrangement drawings coded (– –), and also provide cross references to details of all components, including located ironmongery, required for work in openings.

Assembly information:

Typical details of internal door jamb assemblies may not usually be shown on the same drawing as window or external door assemblies, and this code is not likely to be much used except for typical ironmongery 'sets' or on small projects where the number of drawings must be strictly limited.

Component information:

General purpose balustrades, lintels and builders work ducts and other components which are not integral with the structure nor with any particular service, but which may be used to complete more than one primary element.

Item types, specification, bill of quantities

This code is unlikely to be used as part of an item type code.

Cost planning

The summarised cost of (30) to (37). Definition as above. Building works costs shall be shown separately from external works costs. Building costs may be shown separately from site costs, and coded (39).

Subscribers to BCIS can provide accumulated cost data for superstructure secondary elements group, although there is no SFCA code for it.

(30)

[or use (90.3)]

Search Pattern (30)←→(3–)←→(– –)

Site superstructure secondary elements

Definition:

● *The site equivalents of (31) to (37)*, including gates and light fences.

Sheets and details

Sheets with this code may be produced or information on site superstructure secondary elements given on (3–) or (– –) sheets.

Location information:

Unlikely to be provided unless external works information is not included in sufficient detail on (3–) or (– –) schedules.

Assembly information:

Typical details, schedules etc may show work in openings, for example the hingeing, bolting and locking arrangements for various types of gates.

Component information:

Typical details may show gates etc and any other parts which may be made off site.

Item types, specification, bill of quantities

This code is used with Table 2/3 item type codes on sheets and details coded (30), (3–), (– –) and in section (30) of the specification and bill of quantities.

Cost planning

Definition as above. This cost will usually be included with External Works.

Using SFCA the cost of site superstructure secondary elements will be included at 6.A.3 *Site enclosure and division.*

(31)
Search Pattern
(31)←→(3–)←→(– –)

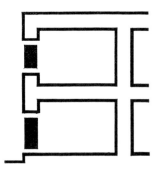

Lintels and work to the reveals of openings will be included under this code for cost planning purposes.

Using SFCA element definitions and codes, the cost of secondary elements in external walls will be included at 2.F *Windows and external doors* and can be divided into
2.F.1 *Windows*
2.F.2 *External doors*

Windows, external doors (secondary elements in external walls)

Definition:
● *Completion on or within openings in external walls structure,* including parts required to form windows, louvres, shutters, sunbreaks, external doors, shop fronts etc, such as sills and thresholds with flashings and damp proof courses, and fanlights and sidelights, linings and trims, sashes, doors, window units, ironmongery and glazing.

Notes:
1 Includes services and fittings only if these are integral in construction with external wall secondary elements.
2 May include lintels unless these are treated as part of external walls.

Sheets and details

Sheets with this code may be produced, or information given on (3–) or (– –) sheets.

Location information:
Setting out information for *openings* is likely to be shown on (21), (2–) or (– –) drawings showing external walls structure, with schedules or drawings coded (31), (3–) or (– –) giving location information on work with wall openings. Any location information on external openings which is shown separately from internal openings may be coded (31).

Assembly information:
Typical details may show jamb conditions etc.

Component information:
Typical details may show windows, doors, frames, linings and any other parts which may be made off site.

Item types, specification, bill of quantities

This code is used with Table 2/3 item type codes on sheets and details coded (31), (3–), (– –) and in section (31) of the specification and bill of quantities.

Cost planning

Definition as above except that the notes do not apply.

(32)
Search Pattern
(32)←→(3–)←→(– –)

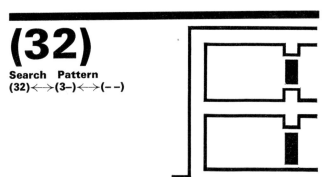

Internal doors, hatches (secondary elements in internal walls)

Definition:
● *Completion on or within openings in internal walls structure,* including parts required to form internal hatches louvres and doors etc, such as thresholds, shutter and blind boxes, frames mullions transomes, barriers and safety rails, fanlights and sidelights linings and trims sashes doors hatch units ironmongery and glazing.

Notes:
1 Includes services and fittings only if these are integral in construction with internal wall secondary elements.
2 May include lintels unless these are treated as part of internal walls.

Sheets and details

Sheets with this code may be produced, or information on secondary elements in internal walls may be given on (3–) or (– –) sheets.

Location information:
Setting out information for *openings* is likely to be shown on (22), (2–) or (– –) drawings showing internal walls structure, with schedules or drawings coded (32), (3–) or (– –) giving location information on work with wall openings. Any location information on internal openings which is shown separately from external openings may be coded with this code.

Assembly information:
Typical details may show jamb conditions etc.

Component information:
Typical details may show hatches, doors, frames, linings and any other parts which may be made off site.

Item types, specification, bills of quantities

This code is used with Table 2/3 item type codes on sheets and details coded (32), (3–), (– –) and in section (32) of the specification and bill of quantities.

Cost planning

Description as above except that the notes do not apply. Lintels and work to the reveals of openings will be included under this code for cost planning purposes.

Using SFCA element definitions and codes the cost of secondary elements in internal walls will be included at 2.H *Internal doors.*

Item types, specification, bills of quantities

This code is used with Table 2/3 item type codes on sheets and details coded (33), (3–), (– –) and in section (33) of the specification and bill of quantities.

Cost planning

Definition as above except that the note does not apply.

Using SFCA element definitions and codes the cost of secondary elements in floors will be included at 2.B *Upper floors.*

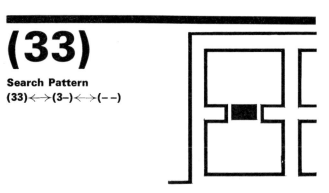

(33)

Search Pattern
(33)←→(3–)←→(– –)

Access floors, traps, stages (secondary elements in floors)

Definition:
● *Completion on or within openings in floor structure,* including parts required to form continuous access floors, traps stages machine bases etc, such as trap doors grills access panels frames (except trimmers), joists boarding trim ironmongery.

Notes:
1 Includes services and fittings only if these are integral in construction with floor secondary elements.

Sheets and details

Sheets with this code may be produced, or information on secondary elements in floors shown on (3–) or (– –) sheets.

Location information:
Setting out information for *openings* is likely to be shown on (23), (2–) or (– –) drawings showing floor structure, with schedules or drawings coded (33), (3–) or (– –) giving any location information and details of secondary elements.

Assembly information:
Typical details may show construction within secondary elements and also how they are fixed into openings or onto the floor structure.

Component information:
Typical details may show trap doors, access panels and any other parts which may be made off site.

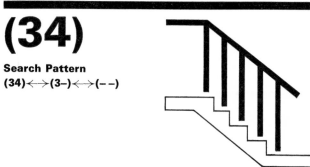

(34)

Search Pattern
(34)←→(3–)←→(– –)

Balustrades (secondary elements in stairs, ramps)*

Definition:
● *Completion of stairs and ramps structure* including parts such as newels, balusters, handrails and centre rails.

Notes:
1 Includes services and fittings only if these are integral with stair secondary elements.

Sheets and details

Sheets with this code may be produced, or information on secondary elements in stairs and ramps may be shown on (3–) or (– –) sheets.

Location information:
Setting out information on stairs and ramps is likely to be given on (24), (2–) or (– –) drawings showing stair structure with schedules or drawings coded (34), (3–) or (– –) giving any location information and details of balustrades, etc.

Assembly information:
Typical details may show junction between sections of balustrades and also how they are fixed to stairs, ramps or other elements.

Component information:
Typical details may show sections of balustrade, handrail, etc, and any other parts which may be made off site.

* The scope of this heading differs from that given in the RIBA Construction indexing manual.

Item types, specification, bills of quantities

This code is used with Table 2/3 item type codes on sheets and details coded (34), (3–), (– –) and in section (34) of the specification and bill of quantities.

Cost planning

Definition as above except that the note does not apply. Instead:
a Include here the cost of balustrades to landings at floor levels where these are associated with stairs or ramps.

Using SFCA element definitions and codes the cost of secondary elements in stairs and ramps will be included at 2.D.3 *Stair balustrades and handrails*.

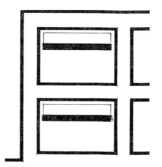

Search Pattern
(35)←→**(3–)**←→**(– –)**

Suspended ceilings (secondary elements under floors and roofs)

Definition:
● *Completion under floors and roofs* including parts such as suspension hangers and runners, fire stops, sound barriers, registers, diffusers.

Notes:
1 Includes services and fittings only if these are integral in construction with suspended ceilings. Does not include ceiling tiles, etc, applied to the suspension.
2 Excludes suspension structure (joists, etc) which is constructionally part of floors or roof.

Sheets and details

Sheets with this code may be produced, or information on suspended ceilings given on (3–) or (– –) sheets.

Location information:
Setting out and located details for suspended ceilings may be shown on schedules or drawings coded (35), (3–) or (– –).

Assembly information:
Typical details may show suspension construction and fixing of suspension to floor and roof structure, as well as fixings for any services pipe work and lighting fittings.

Component information:
Typical details may show special suspension units and any other parts which may be made off site.

Item types, specification, bills of quantities

This code may be used with Table 2/3 item type codes on sheets and details coded (35), (3–), (– –) and in section (35) of the specification and bill of quantities.

Cost planning

Definition as above, with notes as follows:
a Excludes ceiling tiles etc applied to the suspension.
b Excludes suspension structure (joists, etc) which is constructionally part of floors or roof.
c Parts of ceilings which principally provide a source of heat, artificial lighting or ventilation shall be included with the appropriate services element and the cost shall be stated separately.
d Cost of suspended ceilings to soffits immediately below roofs shall be shown separately.

Using SFCA element definitions and codes the cost of suspended ceilings will be included at 3.C.2 *Suspended ceilings*.

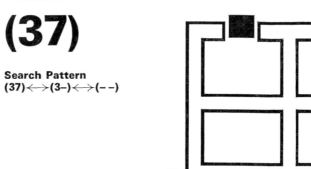

Search Pattern
(37)←→**(3–)**←→**(– –)**

Rooflights, etc (secondary elements in roofs)

Definition:
● *Completion on or within openings in roof structure* including parts required to form lights and traps, dormers and roof windows, pavement lights, etc, such as frames, kerbs (except trimmers), blind boxes, domes, louvres, trim, opening gear, glazing. Also items such as balustrades, snow guards and duckboards.

Notes:
1 Includes services and fittings only if these are integral in construction with roof secondary elements.

Sheets and details

Sheets with this code may be produced, or information on secondary elements in roofs may be shown on (3–) or (– –) sheets.

Location information:

Setting out information for openings is likely to be shown on (27), (2–) or (– –) drawings showing roof structure, with schedules, or drawings coded (37), (3–) or (– –) giving location information and details of work with rooflights, etc.

Assembly information:

Typical details may show rooflights etc (if constructed in-situ) and junctions between them and the roof structure.

Component information:

Typical details may show rooflights and any other parts which may be made off site.

Item types, specification, bills of quantities

This code may be used with Table 2/3 item type codes on sheets and details coded (37), (3–), (– –) and in section (37) of the specification and bill of quantities.

Cost planning

Definition as above except that the notes do not apply.

Using SFCA element definitions and codes the cost of rooflights etc will be included at 2.c.4 *Rooflights*.

(4-)

Search pattern
(4–)←→(– –)

Finishes (main group)

Definition:
● *Applied* finishes including where necessary, the layer of construction which is fixed or applied to the structure before decorating as well as the decoration itself.*

Sheets and details

This code is used for sheets, details, etc, covering two or more specific elements from (40) to (47).

Location information:

Internal wall, floor and ceiling finishes in room spaces may often conveniently be shown on schedules or elevational drawings with this code.

Assembly information:

Sheets (schedules) showing commonly recurring groups of item types codes and annotations with short overcodes, as an aid to the specification of wall floor and ceiling finishes may carry this code.

Component information:

This code is unlikely to be used for component information.

* By means of an operation distinct and separate from the operation of erecting or assembling the structure.

Item types, specification, bills of quantities

This code is unlikely to be used as part of an item type.

Cost planning

The summarized cost of (40) to (47). Definition as above. Building works costs shall be shown separately from external work costs. Building costs may be shown separately from site costs, and coded (49).

Subscribers to BCIS can provide accumulated cost data for finishes group although there is no SFCA code for it.

(40)   [or use (90.4)]

Search pattern
(40)←→(4–)←→(– –)

Site finishes

Definition:
● *The site equivalents of (41) to (47) including parts required to form hard finishes for roads, footpaths, vehicle parks, paved areas, playgrounds; and for soft areas for playing fields planted areas and hedges, such as kerbs, paviors wearing and base course, hardcore, turf, plants, shrubs.*

Sheets and details

Sheets with this code may be produced or information on site finishes given on (4–) or (– –) sheets.

Location information:

Setting out and located details of hard and soft surfaces, etc.

Assembly information:

Typical details may show edgings to hard and soft surfaces, paving types and constructions, etc.

Component information:

Typical details may show tree grids, kerbs and other parts which may be made off-site.

Item types, specification, bills of quantities

This code is used with Table 2/3 item type codes on sheets and details coded (40), (4–), (– –) and in section (40) of the specification and bill of quantities.

Cost planning

Definition as above. This cost will usually be included with External Works.

Using SFCA, the cost of site finishes will be included at 6.A.2 *Surface treatment*.

(41)

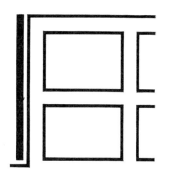

Search pattern
(41)←→(4–)←→(– –)

External wall finishes

Definition:
● *External applied finishes to external walls*, including preparatory work and parts such as battens, applied cladding, tiling, rendering, flashings, cover fillets, decoration.

Notes:
1 Will normally exclude finishes integral with the structure such as facing brickwork.

Sheets and details

Sheets with this code may be produced or information on external wall finishes given on (4–) or (– –) sheets.

Location information:
Location of external finishes to external walls may conveniently be shown on elevational drawings or schedules with this code or on general finishes schedules coded (4–) or general arrangement drawings coded (– –)

Assembly information:
Typical details may show junctions of tiling, etc, with other finishes.

Component information:
Typical details may show flashings, plaques and other parts which may be made off site.

Item types, specification, bill of quantities

This code is used with Table 2/3 item type codes on sheets and details coded (41), (4–), (– –), and in section (41) of the specification and bill of quantities.

Cost planning

Definition as above.

Using SFCA element definitions and codes, the cost of external wall finishes will be included in 2.E *External walls*.

(42)

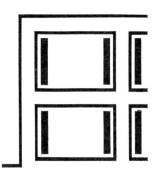

Search pattern
(42)←→(4–)←→(– –)

Internal wall finishes

Definition:
● *Internal applied finishes to internal and external walls* including preparatory work and parts such as battens applied cladding, plasterboard, tiling, plaster or other thick coatings, cover fillets, bands, dadoes, picture rails, decorations.

Notes:
1 Will normally exclude finishes integral with the structure such as facing brick work.

Sheets and details

Sheets with this code may be produced or information on internal wall finishes given on (4–) or (– –) sheets.

Location information:
Location of internal wall finishes may conveniently be shown on elevational drawings or schedules with this code or on general finishes schedules coded (4–).

Assembly information:
Typical details may show junctions of one type of finish with another, and schedules coded (42) or (4–) can show commonly occurring groups of specification items.

Component information:
Typical details may show plywood, leather, tiles, stone and other finishes which may be worked into a final condition off-site.

Item types, specification, bills of quantities

This code is used with Table 2/3 item type codes on sheets and details coded (42), (4–), (– –) and in section (42) of the specification and bill of quantities.

Cost planning

Definition as above except the note does not apply. Instead:
1 Surfaces which are self-finished (eg self-finished partitions, fair faced work) shall be included in the appropriate element.
2 Insulation which is a wall finishing shall be included here.
3 The cost of finishes applied to the inside face of external walls shall be shown separately.

Using SFCA element definitions and codes the cost of internal wall finishes will be included in 3.A *Wall finishes*.

(43)

Search pattern
(43)←→**(4–)**←→**(– –)**

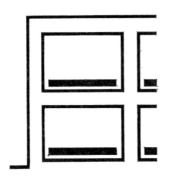

(44)

Search pattern
(44)←→**(4–)**←→**(– –)**

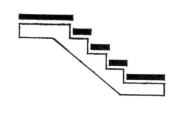

Floor finishes

Definition:
● *Applied floor finishes and floating floors* including preparatory work and parts such as non-structural screed, battens, suspension units, cover strips, skirtings and other edgings, tiles, sheets.

Notes:
1 Will normally exclude stair finishes and structural screeds.
2 Where the floor structure does not otherwise provide a platform or is self finished or the finish is integral with the slab, then the flooring finish will be included with (13) Floor bed or (23) Floors, galleries as the case may be.

Sheets and details

Sheets with this code may be produced or information on floor finishes given on (4–) or (– –) sheets.

Location information:
Location of floor finishes may conveniently be shown on drawings or schedules with this code or on general finishes schedules coded (4–) or general arrangement drawings coded (– –).

Assembly information:
Typical details may show junctions of skirtings and one type of finish with another, floating floors, etc, and schedules coded (43) or (4–) can show commonly occurring groups of specification items.

Component information:
Typical details may show skirting sections and other parts which may be made off-site.

Item types, specification, bills of quantities

This code is used with Table 2/3 item type codes on sheets and details coded (43), (4–), (– –) and in section (43) of the specification and bill of quantities.

Cost planning

Definition and notes as above.

Using sfca element definitions and codes the cost of floor finishes will be included with 3.b *Floor finishes.*

Stair, ramp finishes

Definition:
● *Applied stair and ramp finishes*, including preparatory work and finishes to treads including nosings, risers, landings other than those at floor level, ramps, strings, soffits.

Sheets and details

Sheets with this code may be produced or information on stair finishes given on (4–) or (– –) sheets.

Location information:
Location of stairs and ramps is likely to be shown on drawings coded (2–) or (– –).
Details of finishes for these stairs and ramps may conveniently be shown on general finishes schedules coded (4–) or possibly, in some circumstances, on drawings or schedules coded (44).

Assembly information:
Typical details may show junction of nosings or stair skirtings with other finishes, and schedules coded (44) or (4–) can show commonly occurring groups of specification items.

Component information:
Typical details may show precast terrazzo stair treads for in-situ concrete stairs, and other parts which may be made off site.

Item types, specification, bills of quantities

This code is used with Table 2/3 item type codes on sheets and details coded (44), (4–), (– –) and in section (44) of the specification and bill of quantities.

Cost planning

Definition as above.

Using sfca element definitions and codes the cost of stair and ramp finishes will be included with 2.d.2 *Stair finishes.*

(45)
Search pattern
(45)←→(4–)←→(– –)

(47)
Search pattern
(47)←→(4–)←→(– –)

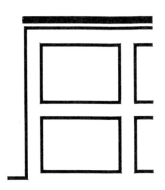

Ceiling finishes

Definition:
● *Applied finishes to suspended ceilings, and to soffits of floors and roofs and sides and soffits of beams not forming part of a wall surface*, including preparatory work and parts such as battens, wiremesh, plasterboard, tiling, plaster or other thick coatings, cornices, coverstrips, coves, decoration.

Sheets and details

Sheets with this code may be produced or information on ceiling finishes given on (4–) or (– –) sheets.

Location information:
Location of ceiling finishes may conveniently be shown on reflected plans coded (45), or combined with other finishes on schedules coded (4–) or on general arrangement drawings coded (– –).

Assembly information:
Typical details may show junctions of cornices or coves with surrounding construction, or joints between ceiling panels.

Component information:
Typical details may show cornices, coves and other parts which may be made off site.

Item types, specification, bill of quantities

This code is used with Table 2/3 item type codes on sheets and details coded (45), (4–), (– –) and in section (45) of the specification and bill of quantities.

Cost planning

Definition as above, but the cost of finishes to soffits immediately below roofs shall be shown separately.

Using SFCA element definitions and codes the cost of ceiling finishes will be included in **3.c.1** *Ceiling finishes.*

Roof finishes

Definition:
● *Applied finishes to roof*, including preparatory work and parts such as roof screeds and insulation, battens, felt, tiling, asphalt and other thick coatings, eaves and verge treatment, flashings, trim and decoration.

Sheets and details

Sheets with this code may be produced or roof finishes may be given on (4–) or (– –) sheets.

Location information:
Location of roof finishes and located details may be shown on drawings with this code showing falls, ridges.

Assembly information:
Typical details may show welting, forming of fillets and drips, flashings to service pipes, etc.

Component information:
Typical details may show any parts which may be made off site.

Item types, specification, bills of quantities

This code is used with Table 2/3 item type codes on sheets and details coded (45), (4–), (– –) and in section (47) of the specification and bill of quantities.

Cost planning

Definition as above.

Using SFCA element definitions and codes the cost of roof finishes will be included in **2.c.2** *Roof coverings.*

(5-)

Search pattern
(5-)←→(- -)

Services (piped & ducted)* (main group)

Definition:
●*Piped and ducted services and integrated service arrangements such as heart units*, including particularly *heat centre** and parts such as boilers and burners, mounting, firing equipment, pressurising equipment, general instrumentation and control, ID and FD fans, gantries, flues, draught stabilizers, fuel conveyors, calorifiers. Cold and treated water supplies and tanks, fuel supply equipment, storage tanks, etc, pipework (water or steam mains) pumps, valves, unions and other equipment, ash removal and soot blowing plant, insulation.
Local heat sources for particular services shall be included with the service to which they apply.

Notes:
1 Builder's works such as boiler houses may be divided and coded by their constituent building elements where convenient. Chimneys and flues which are an integral part of the building structure may usually be included with the appropriate building element.

Sheets and details

This code is for sheets, details, etc, covering two or more specific elements from (50) to (57).

Location information:
On many projects setting out information (eg pipe runs) builder's work schedules and any located details for services may be conveniently divided between two series of sheets with this code. One can show general building services such as drainage, water supply and gas supply, and the other can show refrigeration, central heating and ventilation or air conditioning.

Assembly information:
Typical details of services assemblies will not usually be given this code if they are concerned with a particular service but will be given a specific element code. Details showing the preparation of specific building elements to receive services should usually be given the appropriate building element code and not the services element code. For example, a drawing showing a duct in the floor bed to receive (central heating) pipes would usually be coded (13), not (56). A drawing showing a raised base for a boiler would be coded (33), not (5-). But details showing pipe fixing for several services to several building elements would be coded (5-); and parts such as manholes, which comprise several building elements but—in many cases—relate to only one services element, can be coded (50) or (51), etc, as appropriate.

Component information:
Heat centre components and integrated service arrangements such as heart units.

* (5-) is the only code used both as a main group code and a code for a specific element (Heat centre). The international SfB Development Group has agreed that (**51**) may be used experimentally in project information for **Heat centre** as the equivalent of (**61**) **Electrical centre**. Offices using (**51**) for this purpose should include Refuse disposal with Drainage at (**52**) **Disposal**. This code and heading will then relate directly to SFCA **5C Disposal installations**.

Item types, specification, bill of quantities

This code will sometimes be used as part of an item type code for work in connection with heat centre. Builder's work items in connection with services will be coded as for drawings showing them (see above), but a column may be included in bills of quantities giving the specific services element code as well as the building element code†. This is useful both for cost analysis purposes and on site, as an aid to locating in bills the builder's work items required for particular services.

Cost planning

The summarized cost of (50) to (57) and the specific cost of heat centre. Definition as above except that the note does not apply. Building works costs shall be shown separately from external works costs. Building costs may be shown separately from site costs, and coded (59).
Note that:
a The cost of builder's work shall, where possible, be shown separately. Where tank and boiler room housings and the like are included in the gross floor area, their component parts shall be analysed in detail under the appropriate building elements. Where this is not done the total cost of such items shall be included under the appropriate services element, or here.
b Chimneys and flues which are an integral part of the structure shall be included with the appropriate building element.
c The cost of *heat centre(s)* shall be shown separately from the summarized cost of (50) to (57) and where more than one heat centre is provided each shall be analysed separately.

Subscribers to SFCA can provide accumulated cost data for piped and ducted services main group as defined above although there is no SFCA code for the group as a whole. Using SFCA element definitions and codes the cost of heat centre will be included at 5.E *Heat Source*.

---

(50)   [or use (90.5)]

Search pattern
(50)←→(5-)←→(- -)

Site services

Definition:
●*The site equivalents of (51) to (57)*, including all drainage (other than land drainage) to and including disposal point, connection to sewer or treatment plant. Similarly includes refuse disposal, water service including wells and fire hydrants or dry mains, gas and heating mains and any special piped services. Includes any heat source external to or under the building.

† See Part I, Section 6.

Notes:

1 Including all work under the building or in external works (ie outside the external face of the external wall).

2 Builder's work such as manholes or septic tanks may be divided and coded by their constituent building elements where this is more convenient.

Sheets and details

Sheets with this code may be produced or information on site services elements given on (5–) or (– –) sheets.

Location information:
Setting out information including manhole numbers, builder's work schedules and located details may be shown on sheets coded (50), (5–) or (– –).

Assembly information:
Typical details of services assemblies including pipework, etc. Details showing the preparation of specific building elements to receive services should usually be given the appropriate building element code and not this code. For example, a drawing showing preparation of site walls to carry external heating mains would be coded (20), not (50).

Component information:
Typical details may include traps, gullies and any other parts which may be made off-site.

Item types, specification, bill of quantities

This code is used with Table 2/3 item type codes on sheets and detail coded (50), (5–), (– –) and in section (50) of the specification and bill of quantities. Builder's work items in bills of quantities may be coded as suggested in the note at (5–) Services: Item types.

Cost planning

Definition as above except that the notes do not apply. Instead:

a The cost of builder's work in connection with each type of service and drainage shall, where possible, be shown separately. Where *ancillary buildings* such as boiler houses are included in the gross floor area their component parts shall be analysed in detail under the appropriate building elements. Where this is not done the total cost of such items shall be included under the appropriate services element, or here.

b Work outside the external face of the building will be included in external works for cost planning purposes.

c The cost of *each individual service* shall be shown separately. Where possible the cost of *drainage* shall be divided into surface water drainage, foul drainage and sewage treatment.

Subscribers to sfca can provide accumulated cost data for services in External Works as defined above although there is no sfca code for the group as a whole. Using sfca element definitions and codes the cost of drainage will be included as follows: 6.b *Drainage* 6.c *External services* (apart from drainage) 6.d *Minor building work*. (Ancillary buildings for services.)

(51)

Search pattern
(51)←→(5–)←→(– –)

Refuse disposal ‡

Definition:

● *Refuse disposal* including parts such as refuse ducts, flues, hoppers, chutes and bins, waste disposal (grinding) units*, central vacuum cleaning**, local incinerators† and shredders and their flues, dustbins and bags. For parts under the building or in external works see (50) Site services.

Notes:

1 Builders work in connection with refuse disposal (eg dustbin enclosures) may be divided and coded by its constituent building parts (walls, etc) where convenient.

Sheets and details

Sheets with this code may be produced or information on refuse disposal given on (5–) or (– –) sheets.

Location information:
Setting out information, builder's work schedules and located details may usually be shown on sheets coded (5–) or (– –).

Assembly information:
Typical details may show assembly of chutes, dustbin enclosures, etc (but see note 1 above).

Details showing preparation of building elements to receive refuse disposal assemblies should be coded as indicated in the note at (5–) Services: Assembly information.

Component information:
Typical details may show chutes, hoppers, etc, and other parts which may be made off site.

Item types, specification, bill of quantities

This code is used with Table 2/3 item type codes on sheets and details coded (51), (5–), (– –) and in section (51) of the specification and bill of quantities. Builder's work items in bills of quantities may be coded as suggested in the note at (5–) Services: Item types.

Cost planning

Definitions as above except that the note does not apply. Instead:

a The cost of builder's work shall where possible be shown

* Excluding kitchen waste disposal drainage units, coded (52) in this manual, coded (73) in the *Construction indexing manual*.
** Including central vacuum cleaning, coded (54) in the *Construction indexing manual*.
† Including sanitary incinerators, coded (74) in the *Construction indexing manual*.
‡ This code may be used experimentally for **Heat centre**. See footnote to (5–).

separately. Where plant rooms, etc, are included in the gross floor area their component parts shall be analysed in detail under the appropriate building elements. Where this is not done the total cost of such items shall be included here.
b The costs of *refuse disposal* and *central vacuum cleaning* shall be shown separately.

Using SFCA element definitions and codes the cost of refuse disposal will be included at 5.c.2 *Refuse disposal*, except central vacuum cleaning which will be included at 5.M *Special installations*.

Item types, specification, bill of quantities

This code is used with Table 2/3 item type codes on sheets and details coded (52), (5–), (– –) and in section (52) of the specification and bill of quantities. Builder's work items in bills of quantities may be coded as suggested in the note at (5–) Services: Item types.

Cost planning

Definition as above except that the note does not apply. Instead:
a The cost of builder's work shall, where possible, be shown separately.

Using SFCA element definitions and codes the cost of drainage will be included at 5.c.1 *Internal drainage*.

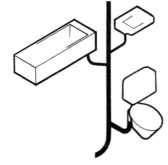

(52)

Search pattern
(52)←→**(5–)**←→**(– –)**

Drainage*

Definition:
●*Soil and waste disposal, chemical and petrol and rainwater disposal*, including parts such as covers, channels, gulleys, gratings, sumps, pumps, rainwater downpipes (but not gutters), soil waste and ventilating pipes, traps, vents. For parts under the building or in external works see (50) Site services.

Notes:
1 Builder's work in connection with drainage above ground may be divided and coded by its constituent building parts where this is convenient.

Sheets and details

Sheets with this code may be produced where necessary or information on drainage may be shown on (5–) or (– –) sheets.

Location information:
Setting out information, builder's work schedules and located details may usually be shown on sheets coded (52) or (5–) which will indicate the positions of sanitary fixtures without giving details of them.

Assembly information:
Typical details may show pipework, etc. Details showing the preparation of building elements to receive drainage assemblies, etc, should be coded as indicated in the note at (5–) Services: Assembly information.

Component information:
Typical details may include channels, gratings, pipes, etc, and other parts which may be made off site.

* This code may be used experimentally for **Disposal**. See footnote to (5–).

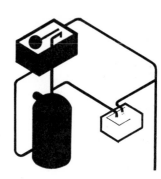

(53)

Search pattern
(53)←→**(5–)**←→**(– –)**

Hot and cold water

Definition:
●*Mains supply, cold water service, hot water services, steam and condensate†*, including parts such as stopcock, water meter, rising main, storage tanks, pumps, pressure boosters, water treatment plant, distribution pipework, valves, storage cylinders, calorifiers, instantaneous water heaters, taps, mixers, insulation. For parts under the building or in external works see (50) Site services.

Notes:
1 Builder's work in connection with hot and cold water services (eg tank house) may be divided and coded by its constituent building parts where this is convenient.
2 Storage tanks or other parts of the water supply system which serve only a particular service at (51) to (57), or a general heat source at (5–), should be included under the appropriate code and not under this code.

Sheets and details

Sheets with this code may be produced or information on hot and cold water services may be shown on (5–) or (– –) sheets.

† Including Steam Service, coded (54) in the *Construction indexing manual* 1968.

Location information:
Setting out information, builder's work schedules and location details may usually be shown on sheets coded (53) or (5–) which will indicate the positions of sanitary fixtures without giving details of them.

Assembly information:
Typical details may show pipework, pipe insulation, tank housing, etc (but see Note 1). Details showing the preparation of building elements to receive pipework, etc, should be coded as indicated in the note at (5–) Services: Assembly information.

Component information:
Typical details may include any parts which may be made off-site.

Item types, specification, bill of quantities

This code is used with Table 2/3 item type codes on sheets and details coded (53), (5–), (– –) and in section (53) of the specification and bill of quantities. Builder's work items in bills of quantities may be coded as suggested in the note at (5–) Services: Item types.

Cost planning

Definition as above except that the notes do not apply. Instead:

a The cost of builder's work shall, where possible, be shown separately. Where tank rooms, etc, are included in the gross floor area their component parts shall be analysed in detail under the appropriate building elements. Where this is not done the total cost of such items shall be included here.
b Storage tanks or other parts of the water supply system which serve only a particular service at (51) to (57) or a general heat source at (5–), should be included under the appropriate code and not under this code. The cost of associated electrical work shall be included with (62) Power.
c The cost of *mains supply* including valves, water meters and rising mains but excluding storage tanks; of *cold water services* (including tanks, pumps, pipework, insulation and taps not included with fixtures); of *Hot and/or mixed water services* (including cylinders, pumps, calorifiers, pipework, insulation, taps not included with fixtures and instantaneous water heaters); and of *steam and condensate*, shall be shown separately.

Using SFCA element definitions and codes the cost of hot and cold water services will be included as follows:
5.D.1 *Mains supply*
5.D.2 *Cold water service*
5.D.3 *Hot water service*
5.D.4 *Steam and condensate*
5.M *Special installations* (Treated water)

(54)

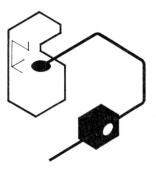

Search pattern
(54)←→(5–)←→(– –)

Gas, compressed air, etc

Definition:
●*Town and natural gas services, propane and butane, medical and industrial gases and compressed air*, including parts such as stop cocks, meters, compressors, storage cylinders, pumps, distribution pipework, taps and general purpose burners. For parts under the building or in external works see (50) Site services.

Note:
1 Builder's work in connection with gas services may be divided and coded by its constituent building parts, where this is more convenient.
2 Parts of the gas supply system which serve only a particular service at (51) to (57) or a general heat source at (5–) should be included under the appropriate code and not under this code.

Sheets and details

Sheets with this code may be produced or information on gas and compressed air services given on (5–) or (– –) sheets.

Location information:
Setting out information, builder's work schedules and located details may usually be shown on sheets coded (5–) or (– –) which will indicate the positions of cookers or other fixtures using gas without giving details of them.

Assembly information:
Typical details may show pipework etc. Details showing the preparation of building elements to receive pipework, etc, should be coded as indicated in the note at (5–) Services: Assembly information.

Component information:
Typical details may include any parts which may be made off-site.

Item types, specification, bill of quantities

This code is used with Table 2/3 item type codes on sheets and details coded (53), (5–), (– –) and in section (54) of the specification and bill of quantities. Builder's work items in bills of quantities may be coded as suggested in the note at (5–) Services: Item types.

Cost planning

Definitions as above except that the notes do not apply. Instead:

a The cost of builder's work shall where possible be shown separately.
b Parts of the gas supply system which serve only a particular service at (51) to (57) or a general heat source at (5–) should be included under the appropriate code, not under this code.

Using sfca element definitions and codes the cost of town and natural gas supply will be included at 5.I *Gas installations*. Medical and chemical gas supply and compressed air are included at 5.M *Special installations*.

Search pattern
(55)⟷(5–)⟷(– –)

Refrigeration

Definition:
●*Cold rooms and refrigerated stores and other refrigeration other than individual refrigerators or refrigeration ancillary to air treatment and air conditioning*, including parts such as cooling towers, compressors, instrumentation and controls, insulation and vapour sealing. For parts under the building or in external works see (50) Site services.

Notes:
1 Builder's work in connection with refrigeration (eg cold room structures) may be divided and coded by its constituent building parts (walls, etc) where this is more convenient.

Sheets and details

Sheets with this code may be produced or information on refrigeration given on (5–) or (– –) sheets.

Location information:
Setting out information, builder's work schedules and located details may usually be shown on sheets coded (5–) or (– –) possibly with located details on a (55) sheet.

Assembly information:
Typical details may show pipework, assembled plant, etc, possibly including special cold room insulation, which may conveniently be shown on a (55) sheet (See Note 1). Details showing preparation of building elements to receive pipework, etc, should be coded as indicated in the note at (5–) Services: Assembly information.

Component information:
Typical details may include any parts which may be made off site.

Item types, specification, bill of quantities

This code is used with Table 2/3 item type codes on sheets

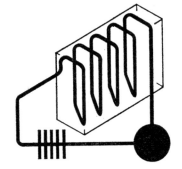

and details coded (55), (5–), (– –) and in section (55) of the specification and bills of quantities. Builder's work items in bills of quantities may be coded as suggested in the note at (5–) Services: Item types.

Cost planning

Definition as above except that the note does not apply. Instead:
a The cost of builder's work shall where possible be shown separately. Where cold rooms, etc, are included in the gross floor area their component parts shall be analysed in detail under the appropriate building elements. Where this is not done the total cost of such items shall be included here.
b The cost of associated electrical work shall be included with (62) Power.

Using sfca element definitions and codes the cost of refrigeration will be included at 5.M *Special installations*.

Search pattern
(56)⟷(5–)⟷(– –)

Space heating

Definition:
●*Space heating by hot water and/or steam*, such as radiators, convectors including skirting heating, fan convectors including unit heaters, panels including ceiling units and floor coils, instrumentation and control, and distribution pipework. Also parts for heating by *ducted warm air* such as ductwork, grills, fans, filters, instrumentation and control; for *electrical built-in systems* such as floor coils, ceiling panels, storage radiators, controlled output storage heaters; for *other centralised systems* such as heat pumps and solar heating; *and local heating* including fireplaces (except flues), radiant heaters, small electrical and gas appliances. For parts under the building or in external works see (50) Site services.

Notes:
1 Builder's work in connection with space heating (eg housing for controlled output storage heater) may be divided and coded by its constituent building parts where this is convenient.

Sheets and details

Sheets with this code may be produced or information on space heating given on (5–) or (– –) sheets.

Location information:
Setting out information, builder's work schedules and located details may usually be shown on sheets coded (56) or (5–).

Assembly information:
Typical details may show pipework, site joinery in connection with fan convectors, etc (see note 1). Details showing preparation of building elements to receive pipework, etc, should be coded as indicated in the note at (5–) Services: Assembly information.

Component information:
Typical details may include any parts which may be made off site.

Item types, specification, bills of quantities

This code is used for the parts defined above with Table 2/3 item type codes on sheets and details coded (56), (5–), (– –) and in section (56) of the specification and bills of quantities. Builder's work items in bills of quantities may be coded as suggested in the note at (5–) Services: Item types.

Cost planning

Definition as above except that the note does not apply. Instead:

a The cost of builder's work shall where possible be shown separately. Where housings, etc, are included in the gross floor area their component parts shall be analysed in detail under the appropriate building elements. Where this is not done the total cost of such items shall be included here.
b The cost of *water and/or steam heating; ducted warm air; electrical built-in systems; other centralised systems;* and *local heating,* shall be shown separately.
c The cost of associated electrical work shall be included with (62) Power.

Using SFCA element definitions and codes the cost of space heating will be included at 5.F *Space heating and air treatment,* as follows:
5.F.1 *Water and/or steam*
5.F.2 *Ducted warm air*
5.F.3 *Electricity*
5.F.4 *Local heating*
5.F.5 *Other heating systems*

(57)

Search pattern
(57)←→(5–)←→(– –)

Air conditioning, ventilation

Definition:
● *Air conditioning (air heating or cooling), including heating with ventilation (air treated locally) and heating with ventilation (air treated centrally)* including parts such as distribution pipework, ducting, grills, instrumentation and control, and heat emission units including heating calorifiers except those which are part of (5–) Heat source.

Also heating with cooling (air treated locally) and heating with cooling (air treated centrally), including parts such as those listed above with the addition of chilled water systems and/or cold or treated water feeds.
Mechanical ventilation (no heating or cooling), including dust and fume smoke extraction and fresh air injection, unit extract fans, rotating ventilators, and instrumentation and controls. For parts under the building or in external works see (50) Site services.

Notes:
1 Builder's work in connection with air conditioning and ventilation (eg plant rooms) may be divided and coded by its constituent building parts where this is convenient.
2 'Air treated locally' indicates air treatment is performed in or adjacent to the space to be treated. 'Air treated centrally' indicates central air heating and cooling with ducting to the space to be treated.

Sheets and details

Sheets with this code may be produced, or information on air conditioning and ventilation may be shown on (5–) or (– –) sheets.

Location information:
Setting out information, builder's work schedules and located details may usually be shown on sheets coded (57) or (5–).

Assembly information:
Typical details may show ducting, housings, etc (see Note 1). Details showing the preparation of building elements to receive pipework, etc, should be coded as indicated in the note at (5–) Services: Assembly information.

Component information:
Typical details may include ducts or any parts which may be made off site.

Item types, specification, bills of quantities

This code is used with Table 2/3 item type codes on sheets and details coded (57), (5–), (– –) and in section (57) of the specification and bill of quantities. Builder's work items in bills of quantities may be coded as suggested in the note at (5–) Services: Item types.

Cost planning

Definition as above except that Note 1 does not apply. Instead:

a The cost of builder's work shall where possible be shown separately. Where plant rooms, etc, are included in the gross floor area their component parts shall be analysed in detail under the appropriate building elements. Where this is not done the total cost of such items shall be included here.

b Show separately the cost of *heating with ventilation (air treated locally); heating with ventilation (air treated centrally); heating with cooling (air treated locally); heating with cooling (air treated centrally), mechanical ventilation (no air treatment).* Where more than one system is used, design criteria specification notes and costs should be given for each.

c State the combination of treatments applied, ie:

Heating	Dehumidification or drying
Cooling	Filtration
Humidification	Pressurisation

and whether inlet extract or recirculation.
High velocity systems shall be identified as:

Fan coil	Induction units 2 pipe
Dual duct	Induction units 3 pipe
Reheat	Induction units 4 pipe
Multi-zone	Any other system (state which)

d In the case of heating with cooling the cost of the cooling plant shall be shown separately. The heat source will be included with (5-).
e The cost of associated electrical work shall be included with (62) Power.

Using SFCA element definitions and codes the cost of air conditioning and ventilation will be included at 5.F *Space heating and air treatment*, as follows:
5.F.6 *Heating with ventilation (air treated locally)*
5.F.7 *Heating with ventilation (air treated centrally)*
5.F.8 *Heating with cooling (air treated locally)*
5.F.9 *Heating with cooling (air treated centrally)*
5.G *Ventilating system (mechanical ventilation)*

(6-)

Search pattern (6-)←→(- -)

Installations (electrical services) (main group)

Definition:
●*Electrical and mechanical services apart from those serving functions already included at (5-) Services.*

Note:
1 Builder's work housing electrical and mechanical services may be divided and coded by its constituent building elements where this is convenient.

Sheets and details

This code is for sheets, details, etc, covering two or more specific elements from (60) to (68).

Location information:
On many projects setting out information, builder's work schedules and located details for electrical services may conveniently be shown on a series of sheets with this code. A separate series may be needed to show electrical centre, power distribution and lighting only.
Lifts, etc, being restricted to a relatively small area of the project, will usually be shown, in detail, on a (66) sheet or sheets.

Assembly information:
Typical details will not usually be given this code if they are concerned with a particular service, but will be given

a specific element code. Details showing the preparation of specific building elements to receive services should usually be given the appropriate building element code and not the services element code. For example, drawings showing holes required in floors for lifts (or other installations) should be coded (23), not (66). See also the note at (5-) Services: Assembly information.

Component information:
This code is unlikely to be used for component information.

Item types, specification, bill of quantities

This code is unlikely to be used as part of an item type code. Builder's work items in connection with services will be coded as for drawings showing them (see above) but a column may be included in bills of quantities giving the specific services element code as well as the building element code*. This is useful both for cost analysis purposes and on site, as an aid to locating in the bills the builder's work items required for particular services.

Cost planning

The summarised cost of (60) to (68). Definition as above except that the note does not apply. Building works costs shall be shown separately from external works costs. Building costs may be shown separately from site costs, and coded (69).
Note that:
a The cost of builder's work shall, where possible, be shown separately. Where switchrooms and the like are included in the gross floor area, their component parts shall be analysed in detail under the appropriate building elements. Where this is not done the total cost of such items shall be included under the appropriate services element, or here.

Subscribers to SFCA can provide accumulated cost data for electrical services main group as defined above although there is no SFCA code for the group as a whole.

(60)   [or use (90.6)]

Search pattern (60)←→(6-)←→(- -)

Site installations (electrical and mechanical services)

Definition:
●*The site equivalents of (61) to (68)*, including electrical services, such as electric mains and power, site lighting, telephones, aerials.

Notes:
a Including all work under the building or in external works (ie outside the external face of the external wall).
b Builder's work such as access pits may be divided and coded by its constituent building elements where this is more convenient.
* See Part I, Section 6.

Sheets and details

Sheets with this code may be produced or information on site installations elements given on (6–) or (– –) sheets.

Location information:
Setting out information including duct runs for electrical site installations, builder's work schedules and located details may be shown on sheets coded (60), (6–) or (– –).

Assembly information:
Typical details of electrical site installations assemblies. Details showing the preparation of building elements to receive electrical installations should be coded as indicated in the note at (6–) Installations: Assembly information.

Component information:
Typical details may include lighting standards and any other parts which may be made off site.

Item types, specification, bill of quantities

This code is used with Table 2/3 item type codes on sheets and details coded (60), (6–), (– –) and in section (60) of the specification and bill of quantities. Builder's work items in bills of quantities may be coded as suggested in the note at (6–) Installations: Item types.

Cost planning

Definition as above except that the notes do not apply. Instead:
a The cost of builder's work in connection with each type of installation shall, where possible, be shown separately. Where *ancillary buildings* such as switch rooms are included in the gross floor area their component parts shall be analysed in detail under the appropriate building elements. Where this is not done the total cost of such items shall be included under the appropriate services or installations element, or here.
b Work outside the external face of the building will be included in External works for cost planning purposes.
c The cost of each individual installation shall be shown separately, particularly *mains* and *lighting* (see below).

Subscribers to sfca can provide accumulated cost data for installations in External works as defined above although there is no sfca code for the group as a whole. Using sfca element definitions and codes the cost of installations in external works will be included as follows:
6.c.5 *Electric mains*
6.c.6 *Site lighting*
6.c.7 *Other mains and services*
6.d *Minor building work* (ancillary buildings for services)

---

(61)

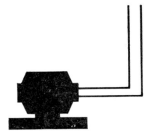

Electrical centre*

Definition:
● *Electrical load centre and mains distribution up to and including consumer units or sub mains distribution boards,* including parts such as meters, generating plant, motors, batteries, converters, transformers, main switchgear, controls and instrumentation, busbar chambers, power factor correction equipment, main and sub main conduit and cabling, stand-by equipment, protective gear, earthing etc. For parts under the building or in external works see (60) Site installations.

Notes:
1 Builder's work in connection with electrical centre may be divided and coded by its constituent building elements where this is convenient.
2 Electrical space heating and air conditioning is included at (56) Space heating or (57) Air conditioning as the case may be.

Sheets and details

Sheets with this code may be produced or information on electrical centre may be given on (6–) or (– –) sheets.

Location information:
Setting out information, builders work schedules and located details may usually be shown on sheets coded (61) or (6–).

Assembly information:
Typical details may show meter cupboards etc (but see Note 1). Details showing preparation of building elements to receive conduit or other electrical centre assemblies should be coded as indicated in the note at (6–) Installations: Assembly information.

Component information:
Typical details may include distribution boards and any other parts which may be made off site.

Item types, specification, bill of quantities

This code is used with Table 2/3 item type codes on sheets and details coded (61), (6–), (– –) and in section (61) of the specification and bill of quantities. Builders work items in bills of quantities may be coded as suggested in the note at (6–) Installations: Item types.

* Included with (62) Power in the *Construction indexing manual* 1968.

Cost planning

Definition as above except that the notes do not apply.
Instead:
a The cost of builders work shall, where possible, be shown separately. Where switch rooms and the like are included in the gross floor area, their component parts shall be analysed in detail under the appropriate building elements. Where this is not done the total cost of such items shall be included here.
b Electrical space heating and air conditioning shall be included with (56) Space heating or (57) Air conditioning as the case may be.
c The cost of standby equipment shall be stated separately.

Using SFCA element definitions and codes the cost of electrical centre installations will be included at 5.H.1 *Electrical source and mains.*

(62)

Search pattern
(62)←→(6–)←→(– –)

Power*

Definition:
●*Power distribution subcircuits from local distribution boards to and including outlet points,* including parts such as wiring, cabling, conduits, switches, sockets, plugs. For parts under the building or in external works see (60) Site installations.

Notes:
1 Builders work in connection with power may be divided and coded by its constituent building elements where this is convenient.
2 Electrical space heating and air conditioning is included at (56) Space heating or (57) Air conditioning as the case may be.

Sheets and details

Sheets with this code may be produced or information on power distribution given on (6–) or (– –) sheets.

Location information:
Setting out information, builders work schedules and located details may usually be shown on sheets coded (62) or (6–).

Assembly information:
Typical details may show assembly of switches, socket outlets etc with other work. Details showing preparation of building elements to receive conduit or other power

* In the *Construction indexing manual* 1968 (62) includes central electrical equipment. This may be coded (61) Electrical centre using this manual.

distribution assemblies should be coded as indicated in the note at (6–) Installations: Assembly information.

Component information:
Typical details may include any parts which may be made off-site.

Item types, specification, bill of quantities

This code is used with Table 2/3 item type codes on sheets and details coded (62), (6–), (– –) and in section (62) of the specification and bills of quantities. Builders work items in bills of quantities may be coded as suggested in the note at (6–) Installations: Item types.

Cost planning

Definition as above except that the notes do not apply.
Instead:
a The cost of builders work shall, where possible, be shown separately.
b The cost of power distribution to the following services and installations should where possible be shown separately: Heat centre, refuse disposal, hot and cold water, gas, refrigeration, space heating, air conditioning, general purpose socket outlets, communications installation, transport installations, security installations, fixtures other than fixtures included in the services or installations listed above.

Using SFCA element definitions and codes, the cost of power distribution from local distribution boards will be included at 5.H.2 *Electrical power supplies.*

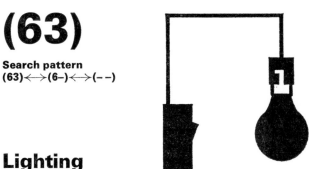

(63)

Search pattern
(63)←→(6–)←→(– –)

Lighting

Definition:
●*Lighting installation,* from the distribution board onwards, including parts such as wiring, cables, switches, lighting fittings and control gear, and sodium, cold cathode, tungsten, fluorescent, mercury lamps, etc. Emergency lighting. For parts under the building or in external works see (60) site installations.

Notes:
1 Builders work in connection with lighting may be divided and coded by its constituent building elements where this is convenient.

2 Translucent panels for suspended ceilings will normally be included with suspended ceilings.

3 Light fittings attached to the outside of the building will normally be coded (63) unless they form an integral part of a site lighting installation.

4 Wiring, switches etc for electrical power for lighting installations may be coded (62) Power.

Sheets and details

Sheets with this code may be produced or information on lighting given on (6–) or (– –) sheets.

Location information:
Setting out information, builders work schedules and located details may usually be shown on sheets coded (63) or (6–).

Assembly information:
Typical details may show assembly of lighting fittings with other types of work. Details showing preparation of building elements to receive lighting fittings or other lighting assemblies or components should be coded as indicated in the note at (6–) Installations: Assembly information.

Component information:
Typical details may include lighting fittings and any other parts which may be made off site.

Item types, specification, bill of quantities

This code is used with Table 2/3 item type codes on sheets and details coded (63), (6–), (– –) and in section (63) of the specification and bill of quantities. Builders work items in bills of quantities may be coded as suggested in the note at (6–) Installations: Item types.

Cost planning

Definition as above except that the notes do not apply. Instead:

a The cost of builders work shall, where possible, be shown separately.

b The costs of *lighting installation* (wiring etc) and of *lighting fittings* including fixing, shall be shown separately. Where lighting fittings are supplied direct by the client, this should be stated. The cost of emergency lighting shall be shown separately. The cost of illuminated signs etc shall be included with fixtures and fittings, not here, and the cost of translucent panels for suspended ceilings will be included with suspended ceilings. The cost of light fittings attached to the outside of the building will normally be included here unless they form part of a site lighting installation.

Using SFCA element definitions and codes, the cost of wiring etc will be included at 5.H.3 *Electric lighting* and the cost of lighting fittings will be included at 5.H.4 *Electric lighting fittings*.

Search pattern
(64)←→(6–)←→(– –)

Communications

Definition:

● *Visual and audio media* such as television, radio, film projection, central dictation and tape recording, intercom, telephone, loudspeaker and public address, staff location, teleprinter, pneumatic message systems, clocks, buzzers, bells in general, including parts such as aerials, control equipment, indicator boards, input equipment, terminal points and equipment. For parts under the building or in external works see (60) Site installations.

Notes:

1 Builders work in connection with communications installations may be divided and coded by its constituent building elements where this is convenient.

2 Wiring etc for electrical power for communications installations will normally be coded (62) Power.

Sheets and details

Sheets with this code may be produced or information on communications systems given on (6–) or (– –) sheets.

Location information:
Setting out information, builders work schedules and located details may usually be shown on sheets coded (64) or (6–).

Assembly information:
Typical details may show assembly of telephone hoods with other work. Details showing preparation of building elements to receive communications equipment etc should be coded as indicated in the note at (6–) Installations: Assembly

Component information:
Typical details may include special loudspeakers, telephone hoods*, and other parts which may be made off site.

Item types, specification, bill of quantities

This code is used with Table 2/3 item type codes on sheets and details coded (64) (6–), (– –) and in section (64) of the specification and bill of quantities. Builders work items in bills of quantities may be coded as suggested in the note at (6–) Installations: Item types.

Cost planning

Definitions as above except that the notes do not apply. Instead:

* Included with (71) Circulation fixtures in the *Construction indexing manual* 1968.

a The cost of builders work shall, where possible, be shown separately.
b The cost of wiring etc for electrical power for communications installations shall be included at (62) Power.
c The cost of *each type of installation* listed in the definition shall be stated separately if possible.
d The cost of bells and alarms forming an integral part of security installations shall be included with (68) Security installations.

Using SFCA element definitions and codes, the cost of communications installations will be included at 5.L *Communications installations*. This will include the cost of all bells and alarms (Note: d above will not apply).

(66)

Search pattern

(66)←→(6–)←→(– –)

Transport

Definition:
● *Lifts and hoists, escalators, conveyors, and other transport systems* (*eg cranes*) including parts such as gantries, trolleys, blocks, hooks cables and ropes, downshop leads, guides, runways, pendant controls, electrical work from and including isolator, cars, buckets, belts, stairways. For parts under the building or in external works see (60) Site installations.

Notes:
1 Builders work in connection with transport installations may be divided and coded by its constituent building elements where this is convenient.
2 Wiring etc for transport installations up to the isolator will be included with (62) Power.

Sheets and details

Sheets with this code may be produced or information on transport installations given on (6–) or (– –) sheets.

Location information:
Setting out information, builders work schedules and located details may usually be shown on sheets coded (66) or (6–).

Assembly information:
Typical details may show construction work to be done on site in association with lifts, hoists, escalators, conveyors etc. Details showing preparation of building elements to receive transport installations should be coded as indicated in the note at (6–) Installations: Assembly information.

Component information:
Typical details may include lift cars and any other parts which may be made off site.

Item types, specification, bill of quantities

This code is used with Table 2/3 item type codes on sheets and details coded (66) (6–), (– –) and in section (66) of the specification and bill of quantities. Builders work items in bill of quantities may be coded as suggested in the note at (6–) Installations: Item types.

Cost planning

Definition as above except that the notes do not apply. Instead:
a The cost of builders work shall, where possible, be shown separately. Where lift motor rooms etc are included in the gross floor area their component parts shall be analysed in detail under the appropriate building elements. Where this is not done the total cost of such items shall be included here.
b The cost of wiring etc for electrical power for transport installations up to the isolator shall be included with (62) Power.
c The cost of *lifts and hoists*, *escalators*, *conveyors* and *other systems* shall be stated separately. The cost of each type of lift or hoist shall be stated separately.

Using SFCA element definitions and codes the cost of transport installations will be included as follows: 5.J.1 *Lifts and hoists* (except window cleaning cradles)
5.J.2 *Escalators*
5.J.3 *Conveyors* (including moving platforms, endless belts, turntables)
5.M *Special installations* (including window cleaning cradles).

(68)

Search pattern

(68)←→(6–)←→(– –)

Security

Definition:
● *Theft prevention and alarm systems* including parts such as surveillance and alarm wiring and equipment, trip wires etc. *Fire prevention and alarm systems* such as sprinkler installations including CO_2 extinguishing system tanks, control mechanism etc, and other fire fighting methods including hose reels, hand extinguishers, asbestos blankets, water and sand buckets, foam inlets, dry risers (and wet risers or ring main piping servicing fire fighting equipment only), fire alarms. *Lightning protection* from finials and conducting

tapes down to and including earthing. For parts under the building or in external works see (60) Site installations.
Notes:
a Builders work in connection with security installations may be divided and coded by its constituent building elements where this is convenient.
b Wiring etc for electrical power for security installations will normally be coded (62) Power.

Sheets and details

Sheets with this code may be produced or information on security installations given on (6–) or (– –) sheets.

Location information:
Setting out information, builders work schedules and located details may usually be shown on sheets coded (68) or (6–).

Assembly information:
Typical details may show hosereel recesses (if constructed on site) and any other construction work done on site in association with security installations. Details showing preparation of building elements to receive this work should be coded as indicated in the note at (6–) Installations: Assembly information.

Component information:
Typical details may include any parts which may be made off site.

Item types, specification, bq

This code is used with Table 2/3 item type codes on sheets and details coded (68), (6–), (– –) and in section (68) of the specification and bill of quantities.
Builder's work items in bills of quantities may be coded as suggested in the note at (6–) Installations: Item types.

Cost planning

Definition as above except that the notes do not apply.
Instead:
a The cost of builder's work shall, where possible, be shown separately. Where housings for security installations are included in the gross floor area their component parts shall be analysed in detail under the appropriate building elements. Where this is not done the total cost of such items shall be included here.
b The cost of wiring, etc, for electrical power for security installations shall be included with (62) Power.
c The cost of *sprinkler installations, other fire fighting installations* and *lightning protection* shall be stated separately where possible. The cost of lightning protection to boiler and vent stacks, etc, shall be stated separately.
d The cost of *theft and fire alarm installations* shall be stated separately.

Using SFCA element definitions and codes the cost of security installations will be included as follows:
5.K.1 *Sprinkler installations*
5.K.2 *Fire fighting installations* (except sprinklers)
5.K.3 *Lightning protection*
5.L *Communications installations* (theft and fire alarms)

(7–)

Search pattern
(7–)←→(– –)

Fixtures (main group)

Definition:
● *Built in or fixed position fittings, not including fittings already included in groups* (5–) *or* (6–).

Notes:
1 May include loose equipment and furniture or plug-in electrical fittings unless these are coded separately in group (8–).

Sheets and details

This code is used for sheets, details, etc, covering two or more specific elements from (70) to (76).

Location information:
Layouts, located details and any builder's work schedules for many types of fixtures may often conveniently be shown on (7–) or (– –) sheets, but sanitary fixtures may need to be shown on a separate series of (74) sheets.

Assembly information:
Typical details are fairly unlikely to be coded (7–) since they will usually be concerned with a particular type of fixture and will be given a specific element code. Details showing the preparation of building elements to receive fixtures should usually be given the appropriate building element code and not the fixtures code. For example, drawings showing the preparation of suspended ceilings to receive curtain tracks should usually be coded (35), not (71); drawings showing the preparation of wall finishes—using pattresses—to receive sanitary fixtures should normally be coded (42) rather than (74) if the pattresses are placed at the same time as the wall finishes.

Component information:
This code is unlikely to be used for component information.

Item types, specification, bill of quantities

This code is unlikely to be used as part of an item type code. Builder's work items for fixtures terminating services will be coded as for drawings showing them (see above), but a column may be included in bills of quantities giving the specific fixtures element code as well as the building element code*. This is useful both for cost analysis purposes and on site as an aid to locating in bills the builder's work items required for particular fixtures.

Cost planning

The summarized cost of (70) to (76). Definition as above except that the note does not apply. Building work costs

* See Part I, Section 6.

shall be shown separately from external works costs. Building costs may be shown separately from site costs, and coded (79).
Note that:
a The cost of builders work shall, where possible, be shown separately.
b Costs may be shown separately as follows:
Fixtures
All fixtures not included in one of the categories below.
Fixed or immovable Works of art
Murals, fixed and/or large sculpture. If items in this class have a significant cost effect on other classes such as internal or external finishes, a note should be included in the appropriate element.
Sanitary fixtures
As defined in (74) Sanitary fixtures.
Unserviced specialist fixed equipment
Non-mechanical and non-electrical fixed equipment (eg gymnasia equipment) which is related to the function of the building.
Serviced specialist fixed equipment
Culinary fixtures as defined in (73), cleaning fixtures as defined in (75), and any other mechanical and electrical fixed equipment related to the function of the building.
c Alternatively, all costs may be shown according to the classes defined under the codes (70) to (76). In this case, the cost of fixed or immovable works of art and of specialist fixtures related to the function of the building shall be shown separately, under the appropriate code.

Using SFCA element definitions and codes note c above will not apply, and the cost of fixtures will be included as follows:
4.A.1 *Fittings, fixtures and furniture* (all fixtures not listed below)
4.A.3 *Works of art*
4.A.4 *Equipment* (unserviced specialist fixed equipment)
5.A *Sanitary appliances* (including slop sinks)
5.B *Services equipment* (serviced specialist fixed equipment)
6.A4 *Site Fixtures*

Sheets and details

Sheets with this code may be produced or information on site fixtures given on (7–) or (– –) sheets.

Location information:
Layouts, builders work schedules and located details.

Assembly information:
Typical details of site fixtures. Details showing the preparation of building elements to receive site fixtures should be coded as indicated in the note at (7–) Fixtures: Assembly information.

Component information:
Typical details may include flower containers and any other parts which may be made off site.

Item types, specification, bill of quantities

This code is used with Table 2/3 item type codes on sheets and details coded (70), (7–), (– –) and in section (70) of the specification and bill of quantities.

Cost planning

See note at (7–) Fixtures: Cost planning.

(71)

Search pattern
(71)←→(7–)←→(– –)

Circulation fixtures

Definition:
●*Built in or fixed position items not normally connected with any main user activity at (72) to (76), including murals, notice boards, signs, entrance mats, ash trays, waste paper receptacles, flower containers, vending machines, blinds, curtain tracks etc*.

Note:
1 May include loose equipment and furniture or plug-in electrical fittings unless these are coded (81).

Sheets and details

Sheets with this code may be produced or information on circulation fixtures given on (7–) or (– –) sheets.

* Telephone booths are coded (64) in this manual.

(70)   [or use (90.7)]

Search pattern
(70)←→(7–)←→(– –)

Site fixtures

Definition:
●*The site equivalents of (71) to (76),* including parts such as fixed notice boards, flower containers, bollards, litter bins, benches, clothes drying equipment, flagpoles, swings.

Notes:
1 Including all work under the building or in external works (ie outside the external face of the external wall)
2 May include loose equipment and furniture or plug-in electrical fittings unless these are coded (80).

Location information:
Layouts, builders work schedules and located details.

Assembly information:
Typical details showing any assembly work for circulation fixtures. Details showing preparation of building elements to receive circulation fixtures should be coded as indicated in the note at (7–) Fixtures: Assembly information.

Component information:
Typical details may show notice boards and any other parts which may be made off site.

Item types, specification, bill of quantities

This code is used with Table 2/3 item type codes on sheets and details coded (71), (7–), (– –) and in section (71) of the specification and bill of quantities.

Cost planning

See note at (7–) Fixtures: Cost planning.

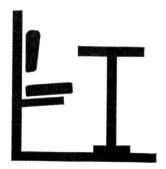

(72)

Search pattern
(72)←→(7–)←→(– –)

General room fixtures

Definition:
● *Built-in or fixed position fixtures for working and relaxing which are not related to user activities at* (73) *to* (76)*, including fixtures such as bunks, fixed seats, benches, tables, desks, computer installations and other fixed machinery and equipment.*

Note:
1 May include loose equipment and furniture or plug-in electrical fittings unless these are coded (82).

Sheets and details

Sheets with this code may be produced, or information on general room fixtures given on (7–) or (– –) sheets.

Location information:
Layouts, builders work schedules and located details.

Assembly information:
Typical details showing any assembly work for general room fixtures.

Details showing preparation of building elements to receive general room fixtures should be coded as indicated in the note at (7–) Fixtures: Assembly information.

Component information:
Typical details may include laboratory benches and any other parts which may be made off site.

Item types, specification, bill of quantities

This code is used with Table 2/3 item type codes on sheets and details coded (72), (7–), (– –) and in section (72) of the specification and bill of quantities.

Cost planning

See note at (7–) Fixtures: Cost planning.

(73)

Search pattern
(73)←→(7–)←→(– –)

Culinary fixtures

Definition:
● *Built-in or fixed position fixtures for culinary purposes apart from general purpose storage at* (76)*, including fixtures such as larders, worktops and integral cupboards, sinks and draining boards, refrigerators, cookers, hot plates, boiling pans, fryers, grills, ovens, hot cupboards, washing up machines, food preparation equipment*†.

Note:
1 May include loose equipment and furniture or plug-in electrical fittings unless these are coded (83).

Sheets and details

Sheets with this code may be produced or information on culinary fixtures given on (7–) or (– –) sheets.

Location information:
Layouts, builders work schedules and located details.

Assembly information:
Typical details showing any assembly work for culinary fixtures. Details showing preparation of building elements to receive culinary fixtures should be coded as indicated in the note at (7–) Fixtures: Assembly information.

Component information:
Typical details may include purpose made kitchen work tops and any other parts which may be made off site.

† Waste disposal units are coded (51) in this manual. Ventilation and extraction units or hoods are coded (57) in this manual.

Item types, specification, bill of quantities

This code is used with Table 2/3 item type codes on sheets and details coded (73), (7–), (– –) and in section (73) of the specification and bill of quantities.

Cost planning

See note at (7–) Fixtures: Cost planning.

(74)

Search pattern
(74)←→(7–)←→(– –)

Sanitary fixtures

Definition:
●*Built in or fixed position fixtures for washing and sanitary purposes apart from general purpose storage at* (76), including fixtures such as baths, wcs, wash basins troughs bidets, urinals, shower cabinets, drinking fountains, towel rails, towel cabinets, mirrors, handdriers, soap dispensers, with traps and other waste fittings, overflows and taps etc as appropriate*.

Note:
1 May include loose equipment and furniture or plug-in electrical fittings unless these are coded (84).

Sheets and details

Sheets with this code may be produced, or information on sanitary fixtures given on (7–) or (– –) sheets. Positions of sanitary fittings, showing the termination of drain runs, waste pipes and water supply pipes will be shown on (52) (53), (5–) or (– –) sheets as appropriate.

Location information:
Layouts, builders work schedules and located details.

Assembly information:
Typical details showing any assembly work for sanitary units or other sanitary fixtures. Details showing preparation of building elements to receive sanitary fixtures should be coded as indicated in the note at (7–) Fixtures: Assembly information.

Component information:
Typical details may include dressing units or mirrors and any other parts which may be made off site.

* Sanitary incinerators are coded (51) in this manual.

Item types, specification, bq

This code is used with Table 2/3 item type codes on sheets and details coded (74), (7–), (– –) and in section (74) of the specification and bill of quantities.

Cost planning

See note at (7–) Fixtures: Cost planning.

(75)

Search pattern
(75)←→(7–)←→(– –)

Cleaning fixtures

Definition:
●*Built in or fixed position fixtures for cleaning purposes apart from general purpose storage at* (76), including fixtures such as washing machines, ironers, dryers, airing cupboards, wash and slop sinks, specialist cleaning plant†.

Note:
1 May include loose equipment and furniture or plug-in electrical fittings unless these are coded (85).

Sheets and details

Sheets with this code may be produced or information on cleaning fixtures given on (7–) or (– –) sheets.

Location information:
Layouts, builders work schedules and located details.

Assembly information:
Typical details showing any assembly work for cleaning fixtures.
Details showing preparation of building elements to receive cleaning fixtures should be coded as indicated in the note at (7–) Fixtures: Assembly information.

Component information:
Typical details may include any parts which may be made off site.

Item types, specification, bq

This code is used with Table 2/3 item type code on sheets and details coded (75), (7–), and (– –) and in section (75) of the specification and bill of quantities,

Cost planning

See note at (7–) Fixtures: Cost planning.

† Vacuum cleaning and disposal system is coded (51) in this manual
Travelling cradles are coded (66).

(76)

Search pattern
(76)←→(7–)←→(– –)

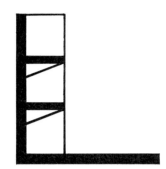

Storage fixtures

Definition:
●*Built in or fixed position fixtures for storage equipment,*
including cupboards, wardrobes, storage walls, shelf and
cupboard units, room dividers, shelving, safes, coathooks,
cloak fittings, lockers.

Note:
1 May include loose equipment and furniture or plug-in
electrical fittings unless these are coded (86).

Sheets and details

Sheets with this code may be produced or information on
storage fixtures given on (7–) or (– –) sheets.

Location information:
Layouts, builders work schedules and located details.

Assembly information:
Typical details showing any assembly work for storage
fixtures.
Details showing preparation of building elements to receive
storage fixtures should be coded as indicated in the note
at (7–) Fixtures: Assembly information.

Component information:
Typical details may include cupboards or any other parts
which may be made off site.

Item types, specification, bill of quantities

This code is used with Table 2/3 item type codes on sheets
and details coded (76), (7–), (– –) and in section (76) of the
specification and bill of quantities.

Cost planning
See note at (7–) Fixtures: Cost planning.

(8-)

Search pattern
(8–)←→(– –)

Loose equipment (main group)

Definition:
●*Loose equipment, furniture and plug in (movable) electrical
fittings.*

Sheets and details

This code is used for sheets, details etc, covering two or
more specific elements from (80) to (86).

Location information:
Layouts for loose equipment—much of which may be
supplied by the client—may often conveniently be shown
on (8–) or (– –) sheets.

Assembly information:
This code is not applicable to loose equipment.

Component information:
This code is unlikely to be used for component information.

Item types, specification, bq

This code is unlikely to be used as part of an item type code.

Cost planning

The summarized cost of (80) to (86). Definitions as above.
Building works costs shall be shown separately from external
works costs.

Note that:
a Costs may be shown separately, as follows:
Furniture and loose equipment
All furniture and loose equipment not included in one of
the categories below.
Movable works of art
Easel pictures, pottery, small sculptures, etc.
Sanitary loose equipment
As defined in (84) Sanitary loose equipment.
Unserviced specialist loose equipment
Loose equipment apart from soft furnishings, which is
related to the function of the building.
Serviced specialist loose equipment
Mechanical and electrical (plug in) culinary loose equipment
defined as in (83), cleaning loose equipment as defined in
(85), and any other loose equipment related to the function
of the building.
Soft furnishings
Curtains, loose carpets or similar soft furnishing materials.
b Alternatively, all costs may be shown according to the
classes defined under the codes (80) to (86). In this case,
the cost of movable works of art, of specialist loose equipment related to the function of the building, and of soft
furnishings, shall be shown separately, under the appropriate
code.

Using SFCA element definitions and codes, note b above will
not apply, and the cost of loose equipment will be included
as follows:

4.A.1 *Fittings, fixtures and furniture* (all furniture and loose
equipment not listed below).
4.A.2 *Soft furnishings.*
4.A.3 *Works of art.*
4.A.4 *Equipment* (Unserviced specialist loose equipment).
5.A *Sanitary appliances* (loose equipment).
5.B *Services equipment* (Serviced specialist loose equipment).
6.A.4 *Site furniture.*

(80)

[or use (90.8)]

Search pattern
(80)←→(8–)←→(– –)

Site loose equipment

Definition:
● *The site equivalents of* (81) *to* (86), including parts such as garden tables and chairs, recreation and gardening equipment.

Sheets and details

Sheets with this code may be produced or information on site loose equipment given on (8–) or (– –) sheets for external works.

Location information:
Layouts

Assembly information:
Not applicable to loose equipment.

Component information:
Typical details may include garden tables or any other parts defined above, all of which may be made off site.

Item types, specification, bill of quantities

This code is used with Table 2/3 item type codes on sheets and details coded (80), (8–), (– –) and in section (80) of the specification and bill of quantities.

Cost planning

See note at (8–) Loose equipment: Cost planning.

(81)

Search pattern
(81)←→(8–)←→(– –)

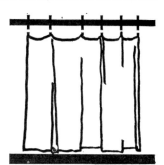

Circulation loose equipment

Definition:
● *Loose equipment not normally connected with any main user activity at* (82) *to* (86), including notice boards, signs, ash trays, waste paper baskets, curtains, pictures, tapestries.

Sheets and details

Sheets with this code may be produced or information on circulation loose equipment given on (8–) or (– –) sheets.

Location information:
Layouts.

Assembly information:
Not applicable to loose equipment.

Component information:
Typical details may include signs or any other parts defined above, all of which may be made off site.

Item types, specification, bill of quantities

This code is used with Table 2/3 item type codes on sheets and details coded (81), (8–), (– –) and in section (81) of the specification and bill of quantities.

Cost planning

See note at (8–) Loose equipment: Cost planning.

(82)

Search pattern
(82)←→(8–)←→(– –)

General room loose equipment, furniture

Definition:
● *Loose equipment and furniture for relaxing and working which is not related to user activities at* (83) *to* (86), including equipment such as beds and bedroom suites, chairs, tables, loose desks, loose platforms etc.

Sheets and details

Sheets with this code may be produced or information on general room loose equipment and furniture given on (8–) or (– –) sheets.

Location information:
Layouts.

Assembly information:
Not applicable to loose equipment.

Component information:
Typical details may include tables or any other parts defined above, all of which may be made off site.

Item types, specification, bill of quantities

This code is used with Table 2/3 item type codes on sheets

and details coded (82), (8–), (– –) and in Section (82) of the specification and bill of quantities.

Cost planning

See note at (8–) Loose equipment: Cost planning.

(83)

Search pattern
(83)←→(8–)←→(– –)

Culinary loose equipment

Definition:
● *Loose equipment for culinary purposes apart from general purpose loose storage units at* (86), including portable cooking and mixing equipment, utensils, tableware.

Sheets and details

Sheets with this code are unlikely to be required, but may be produced if necessary or otherwise culinary loose equipment may be shown on (8–) or (– –) sheets.

Location information:
Layouts.

Assembly information:
Not applicable to loose equipment.

Component information:
Typical details may include any parts defined above, all of which may be made off site.

Item types, specification, bill of quantities

This code is used with Table 2/3 item type codes on sheets and details coded (83), (8–), (– –) and in section (83) of the specification and bill of quantities. It is most unlikely that specification items requiring this code will be included in many projects.

Cost planning

See note at (8–) Loose equipment: Cost planning.

(84)

Search pattern
(84)←→(8–)←→(– –)

Sanitary loose equipment

Definition:
● *Loose equipment for washing and sanitary purposes apart from general purpose loose storage units at* (86), including equipment for personal hygiene.

Sheets and details

Sanitary loose equipment is unlikely to be specified but if it is, sheets coded (84) may be produced or otherwise sanitary loose equipment may be shown on (8–) or (– –) sheets.

Location information:
Layouts.

Assembly information:
Not applicable to loose equipment.

Component information:
Typical details may include any parts defined above, all of which may be made off site.

Item types, specification, bill of quantities

This code is used with Table 2/3 item type codes on sheets and details coded (84), (8–), (– –) and in section (84) of the specification and bill of quantities. It is most unlikely that specification items requiring this code will be included in many projects.

Cost planning

See note at (8–) Loose equipment: Cost planning.

(85)

Search pattern
(85)←→(8–)←→(– –)

Cleaning loose equipment

Definition:
● *Loose equipment for cleaning purposes apart from general purpose storage units at* (86), including floor polishers, vacuum cleaners.

Sheets and details

Cleaning loose equipment is unlikely to be specified but if it is, separate sheets coded (85) may be produced or otherwise cleaning loose equipment may be shown on (8–) or (– –) sheets.

Location information:
Layouts.

Assembly information:
Not applicable to loose equipment.

Component information:
Typical details may include any parts defined above, all of which may be made off site.

Item types, specification, bill of quantities

This code is used with Table 2/3 item type codes on sheets and details coded (85), (8–), (– –) and in section (85) of the specification and bill of quantities. It is most unlikely that specification items requiring this code will be included in many projects.

Cost planning

See note at (8–) Loose equipment: Cost planning.

(86)

Search pattern
(86)←→(8–)←→(– –)

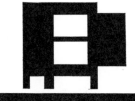

Storage loose equipment

Definition:
● *Loose equipment for storage purposes*, including loose cupboards, chests, shelf units, travel equipment, strong boxes.

Sheets and details

Sheets with this code may be produced or information on storage loose equipment given on (8–) or (– –) sheets.

Location information:
Layouts.

Assembly information:
Not applicable to loose equipment.

Component information:
Typical details may include any parts defined above, all of which may be made off site.

Item types, specification, bill of quantities

This code is used with Table 2/3 item type codes on sheets and details coded (86), (8–), (– –) and in section (86) of the specification and bill of quantities.

Cost planning

See note at (8–) Loose equipment: Cost planning.

Table 2: construction forms

Definitions for purposes connected with project information, of CI/SfB Table 2: Construction forms, as listed in RIBA Construction indexing manual 1968 (with additional codes A, B, C, D).

Codes E to Y, when used for assembly information, code work as fixed in position. Users who wish to check that they have an appropriate code should look at the definition following the code they consider most likely and at the terms below it in *italics*. These terms must be read in context with the SMM work section headings and subheadings which are given in each case, as well as with the definition.

For instance, should small lintels over air bricks in clay brickwork be specified as an integral part of brickwork or coded separately? A check at 'F' shows that F covers *bricks* (in 'Brickwork') including . . . air bricks and the lintels for them . . . . But lintels can, of course, be coded separately from brickwork as 'work with structural units' in their own right. If they are large, with erection likely to be carried out by a gang separate from the bricklayers and forming a separate work package, they should probably be coded separately, at G. A more obvious example is work associated with bar or fabric reinforcement which can be described as part of concrete or as a separately coded operation at H or J. In these and similar cases individual architects and quantity surveyors can decide how best to divide up the work in the light of experience and circumstances. The coding system allows considerable flexibility in this respect.

All labours associated with the items listed are assumed to be included with them.

A
Preliminaries

Definition
● *Conditions for the work, including general administration, plant, labour and operational requirements.*

Assembly information:

Items with this code do not describe building work (ie demolition, excavation, work with formless materials or particular types of assemblies or the particular administrative, plant, labour and operational requirements of these kinds of work. All these subjects will be coded under later headings. They may, however, cover work of a temporary nature which is not to be incorporated in the finished building.

Commodity information:

Items with this code do not describe particular commodities (materials, products and components) which may be brought on site for incorporation in the work, all of which will be coded under later headings. They may, however, cover objects which are not to be incorporated in the finished building such as contractors plant, tools and so on.

B

Demolitions

Definition:
● *Demolitions as distinct from excavations and constructions at C to Y.*

Assembly information:

'De-assembly'. Items with this code cover administration, plant, labour activities and operations associated with demolition such as those listed below:

0 General
1 Protecting
2 Supporting, eg underpinning
3 Handling
4 —
5 Treating, eg cutting, breaking up
6 Removing, clearing out
7 —
8 Cleaning
9 Sundry

Commodity information:

Items with this code do not describe particular commodities (materials, products and components) which may be brought on site for incorporation in the new work, all of which will be coded under later headings. They may, however, cover objects which are not to be incorporated in the finished building such as contractors plant, tools, and demolished items which are to be sold.

C

Earthworks

Definition:
● *Earthworks as distinct from constructions at D to Y.*

Assembly information:

Items with this code cover administration, plant, labour activities and operations associated with earthworks, including preserving turf and soil, excavating, trenching, disposal of excavated material, filling, soiling seeding and turfing etc, disposal of water, planking and strutting etc.

Commodity information:

Items with this code describe particular commodities (materials, products and components) which may be brought on site for incorporation in earthworks. They may also cover objects which are not to be incorporated in the work such as contractors plant, tools.

D*

Search pattern
D←→Y

Formless and basic materials

Definition:
● *Materials which may need to be mixed (pre-assembled) before they are in a state suitable for application as part of constructions in final position, at E to Y.*

Assembly information:

Items with this code include descriptions of mixing (pre-assembly) of formless materials like mortar (concrete mix).

Commodity information:

Items with this code include basic materials and formless bulk materials (requiring mixing with similar materials described separately) which may be used in two or more of the assemblies with capital letter codes which follow. Examples of the former are *timber*, *metal*, and of the latter are *aggregates, lime, cement, mortar, gypsum, resins,* etc.

E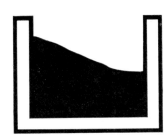

Search pattern
E←→Y

Cast in situ

Definition:
● *Products placed and set in final position.*

Assembly information:
For example

In piling
Concrete piles: (bored piles) *concrete filling* including, reinforcement (unless coded separately under H or J), etc.

In concrete work
Plain concrete: *in-situ concrete* including temporary formwork, treating unset concrete, holes for pipes etc, cast on or hacked finishes, expansion joints, fixing slips, metal clips etc. *Concrete filling* to hollow walls (unless coded under F) etc.

* D is used experimentally in this manual. Users who want to conform strictly to library practice should use Y instead.

Reinforced concrete: *in-situ concrete* including temporary formwork, treating unset concrete, holes for pipes etc, cast on or hacked finishes, bar reinforcement† (unless coded separately under H), fabric reinforcement† (unless coded separately under J). etc.

Hollow-block suspended construction: *in-situ concrete* including blocks, temporary formwork, reinforcement† (unless coded separately under H) fixing slips, etc.

Prestressed concrete: *in-situ concrete* including temporary formwork, reinforcement† (unless coded separately under H or J), wires, cables (unless coded separately under J) etc.

Commodity information*:
Not applicable

sleeves, running mortices with lead, cramps, dowels, plugs etc, centring etc (also dpcs unless coded separately).

Cast stonework: including items as above

Clayware work: including items as above

Commodity information*:
Any commodity of block form which may be brought on site for incorporation in the work, such as *ashlar, blocks, bricks, cobbles, masonry, rubble, setts*. A full list is given at F in the *Construction indexing manual*.

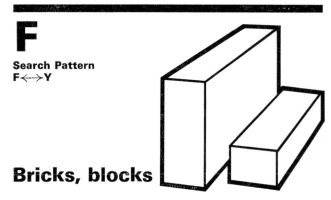

F

Search Pattern
F⟵⟶Y

Bricks, blocks

Definition:
● *Bricks and blocks usually laid in conjunction with each other in large numbers.*

Assembly information:
For example

In brickwork and blockwork
Brickwork, brick facework, brickwork built fair both sides or entirely of facing bricks, brickwork in connection with boilers: *bricks* including mortar and pointing, wall ties, bands, cappings, brick sills, bases etc, tile creasings, and brickwork sundries such as reinforcement (unless coded separately under H or J), air bricks etc including lintels for them, pipe sleeves, flues and flue blocks, chimney pots, centring etc (also dpcs unless coded separately).

Blockwork: *blocks* including mortar and pointing, and blockwork sundries such as reinforcement (unless coded separately under H or J), air bricks etc including lintels for them, pipe sleeves, flues and flue blocks, chimney pots, centring etc (Also damp proof courses unless coded separately).

In rubble walling
Stone rubblework: *stones* including mortar and pointing if any, wall ties or anchors, temporary strutting, and sundries such as pipe sleeves, flues, flue blocks, chimney pots, centering etc (also dpcs unless coded separately,

In masonry
Natural stonework: *stones* including mortar and pointing, wall ties or anchors, temporary strutting, pier caps and chimney caps etc and stonework sundries such as pipe

* Where coded separately from Assembly information.

† Most offices code reinforcement as a separate work package at H and/or J.

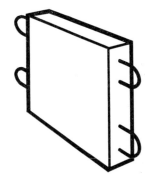

G

Search Pattern
G⟵⟶Y

Large units (structural)

Definition:
● *Special purpose units which are primarily structural, larger than blocks and usually specially shaped with fixings attached.*

Assembly information:
For example

In piling
Wood piling: *wood piles etc*
Cast concrete piling: *cast concrete piles etc*
Steel sheet piling: *sheet steel piles etc*

In concrete work
Precast concrete units: *large units* such as partitions, staircases, kerbs, sills, lintels, including jointing and bedding materials, anchor bolts, rag bolts.

Precast prestressed units: *units* including mortar and jointing, reinforcement wires, temporary supports etc.

In roofing
Roof decking: *decking units* (unless sheeting, coded N) including bearings, flashings, abutments, timber blocks or fillets inserted during fixing, etc.

In carpentry
Structural timber units: *units* such as *trusses* including nails and carpentry sundries such as pads, slips, blocks, plugging and carpenters metalwork such as ties, rods, straps, shoes, heads, bolts, metal connections and screws.

In structural steelwork
Grillages and girders: *compound and latticed girders* and *runway rails* etc including sundries such as rivets, wedging, anchor bolts, gutters in steelwork.

Stanchions, columns and portal frames: *Stanchions* etc including bloom bases and sundries such as rivets, wedging, anchor bolts, gutters in steelwork.

Roof members, braces, struts and rails: such as *trusses, purlins* including sundries such as rivets, wedging anchor bolts, gutters in steelwork.

In metalwork
Composite units: such as *staircases, ladders, landings and gangways, trusses, purlins,* including connections and sundries such as anchor bolts.

Standard units: such as *staircases, ladders, landings, lintels,* including sundries such as anchor bolts.

In fencing
Open type fencing: *posts* etc.

Close type fencing: *posts, infilling units* (complete panels) etc.

Commodity information*

Any commodity of large structural unit form which may be brought on site for incorporation in the work, such as *open web joists, space frames* etc. A full list is given at G in the *Construction indexing manual.*

H

H←→Y

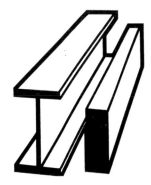

Sections, bars

Definition
● *Lengths of constant or continually repeated cross section other than simple hollow sections*

Assembly information:
For example

In concrete work
Bar reinforcement: *bars* including bands, hooks, tying wire, distance blocks, spacers, links, stirrups, binders etc.

In roofing
Slate or tile roofing: parts such as *lathing, battening, counter-battening* (if not coded under N).

In carpentry
Structural timbers: such as *joists, rafters, purlins, strutting and nogging, cleats, sprockets,* including pins, pipe sleeves and sundries such as pads, slips, blocks, plugging, and carpenters' metal work such as tie rods, straps, shoes, heads, bolts, metal connectors and screws.

* Where coded separately from Assembly information.

Boarding: such as *weather boarding, gutter boarding,* including firrings, gusset ends, drips and cesspools, nails, sundries and carpenter's metal work.

Fillets, grounds, battens and bracketing: such as *tilting fillets and rolls, corner fillets, grounds, skeleton framework, bracketing, cradling around steel work and to form false beams,* including nails, sundries and carpenter's metal work.

In joinery
Flooring: such as *board and strip* flooring (plywood boarding etc coded R), including metal tongues, nosings, bed moulds, margins, access traps, nails, and sundries such as plugging, pelleting, pipe sleeves, and ironmongery such as dowels, cramps, bolts.

Eaves and verge boarding: such as *fascia and barge boards* (plywood boarding etc coded R), including nails, sundries, ironmongery.

Plain linings, casings and partitions: (plywood linings etc coded R) parts such as *stiles, top rails, fillets, mouldings,* including access traps, nails, sundries, ironmongery.

Doors, windows, skylights and lanterns†: parts such as *beads, fillets, mouldings, boarding, stiles, rails, rolls, window boards, nosings, bed-moulds,* including nails, sundries and ironmongery such as flanges, tracks, pulleys.

Frames, sills and kerbs: parts such as *mullions, transomes,* including keys, wedges, nails, sundries and ironmongery such as handrail screws.

Fillets, glazing beads and grounds: such as *weather fillets, condensation fillets, stop fillets, glazing fillets,* grounds including nails, sundries and ironmongery.

Skirtings, architraves, picture-rails and cornices: *skirtings* etc, *dado-rails, wall mouldings, cappings, pelmets, cover fillets,* including bracketing, plinth blocks, nails, sundries and ironmongery.

Shelves, table tops and seats: parts such as *frames, ledges, slats, bearers, legs,* including nails, sundries and ironmongery.

Sinks, draining-boards and backboards: parts such as *frames, ledges, slats, bearers, legs.*

Staircases: parts such as *treads, risers, strings, apron-linings, cappings, mouldings, handrails, balusters, newels,* including nails, sundries and ironmongery.

In structural steelwork
Generally: parts such as *basic sections,* unframed steelwork such as *angles, tees, joists, channels.*

In metalwork
Bars, sections: such as *handrails, core rails, balusters, newels, rails, straps, hangers, brackets,* including lugs and sundries such as bolts.

In plaster work and other floor, wall and ceiling finishes
Suspended plain sheet linings with supporting metalwork:

† Doors, windows, skylights and lanterns etc complete and ready for fixing are coded X, preceded by the appropriate Table 1 code. But the work of making up these and similar components from timber *sections*—if specified—can be coded H on component drawings (despite the fact that they are unlikely to be made up 'in situ'), so that cross reference can readily be made to relevant clauses in the specification.

parts such as *hangers, framing members, trim.*

Fibrous plaster: parts such as *coves, cornices.*

In fencing
Open-type fencing: *boarding* etc.

Close-type fencing: *boarding* etc.

Commodity information*

Any commodity of section, bar form which may be brought on to site for incorporation in the work, such as *angles, bars, battens, beads, boards, channels, extrusions, gaskets, joists, laths, linings, matchboard, mouldings, planks, profiles, rods, strips, trim, weatherboards.* A full list is given at H in the *Construction indexing manual.*

Search Pattern
I⟵⟶Y

Tubes, pipes

Definition
● *Lengths of simple hollow cross section with fittings etc*

Assembly information:
For example

In metalwork
Tubes: *tubes* (unless structural coded G), including lugs and sundries such as bolts.

In plumbing and engineering installations
Gutter work: *gutters,* including fittings such as bends, elbows, junctions, stopped ends, nozzle outlets, and bolts, lugs, brackets, straps.

Pipe work: *pipes,* including fittings such as bends, elbows, springs, offsets, junctions, shoes, reducers, elbows, tees, crosses, unions, and expansion loops, outlets, rainwater heads etc, cowls, terminals, bolts, couplers, sockets, tappings, bosses, flanges, supports, caps and plugs, inspection doors, dampers, traps, thimbles, gratings to roof outlets, flaps, flashing-plates, weathering aprons, cravats (unless coded separately under M). Also *large tubes* (eg for chimneys), including base plates, linings, claddings, anchor-bolts, guy-ropes, ladders, guard rails, painters' hooks, cleaning doors, cowls, terminals.

Ductwork: *ducts,* including fittings such as bends, offsets, diminishing pieces, junction pieces, and extract hoods, including bolts, brackets, hangers, dampers and louvres, access doors, shutters, grilles, diffusers, deflectors, equalisers, cowls, terminals, dampers.

* Where coded separately from Assembly information.

Thermal insulation: *pipe* and *duct* insulation (unless coded separately according to form of insulation at D, K etc).

In electrical installations
Conduits, trunking and tray: *conduit etc,* including conduit fittings such as bends, elbows, tees etc, conduit-boxes, including bushes, lock-nuts, plugs; also *trunking,* trunking-fittings such as bends, crosses, offsets, reducers, tees, including pinracks; *trays,* tray-fittings such as bends, crosses, offsets, tees.

In drainage
Pipework: *pipes,* including pipe-fittings such as bends, junctions, diminishing pipes, channels, including accessories such as gulleys, traps, inspection shoes, fresh air inlets, non-return flaps, gratings, sealing plates.

Commodity information*

Any commodity of tube, pipe form which may be brought on to site for incorporation in the work, such as *chutes, conduits, duct tubes* and *pipes, hoses, pipes,* 'tiles' (for drainage), *tubes* etc. A full list is given at I in the *Construction indexing manual.*

Search pattern
J⟵⟶Y

Wires, mesh

Definition
● *Wire, ropes, cables, mesh etc*

Assembly information:
For example

In concrete work
Fabric reinforcement: *fabric,* including bends, tying wire, distance blocks, temporary strutting etc.

Prestressed concrete: parts such as *wires* and *cables.*

In roofing
Thatch: (*wire netting* only, if not coded K).

In metalwork
Work in wire mesh or expanded metal: *wire mesh, expanded metal.*

In electrical installations
Cables and conductors: such as *electrical cables, earthing and lightning conductors,* including joint boxes, cable termination glands, earth electrodes, supports (saddles, cleats, clips, hangers, suspenders), insulators, rivets, bolts, clamps.

In plasterwork and other floor, wall and ceiling finishes
Lathing: such as metal (*mesh*) *lathing* around columns (unless coded P).

In fencing

Open-type fencing: such as *chain-link, wire mesh, wire fencing.*

Commodity information* :

Any commodity of wire, mesh form, which may be brought onto site for incorporation in the work, such as *cables, chains, chain link, cords, expanded metal, lines, mesh, lathing, ropes, strings, wire netting, wires, yarns.* A full list is given at J in the *Construction indexing manual.*

Search pattern
K ←→ Y

Quilts

Definition
● *Resilient quilts*

Assembly information:
For example

In roofing
Thatch roofing: *thatch,* including wire netting (unless coded J).

In carpentry
Sundries: such as insulating *quilts.*

In plumbing and engineering installations
Thermal insulation: such as detachable *mattresses, sectional insulating coverings.*

Commodity information* :
Any commodity of quilt form which may be brought onto site for incorporation in the work, such as *prefoamed felted material, lagging, quilts, sponge.* A full list is given at K in the *Construction indexing manual.*

L

Search pattern
L ←→ Y

Foils, papers

Definition
● *Sheet materials which can be rolled to a smaller diameter and which are not primarily for decorative purposes*

* Where coded separately from Assembly information.

Assembly information:
For example

In brickwork and blockwork
Damp proof courses: such as *bituminous felt,* including bedding, pointing (unless coded under F).

In roofing
Slate or tile roofing: *underfelting* (unless coded N).

Bitumen felt roofing: *felt,* including integral skirtings, aprons, linings to gutters, channels, sumps, cesspools etc, coverings to kerbs, collars around pipes standards etc.

Commodity information* :
Any commodity of foil, paper form which may be brought onto site for incorporation in the work, such as *building papers, canvas, felts, foils, sacking, scrim* etc. A full list is given at L in the *Construction indexing manual.*

M

Search pattern
M ←→ Y

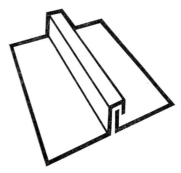

Foldable sheets

Definition
● *Sheets which can be bent to a tight radius without fracture and which will keep their shape when formed*

Assembly information:
For example

In brickwork and blockwork
Damp proof courses: such as *sheet metal,* including bedding, pointing (unless coded under F).

In roofing
Sheet metal roofing, sheet metal flashings and gutters: such as *sheet flashings* and *coverings,* including aprons, weatherings, cappings, linings to gutters, cesspools, sumps, collars around pipes standards etc, soakers, metal slates, including clips, tacks, nails, lead dots. Also underfelting (unless coded separately).

In metalwork
Sheet metal: including *sheet coverings,* linings and nails, screws.

Ductwork: (unless pre-assembled, coded I) parts of folded *sheets* such as bends, offsets.

In plasterwork and other floor, wall and ceiling finishes
Plain sheet finishings: including *coverstrips* (unless sections, coded H).

Commodity information* :
Any commodity of foldable sheet form which may be

brought onto site for incorporation in the work, such as sheets, soakers, strips etc. A full list is given at M in the *Construction indexing manual.*

N

Search pattern
N⟵⟶Y

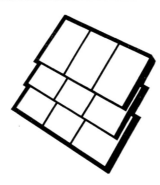

Overlap tiles, sheets

Definition
● *Sheets and tiles designed to be used overlapping each other.*

Assembly information:
For example

In roofing
Slate or tile roofing: *slates, tiles,* including beddings, pointing and finishing with cement fillets, slips, hip-irons, metal slates and soakers (unless coded M), lathing, battening and counter battening (unless coded H), underfelting (unless coded L) etc.

Corrugated or troughed sheet roofing: *sheets,* (unless structural units, coded G), including filler pieces, flashing pieces, ridge and hip cappings etc and bedding, flashings and soakers (unless coded M), expansion joints, barge boards (unless coded H) etc.

Commodity information*:
Any commodity of overlap tile, sheet form which may be brought onto the site for incorporation in the work such as *corrugated sheets, shingles, slates, tiles* etc. A full list is given at N in the *Construction indexing manual.*

P

Search pattern
P⟵⟶Y

Thick coatings

Definition
● *Thick coatings which are applied and set in-situ too stiff to be applied by brush*

* Where coded separately from Assembly information.

Assembly information:
For example

In asphalt work
Mastic asphalt: *asphalt coverings,* including integral skirtings, fascias, aprons, linings, fillers, collars, underlay (unless coded L) etc.

In plumbing and engineering installations
Thermal insulation: (such as *sprayed asbestos*).

In plasterwork and other floor, wall and ceiling finishes
In-situ finishings: such as *granolithic, latex, magnesium oxychloride, terrazzo, plaster, tarmacadam, pitchmastic coverings,* including integral skirtings, bands, margins, kerbs, channels, linings, mouldings, cornices, dividing strips, angle beads.

Beds and backings: such as *floated and trowelled beds, working beds,* including channels, linings, screeded and floated and trowelled backings, working backings.

Commodity information: *
Most thick coatings (pastes) will derive from mixing together various formless bulk materials (coded D) on site, and will not be brought onto the site as ready-to-use commodities.

R

Search pattern
R⟵⟶Y

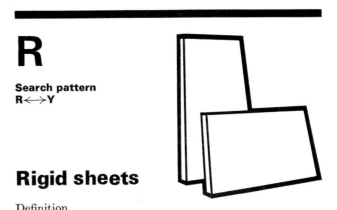

Rigid sheets

Definition
● *Sheets which cannot be bent to a small diameter*

Assembly information:
For example

In roofing
Roof decking: such as *wood wool slabs* (unless reinforced and coded G), including timber blocks inserted during fixing etc.

In joinery
Panelled linings: such as *plywood, blockboard panels,* including sundries, ironmongery.

Doors, windows, skylights and lanterns: parts such as *panels.*

Shelves, table tops and seats: parts such as *panels.*

Sinks, draining boards and backboards: parts such as *panels.*

Fittings and fixtures: parts such as *panels.*

Staircases: parts such as *panels.*

In metalwork
Work in plates: such as *floor plates, chequer plates, duct covers*

In plasterwork and other floor, wall and ceiling finishes
Plain sheet finishings: *sheets* including access panels, etc.

Base boarding: *plasterboards and similar boards* (plaster finish coded P) including hangers (unless coded separately at H), etc.

Suspended plain sheet linings with supporting metalwork *sheets* including hangers (unless coded separately at H) access panels, trim, etc.

Fibrous plaster: such as *slabs, casings, covers, cornices* (unless sections coded H) including grounds, brackets, hangers (unless coded separately at H) access panels.

Self finished partitions: parts such as *slabs*, panels (unless structural, coded G).

In glazing
Glass in openings: *sheet glass* including beads, clips, angle pieces, etc.

Mirrors: *glass in mirrors*

Patent glazing:† *glass or other sheets* including glazing bars, ironmongery, etc.

Commodity information*
Any commodity of rigid sheet form which may be brought on to the site for incorporation in the work such as *boards, panes, panels, plate, sandwich slabs, sheets*. A full list is given at R in the *Construction indexing manual*.

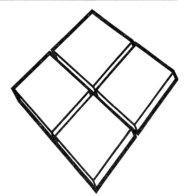

Search pattern
S←→Y

Rigid tiles

Definition
● *Small units which cannot be rolled to a small diameter and which are thin in relation to their length and/or width, including tile skirtings, etc. Usually laid butt jointed in large numbers.*

Assembly information:
For example

In plasterwork and other floor, wall and ceiling finishes
Tile, slab or block finishes: (unless tile coded T) *tiles* such as *precast concrete, terrazzo, mosaic, asphalt, clayware, brick, stone, slate, marble, glass, composition, wood blocks, metal,* etc. including integral skirtings, bedding (if not coded P), screws, clips, anchors, grouting, pointing, dividing strips, etc.

* Where coded separately from Assembly information.

† Coded X in *Construction indexing manual*

Commodity information*
Any commodity of rigid tile form which may be brought on to the site for incorporation in the work. A full list is given at S in the *Construction indexing manual*.

T

Search pattern
T←→Y

Flexible sheets, tiles

Definition
● *Flexible sheets (and tiles cut from them) which can be rolled to a small diameter and which are made primarily for decorative purposes.*

Assembly information:
For example

In plaster work and other floor, wall and ceiling finishes
Tile finishings: such as *plastics, linoleum, cork, rubber tiles* including bedding and accessories, etc.

Plain sheet finishings: such as *plastics, linoleum, cork, rubber sheets* including bedding and accessories, etc.

Commodity information*
Any commodity of flexible sheet, tile form which may be brought on to the site for incorporation in the work such as *carpets, sheets, tiles*. A full list is given at T in the *Construction indexing manual*.

U

Search pattern
U←→Y

Papers, fabrics

Definition
● *Thin flexible sheets made for decorative purposes.*‡

Assembly information:
For example

In painting and decorating
Paperhanging: *paper* including border strips, scrim, etc.

‡Decorative surfaces are surfaces designed with a special regard to their visual appearance and other qualities as the contact layer between the user and the building.

Commodity information*

Any commodity of paper, fabric which may be brought on to the site (often as a roll) for incorporation in the work, such as *cloths, fabrics, finishing papers, linen, textiles, wallpapers,* etc. A full list is given at U in the *Construction indexing manual.*

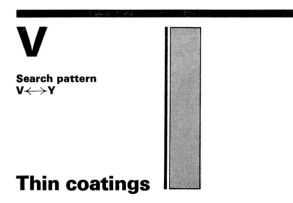

V

Search pattern
V◀─▶Y

Thin coatings

Definition
● *Thin coatings which are surface applied and set in their final position. Normally applied by brush.*

Assembly information:
For example

In painting and decorating
Painting and similar work: such as *paint, lime **whiting**, distempering, staining, graining, varnishing* including knotting, stopping, priming, scrim, undercoating

Polishing: *polish*

Signwriting: *paint* including gold leaf, etc.

Commodity information*
Any commodity to be applied as thin coating form (liquids) which may be brought on to the site, often in a tin, for incorporation in the work such as *dressings, emulsions, films, finishing coats, glazes, lacquers, paints, polishes, priming, seals, undercoats, varnish.* A full list is given at V in the *Construction indexing manual.*

X

Search pattern

X◀─▶Y

Components

Definition
● *Complex single purpose nonstructural products manufactured off site.*
● *Manufactured articles finished and complete in themselves, intended to be non-structural parts of a completed building or structure.*

* Where coded separately from Assembly information.

Assembly information:
For example

In joinery
General: work with components of timber (shop joinery) in general, including jointing. Particular components—windows, etc—will normally be classified and coded primarily by Table 1 and secondarily by X.

In ironmongery: *sets, gearing,* including bolts, screws, etc.

In metalwork
General: work with components of metal in general, including jointing. Particular components—windows, etc—will normally be classified and coded primarily by Table 1 and secondarily by X.

In plumbing and engineering installations
General: work with components in general including jointing. Particular components—baths, etc—will normally be classified and coded primarily by Table 1, secondarily by X.

Commodity information*
Any component as defined above, including fixings such as *ties, bolts,* etc. Examples are given at X in the *Construction indexing manual*

Y

Constructions, products

Definition
● *Two or more specific construction forms E to X*

Assembly information:

This code is used for work involving any two or more of the assembly forms D to X. Clauses requiring this code should be avoided as far as possible. It may be necessary to use it, for example, for clauses referring to 'joinery' covering work with composite constructions consisting of sections, rigid sheets and pre-assembled components.

Commodity information*
Items with this code cover any two or more of the product (commodity) forms D to X. The use of clauses requiring this code should be avoided as far as possible.

Table 3: Materials

Codes and headings for purposes connected with project information, of CI/SfB Table 3: Materials, as listed in RIBA Construction indexing manual 1968 (with additional codes for administration, plant labour and operations)

Groups a to d: administration, plant, labour and operational (labour plus plant) activities

*Included in *Construction indexing manual* Table 4, not Table 3
†Included in *Construction indexing manual* (Ag). *Construction indexing manual* (A1) is Founding, taking over, establishing
‡Included in *Construction indexing manual* (Aj). *Construction indexing manual* (A2) is Financing, accounting
§Divided in *Construction indexing manual* between (A2) Financing, accounting and (A4) Cost planning, tenders
‖The terminology differs from that used in *Construction indexing manual*, but the meaning of these headings is basically unchanged

a ADMINISTRATION*
a1 **Communications**†
a2 **Controls, constraints**‡
a3 **Design**
a4 **Finance, tender**§
a5 **Production**
a7 **Quality**
a8 **Appraisal, feedback**
a9 **Sundry administrative matters**

b AIDS, TEMPORARY WORKS, PLANT*
b1 **Aids for protecting, storing** ‖
b2 **Aids for supporting** ‖
b3 **Aids for handling** ‖
b4 **Aids for making** ‖
b5 **Aids for treating** ‖
b6 **Aids for placing** ‖
b7 **Aids for making good** ‖
b8 **Aids for cleaning** ‖
b9 **Sundry aids** ‖

c LABOUR* ‖
c1 **Labour for protecting, storing** ‖
c2 **Labour for supporting** ‖
c3 **Labour for handling** ‖
c4 **Labour for making** ‖
c5 **Labour for treating** ‖
c6 **Labour for placing** ‖
c7 **Labour for making good** ‖
c8 **Labour for cleaning** ‖
c9 **Sundry labours** ‖

d OPERATIONS (labour + aids)* ‖
d0 **Protecting, storing** ‖
d2 **Supporting** ‖
d3 **Handling** ‖
d4 **Making** ‖
d5 **Treating** ‖
d6 **Placing** ‖
d7 **Making good** ‖
d8 **Cleaning** ‖
d9 **Sundry operations** ‖

Groups e to o: materials in formed products

e NATURAL STONE
Artificial stone see f3
Stone aggregate, gravel see p1
e1 **Granite and igneous**
e2 **Marble**
e3 **Lime stone (other than marble)**
e4 **Sandstone**
Gritstone, freestone etc
e5 **Slate**

f FORMED (PRECAST) CONCRETE ETC
Aggregates see p
Cements see q, r
Mortars and concrete in general see q, r
f1 **Sandlime concrete**
Calcium silicate, flint lime, slag and lime etc
f2 **Heavyweight concrete (precast)**
Precast concrete apart from the types below
Heavyweight concrete and mortar in situ and in general see q4
f3 **Terrazzo (precast) etc**
Terrazzo in situ and in general see q5
cast stone (artifical stone; reconstructed stone etc)
Granolithic
f4 **Lightweight concrete (precast)**
Lightweight concrete in situ and in general see q6
Aerated concrete (cellular), foamed
f5 **Lightweight aggregate**
Concrete (precast) including sawdust concrete
Lightweight aggregate concrete in situ and in general see q7
f6 **Asbestos-based materials (preformed)**
Asbestos fibre see m1
Asbestos-based materials in situ see q9
Asbestos cement; bitumen bonded asbestos cement; asbestos combined with silica and hydrated lime, etc
f7 **Gypsum (preformed)**
Gypsum plaster in general see r2
Fibrous
f8 **Magnesium based materials (preformed)**
Composition in situ and in general see r3
Synthetic bonded mortars, resin cement in situ and in general see r4

g CLAY, IN GENERAL
Clay aggregate see p3
g1 **Adobe, cob, pise**
Rammed earth; diatomaceous earth (diatomite), kieselguhr, moler earth etc
Earth fill, earth in general see p1
g2 **Fired clay**
g3 **Faience**
Glazed fireclay; ceramic; salt glazed ware (glazed vitrified clay); semi-vitreous; stoneware; terracotta; vitreous; etc
g6 **Heat-resistant material**
Refractory ware, fireclay

h METAL IN GENERAL
Anti-corrosive materials see u
h1 **Cast iron**
Malleable, including vitreous enamelled
h2 **Steel**
Black; blue; bright; high tensile; mild; etc
Including: copper-covered; galvanised; plastics-coated; sherardized; tin plate; vitreous enamelled
h3 **Steel alloys**
(Including stainless steel); heat-resisting steel
h4 **Aluminium alloy**
(Including aluminium); aluminium copper; aluminium silicon; aluminium zinc; etc. Including: anodized; plastics-coated; pre-painted
h5 **Copper**
Copper and hessian
h6 **Copper alloy**
Aluminium bronze (copper aluminium); brass; bronze; copper nickel; copper silicon (silicon bronze); german silver (nickel silver); gunmetal; phosphor bronze; etc
h7 **Zinc**
h8 **Lead**
Lead and bitumen; lead and hessian; white metal; etc
h9 **Tin, chromium, nickel etc**

i WOOD (INCLUDING ROT-PROOFED) IN GENERAL
Wood fibre, particles see j1
Paper see j2
Wood aggregate, fill see p5
Protective materials see u3
i1 **Timber (unwrot)**
i2 **Wrot soft wood**
Cedar; fir; hemlock; larch; pine; poplar; redwood; spruce; whitewood; etc
i3 **Wrot hardwood**
(not listed)
i4 **Laminated wood, plywood**

j NATURAL FIBRES ARD CHIPS, LEATHER*
Including mixtures of natural fibres, synthetic fibres and leather
Wood see i
Wood wool see j8
Mineral fibres see m1
Synthetic fibres see n
j1 **Wood fibre, wood particles**
Bark; bonded fibre; etc

j2 **Paper**
Bituminized paper; kraft paper; metal-backed paper, etc
j3 **Vegetable fibres**
Bamboo; coir; cotton; eelgrass; jute; flax; hemp; reeds; rushes; seagrass; sisal; straw; cork; etc
j6 **Animal fibres and leather**
Including animal hair; wool; etc
j7 **Mixed natural/synthetic fibres**
Wool/synthetic fibre
j8 **Wood wool**

m MINERAL FIBRES IN GENERAL
Mineral fibre fill (all types) see p7
m1 **Mineral fibres**
Asbestos fibre
Asbestos-based materials see f6, q9
Glass fibre
Glass see o
Mineral fibre including: rock; slag

n PLASTICS ETC
Protective materials in general see u
Paints see v
n1 **Asphalt (preformed)**
Asphalt, bitumen in situ and in general see s
Limestone aggregate; natural rock; asphalt aggregate; etc
n2 **Impregnated fibre and felt**
Bitumen bonded asbestos cement see f6
Bitumen lead see h8
Bituminized paper see j2
Bituminous felt; bitumen polythene; pitch fibre; etc
n4 **Linoleum**
n5 **Rubbers (natural and elastomers)**
n6 **Plastics in general**
Including: rubbers if not described separately; synthetic fibres
Synthetic bonded mortars see r4
n7 **Cellular plastics**
Subdivide like n6
Expanded plastics; foamed plastics etc
n8 **Reinforced, laminated plastics**†
Subdivide like n6
Composite plastics; plastics laminated with other materials (reinforced plastics); etc

o GLASS*
Glass fibre see m1
o1 **Clear, coloured**
o2 **Translucent, coloured, foamed**
o3 **Opal, opaque, coloured, foamed**
o4 **Wired (all types)**
o5 **Multiple glazed**
All types
o6 **Heat, X-ray absorbing, rejecting**
All types
o7 **Mirrored**
o8 **Toughened (clear and opaque)**
All types
o9 **Cellular, foamed in general**

*The International Basic Tables do not give a detailed subdivision for o and j covers international Basic Table headings j and k

Groups p to s: materials in formless products

p LOOSE FILL, AGGREGATES IN GENERAL
Stone in blocks see e
p1 **Natural fills, aggregates**
Crushed granite; ballast; earth; gravel, hoggin; pumice aggregate; roadstone; sand; shales; shingle; stone aggregate; etc
p2 **Artificial (processed) aggregates (heavy)**
Air-cooled slag; blast furnace slag (air cooled); crushed concrete; bricks; hardcore; etc
p3 **Artifical (processed) aggregates (light)**
Blast furnace slag (foamed); clinker (breeze); exfoliated vermiculite; expanded clay; expanded (foamed) slag; expanded mica; expanded perlite; expanded shale; expanded slate; foamed slag; furnace clinker (breeze); sintered pulverize fuel ash; etc
p4 **Ash**
Fly ash (pulverised fuel ash); furnace bottom ash; etc
p5 **Shavings**
Wood see j
p6 **Powder**
Crusher dust; granulated blast furnace slag; sawdust; etc
p7 **Organic, mineral fibre loose fills**
Organic fibres see j
Mineral fibres see m
p8 **Plastics fills**
Subdivide like n6

q   CEMENT, MORTARS AND MASS (IN SITU) CONCRETE
Aggregate see p
Admixtures for concrete in general see u2
q1   Lime
Calcium silicate ; hydrated ; hydraulic ; lime putty ; slaked ; etc
q2   Cement
Portland cement in general (air-entrained ; low heat ; masonry cement ; quick-setting ; rapid-hardening ; sulphate resisting ; waterproof ; white ; etc
Cements containing granulated blast furnace slag (Portland blast furnace ; slag cement ; super sulphated ; etc)
High alumina cement (ciment fondu)
Special cements ; expansive cements ; oil well cements ; etc
q4   Mortar, heavyweight concrete in situ and in general, plaster, concrete
Formed (precast) concrete see f
Gypsum (preformed) see f7
Gypsum plaster in general see r2
Synthetic bonded mortars see r4
Cement lime plaster ; cement plaster ; mortar ; lime plaster ; mortar ; etc
q5   Terrazzo etc ; concrete with special aggregate, in situ and in general
Precast terrazzo see f3
Granolithic with special aggregates (aluminium oxide aggregate ; carborundum aggregate ; flint aggregate ; metal aggregate ; quartz aggregate ; etc)
q6   Lightweight concrete ; lightweight concrete in situ and in general
Precast lightweight concrete see f4
Aerated concrete ; cellular ; foamed ; etc
q7   Lightweight aggregate concrete in situ and in general including sawdust concrete
Precast lightweight aggregate concrete see f5
q9   Asbestos-based materials in general
Asbestos-based materials (preformed) see f6
Asbestos fibre see m1
Asbestos fibre loose fill see p7

r   GYPSUM, SPECIAL MORTARS ETC
Plastics in general see n6
Adhesives in general see t3
r1   Clay mortar, chemically resistant mortar, fire-resistant mortar
Cement glaze ; refractory concrete ; refractory mortar ; etc
r2   Gypsum
Alabaster ; anhydrous ; hardwall ; hemihydrate (plaster of paris) ; Keenes cement ; Parian cement ; etc
r3   Magnesium based materials
Cement-rubber latex ; cement wood ; compositions ; etc
r4   Synthetic bonded mortars : plastics binders
Acrylic, epoxy ; polyester ; polyurethane ; polyvinyl acetate (PVA) ; etc

s   BITUMINOUS MATERIALS
Asphalt (preformed) see n1
Bitumen impregnated materials see n2
Adhesives in general see t3
Protective materials in general see u
s1   Bitumen, pitch, tar, basic materials, also paints and emulsions
Binder for coated macadam ; bitumen emulsion ; bitumen solution ; bituminous paints ; coal tar pitch ; petroleum bitumen ; Trinidad Lake asphalt ; etc
s4   Mastic asphalt : small or no aggregate
Pitch mastic
s5   Rolled asphalt, bitumen macadam, tar macadam ; large aggregate
Cold asphalt ; dense coated macadam ; dense tar surfacing ; etc

Groups t and u : fixing and protective materials

t   FIXING AND JOINTING AGENTS, COMPOUNDS
Bituminous materials in general see s
t1   Welding material
t2   Soldering material
t3   Adhesives, bonding agents
Animal glues (bitumen ; blood albumen glues ; casein glues ; etc)
Vegetable glues (cellulose and starch derivatives ; rubber ; other vegetable derivatives)
Synthetic rubbers (polychloroprene ; polysulphide, polyurethane ; etc)
Thermoplastics ; polyvinyl acetate (PVA) ; synthetic resins
Thermosets (phenol formaldehyde ; urea formaldehyde ; etc)

t4   Putty, mastics, jointing materials etc
Bitumen-asbestos mastic ; joint fillers in general
Synthetic rubber-based sealants (butyl putty ; polysulphide ; polyurethane ; etc)
t5   Fastenings in general
t6   Permanent fastenings
Anchorage devices (**plugs, dowels, fixing slips, etc**), which accept **fixing** devices ; fixing devices (**nails, screws**, etc) ; joining and attachment devices (**clips, connectors, ties, cramps**, etc)
t7   Ironmongery, hardware in general

u   PROTECTIVE MATERIALS
Sprayed concrete see q4
Resin cement see r4
Bituminous materials in general see s
u1   Anti-corrosive materials
Treatments in general
Paints see Vv
Paint materials see v
Metallic protection applied by : anodizing ; cementation ; chromium plating ; electroplating ; galvanising ; hot dipping ; spraying ; etc
Non-metallic protection applied by : nitriding ; oxide film formation ; phosphate processes ; vitreous enamelling ; chlorinated rubber ; plastics coatings, etc
u2   Concrete admixtures in general
Workability aids (flocculating (thickening) additives ; plasticising mineral additives ; water reducing agents ; etc)
Modifiers of mechanical properties (admixtures to improve bonding ; hardening accelerators ; setting accelerators ; setting retarders ; etc
Surface hardeners see also u5
Modifiers of physical properties (agents to reduce heat of hydration ; anti-freezing agents ; colouring modifiers ; admixtures ; expansion producing agents ; frost-resistance improvers ; 'waterproofers' ; water retaining agents ; etc)
Modifiers of chemical, biological properties (corrosion inhibiting agents, fungicidal, germicidal and/or insecticidal agents ; improvers of resistance to aggressive chemicals modifiers of alkali-aggregate reaction ; etc)
Additives to improve grouts and/or facilitate pumping of concrete ; air content modifiers (air-entraining agents, anti-foaming agents ; foam forming in situ ; gas forming in situ ; etc)
u3   Materials
Treatments for prevention of insect attack etc and rot-proofing materials in general ; creosote ; wood preservatives ; etc
u4   Flame-retardant materials
Treatments in general : means for improving fire resistance
u5   Surface treatment materials
Treatments in general
Paint materials see v, see also V
Lacquers and varnish see v4
Hardeners ; polish ; sealers ; etc
u6   Water-repellent materials
Treatments in general (silicones, surface waterproofers ; etc)

Groups v and w : paints and chemicals

v   MATERIALS FOR PAINTS ETC
Bituminous materials see s
Protective materials in general see u
v1   Stopping, paint fillers etc
Knotting
v2   Pigments, stains etc
v3   Oils
Boiled ; castor ; linseed ; tung ; etc
v4   Varnish
Varnish and lacquers ; finishes other than paint (copals ; epoxy resins ; polyurethane ; shellac ; etc)
v5   Paint
Complete paint systems other than varnish, emulsion and cement paints
Oil and synthetic resin-based paints (flat oil finishing paints ; gloss paints ; stove enamelled paints ; synthetic enamel paints ; etc)
v6   Emulsion paints
Alkyd based ; polyvinyl acetate (PVA) based
v8   Cement paint, lime wash
Distempers ; lime whiting ; textured cement paints ; water paints ; whitewash ; etc
v9   Metallic paints

w   OTHER CHEMICALS
w1   Rust-removing agents
w2   Solvent, thinner, drying agent, emulsifying agent etc
Petrol ; POL ; paint removers ; paraffin ; turpentine ; oils in general ; etc

w4 Water
w5 Acids and alkalis
w6 Fertilisers, sprays, etc
w7 Soaps, detergents, cleaning powders

Group x : plants

x   PLANTS
x1   Trees
x2   Shrubs
x3   Non-woody plants
Alpines ; bulbs ; herbaceous plants ; water plants
x4   Special plants
Displays ; indoors ; plant combinations ; rareties ; specimens
x5   Turf grasses and plants

Group y : materials in general

y   MATERIALS IN GENERAL
Includes two or more specific classes e/x eg : sections—wood Hi ; sections—metal Hh but sections : wood and metal Hy

Part II, Section 2: Examples

This section shows examples of an office manual, drawings and other documents. Part I of this manual has inevitably been lengthy, because it provides those with special responsibility for data co-ordination with reasonably thorough answers to most of the problems which may arise in producing effectively integrated documentation.
But staff in most offices are unlikely to read Part I in detail, and offices are encouraged to produce their own manuals, tailored to their own particular use of the system and short enough to be read by all staff.

Such a manual can act as an index to Part I of this manual if it uses the same main Section numbers. It can also refer to or include the examples of documents which follow and the 'brief explanation' (see next Section) as an appendix.
Typical headings for an office manual of this kind are given below, with sample and outline text for a section on drawings. The text refers to the example drawings which follow, and has been written as if for a small office carrying out small to medium size projects. The present manual is referred to throughout as RIBA PM.

MESSRS. T.Z. ATKINS CI/SfB PROJECT MANUAL

Section 1. Office policy

[Manual can make reference to 'Brief explanation' (RIBA Project Manual, Part II, Section 3) which can be attached as an appendix, as a brief description of the system; also give a short statement of the reasons for using CI/SfB in the office for project information; purposes for which it is or may be used; general routines for dealing with consultants, contractors and others, as they affect the classification and coding of documents.]

Section 2. Basic principles

[Very brief description of 'search pattern', 'cross reference' and 'sortation'; classification and coding; identification and coding. Kept short by frequent reference to RIBA PM Part I, para 2.1, 2.2 and 2.3.]

Section 3. Facets in use

[Complete list of all codes to be used in the office on project information eg:]

Project Code (see RIBA PM Part I Para 3.5):

on all project documents:	Two digits from CI/SfB Table 0 followed by a point, then an identification number for the project.

Process facet (see RIBA PM Part I Para 3.1):

on documents showing location:	Uncoded
on documents showing assembly:	Code A
on documents showing commodities:	Code C

Project division (see RIBA PM Part I Para. 3.2):

'Complete project'	Uncoded
Blocks	1 to 8 for small projects. External works use 9. Plant housings and ancillary buildings should normally be given codes as separate blocks.
Levels	1 to 8. Single storey projects will not be coded.
Zones	1 to 8. Used on projects involving cross wall construction.
Rooms	1 upwards.

CI/SfB Table 1: Elements (see RIBA PM Part I Para 3,3 and Definitions, PM Part II Section 1):

[Insert copy of matrix from 'Brief explanation'; or refer to it.]

CI/SfB 2/3: Construction Form/Material (see RIBA PM Part I para 3,4, and Definitions in Part II, Section 1):

[Insert copy of lists of codes from 'Brief explanation', or refer to these.]

Section 4. Drawings and schedules

All the types of codes listed above will be used on drawings and schedules. The method of using them is illustrated by the examples of specimen drawings and schedules in RIBA PM Part II Section 2.

Location drawing and detail coding (see RIBA PM Part I para 4,25)

Drawing and detail numbers:

The codes 'L' and (--) will not be shown on drawings or details produced by this office, unlike those illustrated in PM Part II Section 2, but the words 'GENERAL ARRANGEMENT' should always appear in the title of 'L(--)' type drawings and the words 'LOCATION' or 'SETTING OUT' in the title of all other 'L type' drawings.

Most general arrangement drawings for small jobs will therefore have drawing numbers (see RIBA PM Part I Para 4,24) such as 2-5, in which 2, 3, 4 and 5 all indicate separate plans, sections and elevations shown on the sheet. (See RIBA PM Fig. 18). Spare codes should be left if there is any likelihood that further plans, sections or elevations will be added to the sheet later. Drawing numbers for location drawings should start at 1 and should not usually exceed two digits, although they can run up to 199 within each Table 1 code if necessary.

Drawings with specific Table 1 element codes such as (27) Roof should only be produced when more general drawings, such as (2-) Superstructure would otherwise be too congested with information. If this is not followed the number of location drawings will get out of hand.

Cross references:

The following cross reference symbols may be used on location drawings. It will be helpful if consultants can agree to adopt the same conventions for use both on their own drawings for a project and on copy negatives sent to them for completion.

(7-)2   on a plan indicates that detail (7-)2 shows fixtures in plan in more detail. (See RIBA PM drawing (1(--)1, room space 1/11 Cloaks).

5   on a plan indicates that detail 5 shows an elevation in the direction pointed by the arrow. (See RIBA PM drawing L(--)1).

22   on a plan, section or elevation indicates that detail 22 shows a section taken where indicated by the arrow. (See RIBA PM drawing L(--)1 and others).

A(27)222   on a plan, section or elevation indicates that detail A(27)222 shows an assembly section (i.e. 'typical section' without reference to location) taken where indicated by the arrow (see RIBA PM drawings L(--)2-5 and L(1--)1).

A(21)301   on a plan, section or elevation indicates that detail A(21)301 shows the assembly, almost certainly to a larger scale. (See RIBA PM drawing L(2-)1A).

(72):Fixed seating   on any drawing is a reminder to users that further information on fixed seating will be found on drawings coded (72) or (7-) and in section (72) of the specification and bill of quantities (see RIBA PM drawing L(--)1).

(27)Ri4.3 Plywood fascia   on any drawing coded (27), (2-) or (--) cross-refers to full descriptions of the plywood fascia in clauses numbered Ri4.3 and/or (27)Ri4.3 in the specification and bill of quantities. (See RIBA PM Part I Para 4.3, also drawing L(--)2-5 and others.

(31)8   indicates that further information about a particular external door opening is to be found on drawings coded (31) or (3-).

Assembly drawing and detail coding (see RIBA PM Part I Para 4.25)

Assembly drawings should be drawn for re-use. Space should usually be left on each drawing for possible additional details of the same type so that, for example, door jamb details are kept together. But this principle should not be taken so far that site staff have to refer to numerous assembly drawings for each opening.

Drawing and detail numbers:

Every assembly drawing and detail will be prefixed A, and identification codes will run from 201 to 399 within every Table 1 code. The word 'ASSEMBLY' will always appear in the title. (See RIBA PM drawing A(31)205-210).

Cross references:

As for location drawings, except that the first three symbols in the list above and cross reference symbols like (31)8, should not be given on assembly drawings.

Component drawing and detail coding (see RIBA PM Part I Para 4.25)

Component drawings should be drawn for reuse. Space should usually be left on each drawing to add brief specification notes about any alternative version of the component which may be required (with a slightly different material specification for example, and/or with different overall dimensions).

Drawing numbers:

Every component drawing and detail should be prefixed C, and identification codes should run from 401 upwards within every Table 1 code. The word 'COMPONENT' will always appear in the title (see RIBA PM drawings C(31)443 and 449).

Cross references:

Very few cross references should appear on component drawings. Each component drawing should normally include all the information required for manufacture of the component, except that item type codes such as (27)Ri4.3 can sometimes be used to cross refer to suitable clauses in the specification, where these exist. This is particularly important in the case of some units like the boiler house door frame shown in RIBA PM drawing C(31)449 which may be designed by this office as a component but actually built by the contractor as an on-site assembly.

Sortation (RIBA PM Figs. 32 and 33)

Location drawings for each project should normally be issued to the contractor arranged primarily by project division, with the drawings for each block kept together; they should be arranged secondarily by Table 1. Assembly and component drawings should be in separate sets, each arranged primarily by Table 1.

Sizes (RIBA PM Part I Para 4.28)

Only 'A' sizes should be used in the office, as follows:

Location drawings   Not larger than A1
Assembly, component drawings   A3

Item type coding

/Brief reference to RIBA PM Part I Para 4.3.7

Section 5. Specification information

/Procedures for using specification library and use of the definitions in RIBA Part II.7

/The remaining sections can continue to follow the arrangement of the RIBA project manual, i.e.:7

Section 6. Measured information

Section 7. Computer methods

Section 8. Cost planning

Section 9. Briefing information

Section 10. Correspondence

Section 11. Design details

Section 12. Drawings programme

Section 13. Feedback

Appendix 'Brief Explanation'

Project documents

The examples of project documents on the following pages show one possible result from using CI/SfB methods. The drawings and specification are by Wilf McCann, and the cost plan, taking-off sheet and bq page are by Malcolm Talbot

(99) BUILDING COST

CI/SfB	ELEMENT	SPECIFICATION	ELEMENT 377 m² £	ELEMENT per m² £	TOTAL 377 m² £	TOTAL per m² £
(31).	EXTERNAL OPENINGS	Landscape timber windows, standard sections, part glazed part infill panels, hardwood sills, glazing, with softwood doors to suit.	1300	3·45		
(32).	INTERNAL OPENINGS	Internal doors, 'Poplar' flush in softwood linings and architraves, with average quality iron-mongery.	271	0·72		
(37).	ROOFLIGHTS	1200 x 1200 mm Double skin rooflight with timber linings. (3 No)	151	0·40		
(39).	SECONDARY ELEMENTS SUMMARY				1722	4·57
(41).	EXTERNAL FINISHES	Decoration externally to be three coats oil paint on softwood. Two coats of polyurethane on hardwood sills.	108	0·29		
(42).	INTERNAL FINISHES	Walls to be covered with two coats plaster with fair face finish to storage areas. Walls painted with two coats of emulsion, and two coats oil on woodwork.	633	1·68		
(43).	FLOOR FINISHES	6 mm pvc tiles on 50 mm screed to Hall and Teaching areas, carpet to Quiet areas, ceramic tiles on screed to all Toilet areas, softwood skirtings.	818	2·17		
		carried forward	1559	4·14		

721.01.R2

- 3 -

OUTSIDE TEACHING AREA

PLAYGROUND

VIEW FROM SOUTH

1 Perspective sketch of Lanchester RC School extension, sheet size A2. All the specimen documents which follow, illustrating how CI/SfB can be applied to project documentation, are for this project. The title strip has been left off this reproduction to save space; the drawing number of the sheet would fall in the (– –) group, as it contains information on the project as a whole

2 Cost plan on A4 sheet. Most offices would use the sheet turned at right angles to allow more horizontal space for setting out the columns

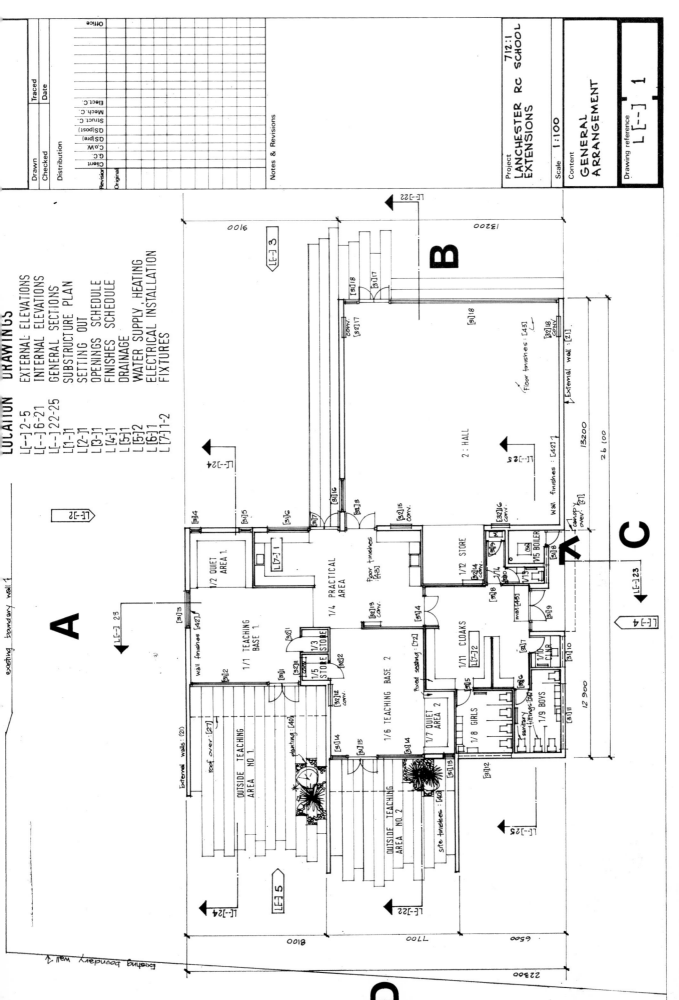

3 General arrangement L(--)1, size A2, the key drawing for building works (external works and overall site layout are not numbered or illustrated in this set of examples). Anyone requiring detailed information on the arrowed boiler house door opening will be led by the (31) ← → (3-) ← → (--) search pattern to the L(3-)1 openings schedule (See **7**)

4 *External elevations: (location) L(– –) 2–5, size A2. Item codes like (27) Ri4·3 plywood fascia cross refer direct to the* *specification and bq. More detailed drawings showing the fascia will be coded (2–) and/or (27)*

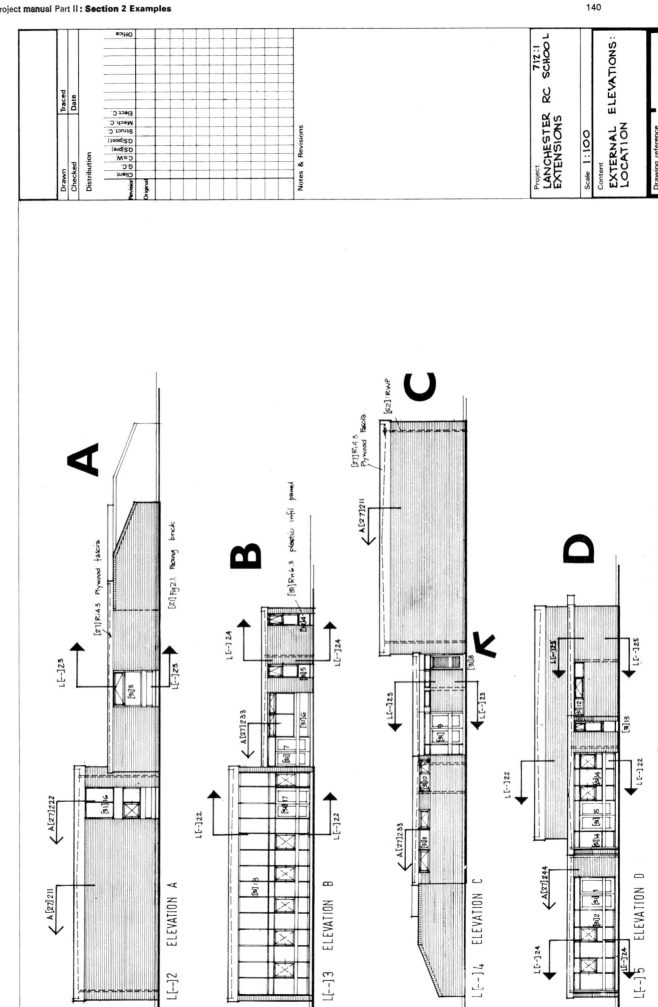

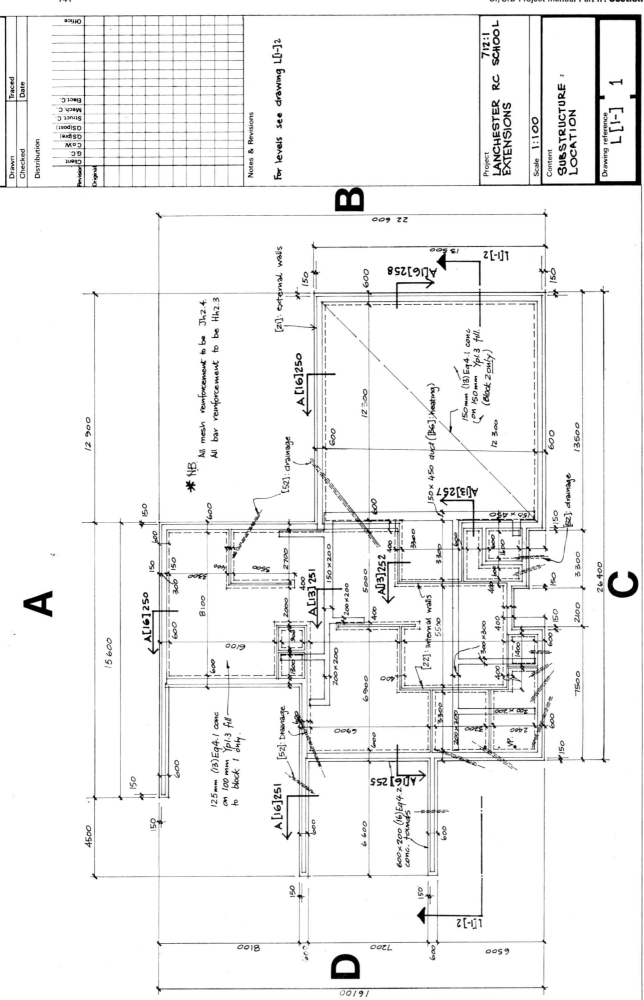

5 *Substructure: location L(1–)1; size A2. The letters A, B, C, D on this drawing and the previous drawings are direction indicators for elevations and schedules. Cross*

references to assembly details all have three digit identification codes like 250, 251, 252, unlike location cross references which have one or two digits

6 *Primary elements: setting out L(2–)1A; size A2. This drawing shows one method of signalling an alteration. It includes item type codes beginning with 2, such as (21)Ff 4.3,*

which conform to the search pattern; and also 'code reminders' like (52) RWP, which may appear on any drawings without regard to the search pattern

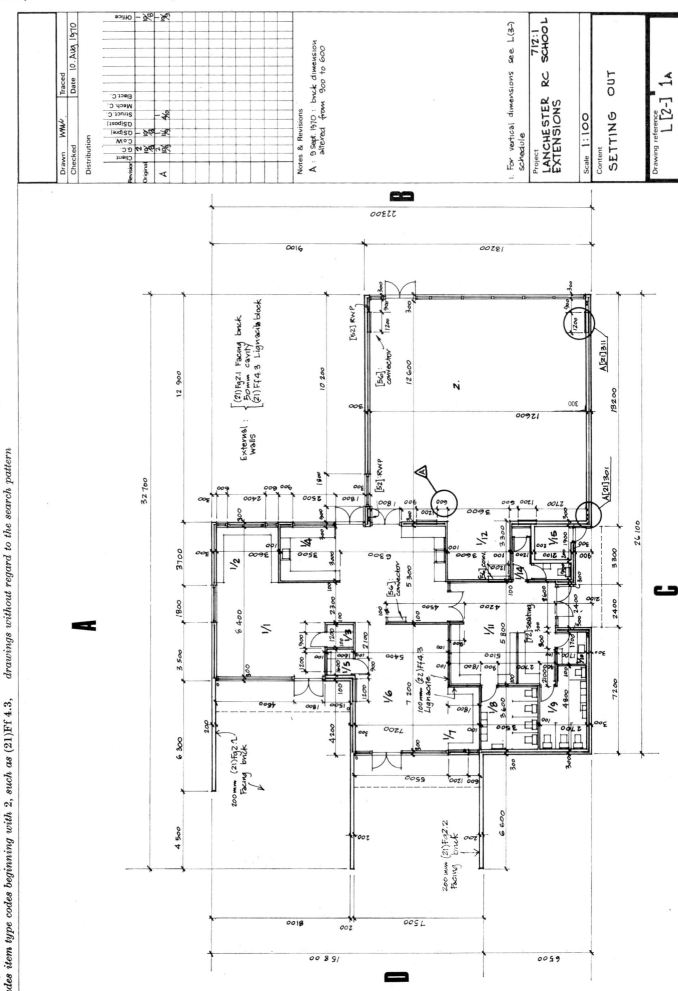

Secondary elements: Openings schedule L(3-)1

Distribution column headers: Client · GC · CoW · QS(pre) · QS(post) · Struct.C · Mech.C · Elect.C · Office · (Original / Revision)

Drawn | Traced
Checked | Date

REF	SPACE	WIDTH¹	HEIGHT¹	TYPE²	GLAZING	GLAZING	TYPE²	Head / lintel detail	JAMB A⁵	JAMB B⁵	HEAD⁵	THRESHOLD⁵
	[31]: EXTERNAL OPENINGS											
(31)1	Teaching base 1	1800	2400	C(31)400	Rol.1 glass	Rol.1 glass	300	300×300 RC lintel type (31)Gf2.1	A(31)200	A(31)200	(A(31)200)	A(31)205
(31)2	do.	6400	2400	C(31)401	Rol.1 glass	Rol.1 glass	C(31)401	do	A(31)200	A(31)200	A(31)200	A(31)205
(31)3	do.	1800	2400	C(31)420	Rol.1 glass	Rol.1 glass	C(31)420		A(31)210	A(31)210	A(31)200	A(31)205
(31)4	Quiet area 1	600	2400	C(31)420	Rol.1 glass	Rol.1 glass	C(31)420	300×600 do	A(31)210	A(31)210	A(31)200	A(31)205
(31)5	do	600	2400	C(31)420	Rol.1 glass	Rol.1 glass	C(31)420	do	A(31)210	A(31)210	A(31)200	A(31)205
(31)6	Practical area	2500	2400	C(31)420	Rol.1 glass	Rol.1 glass	C(31)420	300×300 do	A(31)210	A(31)210	A(31)200	A(31)206
(31)7	do	1800	2100	C(31)400	Rol.1 glass	Rol.1 glass	C(31)400		A(31)211	A(31)211	A(31)200	A(31)206
(31)8	Boiler room	900	2400	C(31)443	—		C(31)449	300×100 (31)HH23 steel lintel	A(31)206	A(31)205	A(31)214	A(31)225
(31)9	Cloaks	2400	2400	C(31)443	Rol.1 glass		C(31)443	do	A(31)210	A(31)210	A(31)200	A(31)216
(31)10	Cleaner Store	1800	600	C(31)443	Rol.2 glass		C(31)443		A(31)210	A(31)210	A(31)200	A(31)211
(31)11	Boys toilets	3600	600	C(31)443	do		C(31)443	2 No 300×100 do	A(31)210	A(31)210	A(31)204	A(31)241
(31)12	Girls toilets	3000	600	C(31)443	do		C(31)443	do	A(31)210	A(31)210	A(31)204	A(31)241
(31)13	Quiet area 2	600	2400	C(31)420	Rol.1 glass	Rol.1 glass	C(31)420	300×60 RC lintel type (31)Gf2.1	A(31)200	A(31)200	A(31)202	A(31)205
(31)14	Teaching base 2	5500	2400	C(31)401	Rol.1 glass	Rol.1 glass	C(31)401	do	A(31)200	A(31)200	A(31)202	A(31)205
(31)15	do	1800	2400	C(31)400	Rol.1 glass	Rol.1 glass	C(31)400		A(31)200	A(31)200	A(31)202	A(31)205
(31)16	Hall	1800	2400	C(31)420	Rol.2 glass	Rol.2 glass	C(31)420		A(31)210	A(31)210	A(31)202	A(31)205
(31)17	Hall	1800	2400	C(31)400	Rol.1 glass	Rol.1 glass	C(31)400	300×300	A(31)200	A(31)200	A(31)202	A(31)205
(31)18	Hall	13200⁴	4200	C(31)400	Rol.3 glass	Rol.1 glass	C(31)400	[27] Roof beam	A(31)200	A(31)200	A(31)202	A(31)205
	[32]: INTERNAL OPENINGS											
(32)1	Teaching base 1	900	2400	C(32)420	Rol.4 glass		C(32)430		A(32)201	A(32)202	A(32)203	A(32)204
(32)2	Teaching base 2	900	2400	C(32)420	do		C(32)430		do	do	do	do
(32)3	Hall	1800	2400	C(32)420	Rol.4 glass		C(32)480		A(32)205	do	A(32)205	A(32)205
(32)4	Cloaks	2200	2400	C(32)420	do		C(32)430		A(32)207	A(32)207	A(32)203	A(32)204
(32)5	Girls toilets	900	2400	C(32)420	do		C(32)430		A(32)201	A(32)202	A(32)203	A(32)204
(32)6	Boys toilets	900	2400	do	do		do		do	do	do	do
(32)7	Cleaner	900	2400	do	do		do		do	do	do	do
(32)8	Staff cloaks	900	2400	do	do		do		do	do	do	do
(32)9	Staff cloaks	900	2400	do	do		do		do	do	do	do
(32)10	Staff WC	900	2400	do	do		do		do	do	do	do
(32)11	Teaching base 1											
(32)12	Teaching base 2											
(32)13	Practical area			FOR DETAILS OF CONVECTOR RECESSES SEE L[5-]3					A[2-]3;1-4			
(32)14	Store			FOR CONVECTOR SCHEDULE SEE								
(32)15	Hall											
(32)16	Hall											
(32)17	Hall											
(32)18	Hall											

Notes & Revisions

1. 5mm has been allowed for all joints between components and structure.
2. Type references refer to the relevant drawing number.
3. References in these columns refer to the relevant details in the book of assembly conditions.
4. This window sectionalised. (7 No 1800 units)

Project: **LANCHESTER RC SCHOOL EXTENSIONS**
Scale: 712:1   1
Content: **OPENINGS SCHEDULE: LOCATION**
Drawing reference: **L[3-]1**

7 Secondary elements: Openings schedule L(3-)1; size A2.
This schedule is a convenient substitute for a location plan.
Details for door (31)8 are shown arrowed and lead to door and frame component details C(31)443 and 449 and jamb assembly details A(31)205 and 206 (see 11 to 13)

8 *Finishes schedule: location L (4-) 1; size A2.*
Consists almost entirely of item type codes cross-referring
direct to the specification and bg, since component and
assembly details are not required

SPACE		[42] INTERNAL WALLS								[43] FLOOR		[44] STAIR		[45] CEILING		NOTES
		WALL A		WALL B		WALL C		WALL D								
REF	NAME	PREP	FINISH	PREP	FINISH	PREP	FINISH	PREP	FINISH	PREP	FINISH	PREP	FINISH	PREP	FINISH	
1/1	Teaching base1	Rm1.1 pinboard	Vv6.3 paint							50mm Pr4.1 screed	6mm Tn8.1 tiles			12mm Rf7.1 plasterbd	Vv6.1 paint	
1/2	Quiet area 1	do	do							do	T16.1 carpet			Sm1.1 ac. tiles	—	
1/3	Store	F.F blockwk	Vv6.2 paint							do	6mm Tn8.1 tiles			12mm Rf7.1 plasterbd	Vv6.1 paint	
1/4	Practical area	do	do							15mm Pr4.2 screed	15mm Sf8.1 tiles			Sm1.1 ac. tiles	—	
1/5	Store	do	do							50mm Pr4.1 screed	6mm Tn8.1 tiles			12mm Rf7.1 plasterbd	Vv6.1 paint	
1/6	Teaching base 2	Rm1.1 pinboard	Vv6.3 paint							do	do			do	do	
1/7	Quiet area 2	do	do							do	T16.1 carpet			Sm1.1 ac.tiles	—	
1/8	Girls toilet	Pr2.2 plaster	Vv6.1 paint							15mm Pr4.2 screed	15mm Sf8.1 tiles			12mm Rf7.1 plasterbd	Vv6.1 paint	
1/9	Boys toilet	do	do							do	do			do	do	
1/10	Cleaner	do	do	Rm1.1 pinboard	Vv6.3 paint					do	do			do	do	
1/11	Cloaks	do	do							50mm Pr4.1 screed	6mm Tn8.1 tiles			do	do	
1/12	Chair store	do	do							15mm Pr4.2 screed	15mm Sf8.1 tiles			do	do	
1/13	Staff toilets	do	do							do	do			do	do	
1/14	Staff cloaks	do	do							do	do			do	do	
1/15	Boiler room	Fair faced	Fair faced	brickwork						concrete bed (ib)	—			2No.6mm layers Rf6.2 asbestos	—	
2	Hall	Pr2.2 plaster	Vv6.1 paint	glazed screen		Pr2.2 plaster	Vv6.1 paint	Pr2.2 plaster	Vv6 paint.	15mm Pr4.2 screed	15mm Sf8.1 tiles			12mm Rf7.1 plasterbd	Vv6.1 paint.	

Distribution: Client, G.C, C.o.W, QS(pre), QS(post), Struct.C, Mech.C, Elect.C, Office

Drawn · Checked · Traced · Date
Revision · Original
Notes & Revisions

Project: LANCHESTER RC SCHOOL EXTENSIONS   712:1
Scale —
Content: FINISHES SCHEDULE: LOCATION
Drawing reference L[4-] 1

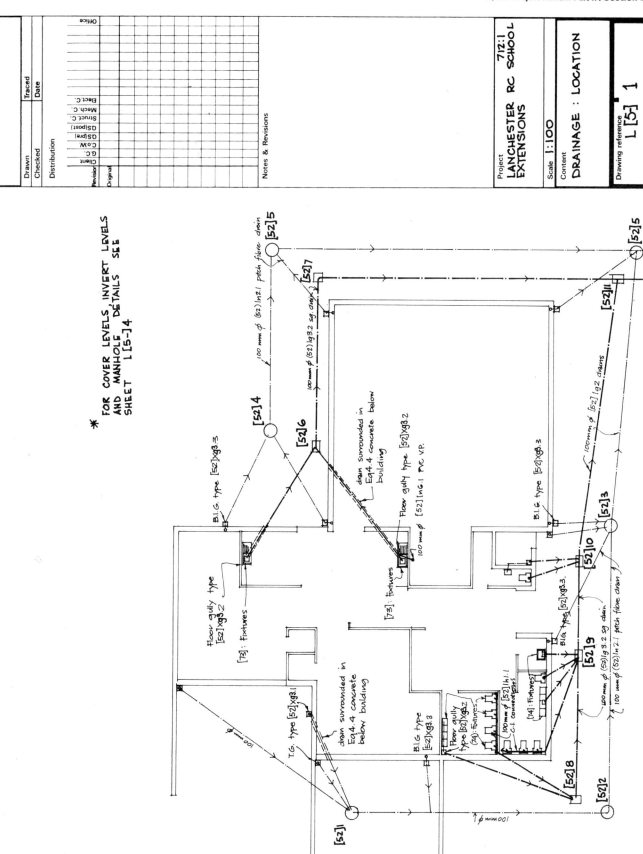

9 *Drawing: location L(5–)1; size A2. Could have been numbered L(52) rather than L(5–), but in view of the small number of services drawings it was decided to code them all* (5–), *namely L(5–)1 Drainage: location; L(5–)2 Water supply, heating: location; L(5–)3 Convector schedule: location; and so on.*

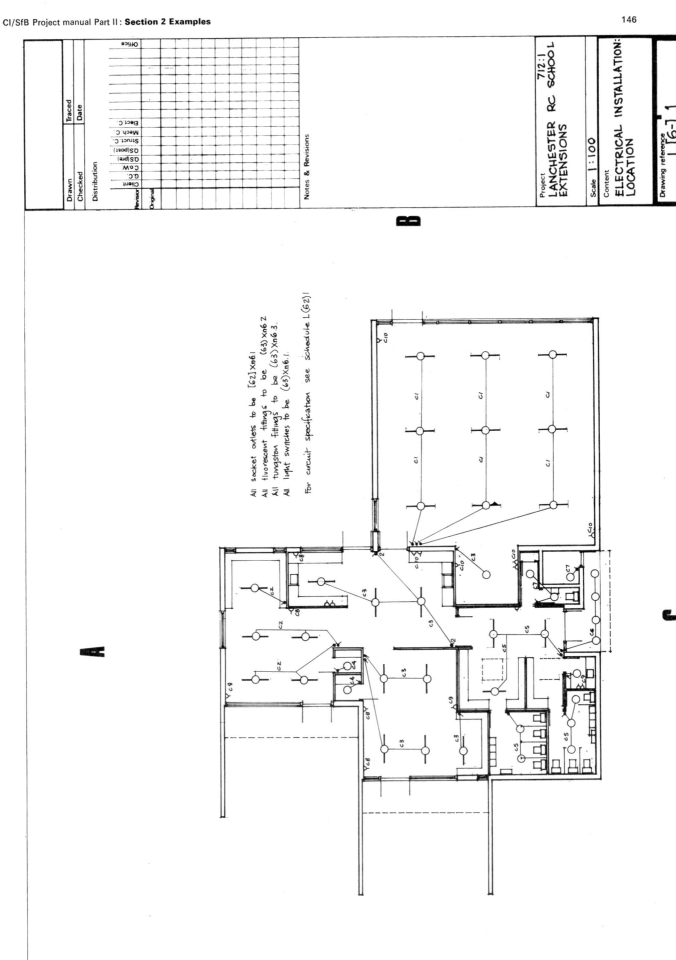

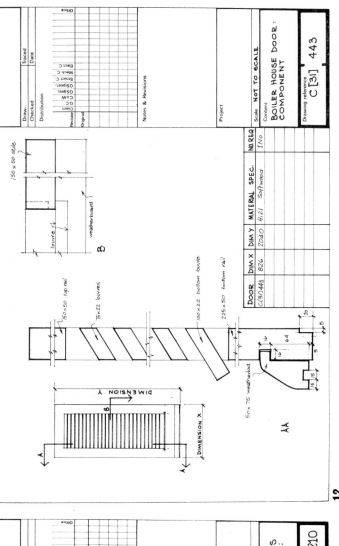

11 External openings jamb conditions: assembly A(31) 205–210; size A3. The assembly details include an item type code for the bitumen dpc but not for the material of the frame (shown on the relevant component drawing), or the brickwork. This—since brickwork is used throughout the project—can be conveniently shown on setting out or other location drawings

12 Boiler house door: component C(31)443; size A3. This component as a whole (ie as a single commodity which can be bought in by the manufacturer) will be coded (31)Xi2 in the specification and bq, but the individual parts which make it up can be separately coded Hi2, Vv5 etc. The drawing shows item type code Hi2.1 softwood but not Vv5 paint. Paint specification is so variable from project to project that it is better shown in the specification, with colours indicated on a (3–) or (––) colour schedule

13 Boiler house door frame: component C(31)449; size A3. This unit, drawn as a component to be manufactured then fixed in position, has been taken off (see **14**) as individual lengths of timber each to be fixed and housed together in situ. This does not matter, since the Hi2.1 refers to general specification clauses which cover the fixing of timber sections to surrounding materials as well as to each other. Any special clauses about the finishing, protection and fixing of the door frame components (as distinct from clauses about wood sections generally) will be in the specification at (31)X

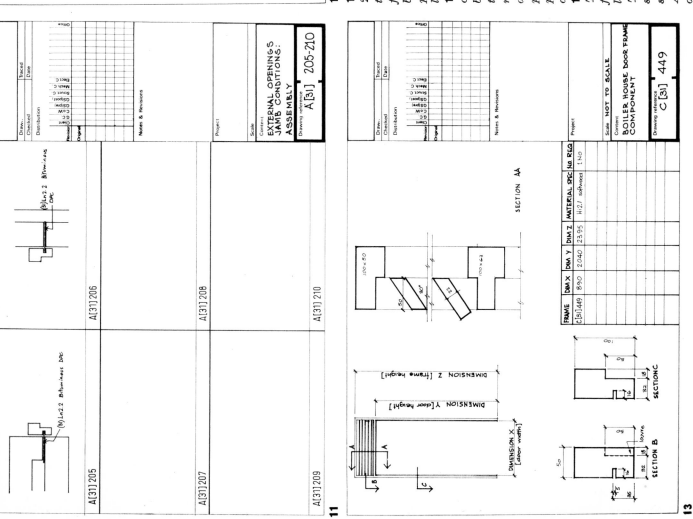

11

12

13

15a — Hi (continued)

Hi Wood Sections

For blockboard, plywood, laminated timber generally, see Ri4.
For ironmongery see Xt7.
For on site painting see Vv5.

Design sizes

Materials and workmanship (except for references to sizes) must comply with CP 112. Sawn timber must be sawn to the sizes given. Where 'finished' sizes are given for wrought timber the notation 'finished' follows each dimension to which it applies. All other sizes are nominal and are subject to an allowance of not more than one-eighth inch for each wrought face and these will be preceded by the notation "ex".

Protection, storage

All timber must be adequately protected against the weather and stored under dry conditions.

Placing

Carpentry includes its fixings by any means (bolts measured separately at Xt6). Work described as "plugged" must be secured by fixing to hardwood slips or pallets; other fixings including dowels must be of hardwood unless otherwise specified.

Hi1 Sawn timber

Treating

Whenever specified, timber is to be pretreated with "——" by open tank cold dipping to a minimum absorption of 2.5oz. per cubic foot in the outer zone. This treatment must be carried out by an authorised agent of "——" Laboratories Ltd.

All cross cuts, morticing, drilling, etc. executed after this treatment must be liberally treated with "——" 10% solution by brushing.

The Contractor must ensure the "——" treated timber has a moisture content between 12% and 18% of its dry weight at the time of fixing.

Placing

Structural timbers must extend in one piece across their support. Where notching is required over supports, the depth of the notch must not exceed 2/5ths depth of timber. Where structural timbers are drilled for the passage of pipes, conduit, etc.

15b — Hi1 (continued)

these cuts should be made as near the neutral axis (usually the centre of the timber) as possible and must not exceed 1/3rd of the depth of the timber. Notching on the top or bottom faces of structural timbers will not be allowed without the permission of the Architect.

Commodities

All sawn timber must comply with BS 1860 Part 1.

Pins, spikes, nails, screws and similar fixings must be of sherardised steel.

Sawn structural timber to CP112 grade 50 treated with "——".

Hi2 Wrot Softwood

Making

Prices for joinery must include for slightly rounding all exposed arrises and leaving all exposed surfaces smooth faced (not machine planed only).

Placing

All framed work must be prepared and knocked together loosely as soon as possible after the Contract has been signed but should not be glued until ready for use. Butt glued joints are to be crosstongued.

Timber which is selected and kept clean and is described as screwed must be secretly fixed or countersunk screwed and pellated. Where timber is fitted with nails or is described as screwed in, the heads must be punched in or countersunk and the holes stopped with an approved filler.

Commodities

Wrot softwood must comply with BS 1186. Glues must comply with BS 1186, Part 2 and where joinery fittings are to be exposed to damp or wet conditions must also be weather and boil proof (Class WBP).

Hi2.1 External wrot softwood (not treated with "——") must be Swedish Finnish or Russian Redwood in unsorted quality of first class production; or Douglas Fir equal to No.2 quality. If the Contractor wishes to use any other type of timber he must obtain the written approval of the Architect.

Hi2.2 Internal wrot softwood (not treated with "——") must be Swedish Russian or Finnish Whitewood (unsorted) Western Hemlock (No. 2 clear) or Parana Pine (prime). If the Contractor wishes to use any other type of timber he must obtain the written approval of the Architect.

SECONDARY ELEMENTS IN EXTERNAL WALLS: WROT SOFTWOOD — (31)Hi2.1

Item		Qty.	Unit	Rate	£ s d
	Boiler House Door Frame				
1.	22 x 75 mm louvre, twice splayed	20	m		
2.	22 x 100 mm ditto, once splayed	2	m		
3.	50 x 100 mm door frame, rebated, and plugged to concrete	1	m		
4.	50 x 100 mm ditto, grooved, and fixed to blockwork	1	m		
5.	50 x 100 mm ditto, stop rebated and grooved, do.	4	m		
6.	63 x 100 mm transom, twice rebated	1	m		
7.	House end of louvre to softwood frame	10	no		
8.	Protection				
	Allow for protecting the work in this section				
	TOTAL TO COLLECTION			Item	£

(The information contained on this sheet has been extracted from a bill page to exemplify the work and items involved in assembling and fixing the individual sections which make up the boiler house door frame.)

14

Taking-off sheet (handwritten) for boiler house door frame.

14 *Taking-off sheet for boiler house door frame as individual lengths of timber fixed in position*

15a, b *Specification pages for Hi wood sections*

16 *Bq page for (31) Hi2.1 showing work in connection with boiler house door frame* **13.** *Alternatively, the door frame, like the door, could have been taken off in its entirety as a component (ie as drawn) and coded Xi2. All work involved in its manufacture and fixing would then be found at bill section (31)Xi2. This would of course still leave the contractor free to assemble it himself on site if he wished to do so*

Part II, Section 3: Brief explanation

This short explanation of CI/SfB based methods of data co-ordination is intended for contractors and others who do not require the very detailed explanation given in Part I of this manual.

CI/SfB based data co-ordination methods

CI/SfB is the basis of a system which can be used by all members of the building team for arranging and cross-referencing information on drawings, specifications, bills of quantities, etc.

It is the UK version of the international SfB classification system, which took its name from the initials of the Swedish committee which originally produced it. SfB was introduced into the UK in 1961 as a method of organising building industry libraries; most people are aware of the SfB reference on the top right hand corner of trade literature. In 1968 the RIBA developed the system further and added 'CI' to distinguish the new development from the original SfB. CI stands for Construction Indexing (system), hence CI/SfB. In April 1969 the council of the RIBA recommended architects to use the system for organising project drawings and other documents and in August 1970 the *Architects' Journal* published for RIBA Services the *Project information manual*, explaining how the system could be used in conjunction with other codes for this purpose.

How it works

CI/SfB contains five main tables or coded lists of items. Three of these are used on this project; these are:

Table 1: Elements (parts)

This lists building parts such as doors, windows and heating systems and gives each part a code consisting of two numerals which are enclosed in brackets to distinguish them from codes used for other purposes. These codes are always given with information concerning the part. For example, windows are coded (31) and all drawings, specifications and measured information concerning windows will be coded (31) or given a related code.

A full list of these codes is shown on the next page.

Tables 2 and 3: Building products and materials

These are used together to code building products first by their form or shape, eg bricks, tubes and sheets, and second by their material, eg wood, glass.

Different forms of products are coded by capital letters eg F: blocks, R: sheets, and the materials of which they are made are given a lower case letter usually followed by a number eg: g2 clay, heavy burnt; i4 wood, laminated. For example:

> Ri4 = sheet, plywood
> Rj3 = sheet, wood wool
> Ro1 = sheet, float glass

Where computers are used the lower case letter will usually be printed as a capital.

All three tables of codes may be used together on drawings and in the bill of quantities, eg:

(21)Fg2 = external walls: brick, clay, heavy burnt
(27)Hi2 = roofs: sections, softwood
(43)Sg2 = floor finishes: tile, clay, heavy burnt (ie quarries)

A list of the principal codes from these tables is shown on the next page.

How to use CI/SfB

Architects, structural and mechanical and electrical consultants, and quantity surveyors normally organise the documents they produce in different ways. For example, consultants often use a drawing numbering system which bears no relationship to that used by the architect or other consultants, and bills of quantities and drawings are difficult to use together because they are not cross referenced. The CI/SfB tables provide standard lists of codes and headings which can be used for organising project documents. CI/SfB automatically cross references information dealing with the same subject, no matter who has produced it.

An automatic cross-referencing system

The short codes used in CI/SfB may appear complicated and confusing at first sight and most people would prefer to write or read 'clay brick external walls' rather than (21)Fg2. However, codes are not used alone without written descriptions, and there are good reasons why these particular symbols should be used. When used beside a written heading or short description they show where other, more detailed, information may be found. It is not necessary to understand the meaning of the codes to use this facility. For example, a typical code and note on a drawing such as (31) windows provides a key to all other information on windows. Drawings coded (31) will give detail of windows; (31) in the bills of quantities and the cost plan will give the cost of windows; (31) in the client's brief will give design requirements for windows. It is not necessary to memorise or even become familiar with the codes to gain advantage from using them.

Element summaries

It is often inconvenient, and sometimes impossible, to produce drawings which deal only with one element. For example, a drawing may give detailed information on both (21) external walls and (22) internal walls. But if it is numbered (21) external walls, it will not be found by someone looking for full information on internal walls or partitions, because information on this subject is coded (22). Similarly, if it is coded (22) it will not be found by someone

CI/SfB *Table* 1 (*Elements*)

(– –)
Project

Substructure	Superstructure			Services		Fittings	
(1–) **Substructure**	**(2–)** **Primary** **elements**	**(3–)** **Secondary** **elements**	**(4–)** **Finishes**	**(5–)** **Services**	**(6–)** **Installations**	**(7–)** **Fixtures**	**(8–)** **Loose** **equipment**
(10) (1–) (– –) Site substructure	(20) (2–) (– –) Site primary elements	(30) (3–) (– –) Site secondary elements	(40) (4–) (– –) Site finishes	(50) (5–) (– –) Site services	(60) (6–) (– –) Site installations	(70) (7–) (– –) Site fixtures	(80) (8–) (– –) Site loose equipment
(11) (1–) (– –) Excavations	(21) (2–) (– –) External walls	(31) (3–) (– –) External openings	(41) (4–) (– –) External finishes	(51) (5–) (– –) Refuse disposal	(61) (6–) (– –) Electrical source	(71) (7–) (– –) Circulation fixtures	(81) (8–) (– –) Circulation loose equipment
	(22) (2–) (– –) Internal walls	(32) (3–) (– –) Internal openings	(42) (4–) (– –) Internal finishes	(52) (5–) (– –) Drainage	(62) (6–) (– –) Power	(72) (7–) (– –) General room fixtures	(82) (8–) (– –) General room loose equipment
(13) (1–) (– –) Floorbeds	(23) (2–) (– –) Floors	(33) (3–) (– –) Floor secondary element	(43) (4–) (– –) Floor finishes	(53) (5–) (– –) Water supply	(63) (6–) (– –) Lighting	(73) (7–) (– –) Culinary fixtures	(83) (8–) (– –) Culinary loose equipment
	(24) (2–) (– –) Stairs	(34) (3–) (– –) Balustrades to stairs	(44) (4–) (– –) Stair finishes	(54) (5–) (– –) Gas	(64) (6–) (– –) Communications	(74) (7–) (– –) Sanitary fixtures	(84) (8–) (– –) Sanitary loose equipment
		(35) (3–) (– –) Suspended ceilings	(45) (4–) (– –) Ceiling finishes	(55) (5–) (– –) Refrigeration		(75) (7–) (– –) Cleaning fixtures	(85) (8–) (– –) Cleaning loose equipment
(16) (1–) (– –) Foundations				(56) (5–) (– –) Space heating	(66) (6–) (– –) Lifts transport	(76) (7–) (– –) Storage fixtures	(86) (8–) (– –) Storage loose equipment
(17) (1–) (– –) Piles	(27) (2–) (– –) Roofs	(37) (3–) (– –) Rooflights	(47) (4–) (– –) Roof finishes	(57) (5–) (– –) Ventilation			
	(28) (2–) (– –) Frames				(68) (6–) (– –) Security		

Above: matrix of CI/SfB *Table* 1 *codes. These codes refer to building elements (parts), or groups of elements. A document containing information exclusively on internal wall finishes, for example, would be given the specific code* (42). *A document containing information on both internal wall finishes* (42) *and ceiling finishes* (45) *would be given the code* (4–). *If it also contained information on, say, suspended ceilings structure* (35) *it would receive the general project code* (– –)

CI/SfB *Tables* 2 *and* 3 *Construction form and materials*

Table 2		Table 3	
A	Preliminaries*	a	Administrative activities†
B	Demolitions*	b	Aids, temporary works, plant†
C	Excavation*	c	Labour†
D	Formless materials*	d	Operations†
E	Cast in situ	e	Natural stone
F	Brick, block	f	Formed concrete, etc
G	Structural unit	g	clay
H	Section, bar	h	metal
I	Tube, pipe	i	wood
J	Wire, mesh	j	Natural fibre
K	Quilt	k	—
L	Foil, paper (except finishing paper)	l	—
M	Foldable sheet	m	Mineral fibre
N	Overlap sheet, tile	n	Plastics, etc
O	—	o	Glass
P	Thick coating	p	Loose fill
Q	—	q	Cement, concrete
R	Rigid sheet	r	Gypsum, etc
S	Rigid tile	s	Bituminous material
T	Flexible sheet, tile	t	Fixing, jointing agents
V	Thin coating including paint	v	Painting material
W	—	w	Other chemicals
X	Components	x	Plants
Y	Construction, products in general	y	Materials in general
Z	—	z	—

*Not part of CI/SfB Table 2
†Based on CI/SfB Table 4

The above table shows CI/SfB *Table* 2 (*Construction form*) *and Table* 3 (*Materials*). *These are always used together; sheet glass would therefore be coded* Ro, *and a clay brick* Fg. *Such a code could then be combined with an element code*

looking for full information on external walls. In order to cope with this problem CI/SfB uses some codes to summarise others. For example, if specification information on external and internal walls is shown on one drawing, it will be coded (2—).

Some drawings cover almost all parts; examples of these are block plans, general cross sections of the building and general room layouts. In these cases a general summary number is used and this is (– –), spoken 'dash-dash'. This means that there are only three places where information on any one subject can be found in any document or set of drawings.

As an example, suppose all information on space heating services is required. (56) is the code for heating. If there are any drawings dealing with heating alone (such as heater unit details) these will be coded (56); if information on space heating has been included with other piped services information (perhaps with drainage on a general services drawing), then the drawing will be coded (5–); if a general layout

from Table 1 (*see above*) *to indicate in what part of the building the product occurs; eg a clay brick forming part of an external wall would be coded* (21)Fg; *or a document containing information on clay tiles occurring in both internal floor and stair finishes would be coded* (4–) Sg

drawing such as a traditional '$\frac{1}{8}$ scale' shows information on piped services as well as on other subjects, then it will be coded (– –).

This may appear complicated at first sight, but all relevant summary numbers are given in the squares showing the Table 1 codes in the matrix on the previous page.

The square showing (56), for example, also includes (5–) and (– –) and these three references show where *all* information will be found on *all* documents dealing with heating services. If, after looking through documents carrying these codes, the information has not been found, then it is reasonable to conclude that it is not included in the set of project documents at all.

Advice and improvements

After a few hours' use, the user gets increased benefit from the system; he will be able to find information more quickly and in a form which will be more useful to him. It is likely that more and more architects will be introducing the system into their offices. There should also be an increase in CI/SfB structured bills of quantities. Success will depend on the willingness of those using the system to contribute to its development. If you find any difficulty in using it or can suggest any improvements please have a word with the architect, who will either answer your questions or pass your comments on to RIBA Services. RIBA Services will advise on the use and development of the system.

Index to tables 1 and 2/3

Users unfamiliar with CI/SfB may initially have difficulty in knowing where to look for a particular bit of information (on 'Roofs', or 'Windows', or 'Anchor bolts', for example) in a set of drawings, specifications, or bills of quantities arranged in accordance with this system. To help them, this index lists the Tables 1 and 2/3 codes for a wide variety of building elements, products, components and materials. It consists largely of simple terms, such as 'Roof (27)'; or 'Decking G', which can be looked up separately. It was decided not to include compound terms involving Tables 1 and 2/3 together, like 'Roof decking (27) G', or 'Roof decking, precast concrete (27) Gf2', for this would have made the index inordinately long and unwieldy.

The index is not intended to be exhaustive; rather, it is a practical aid for everyday use. Note that:

1 All items with a bracketed code may be found in one of three places on the drawings, specifications, bqs and so on: either under the specific code given in this index (eg (31) for windows); or under the appropriate main group code (which is (3–) in the above case); or under the code for the project in general (– –).

2 Items will be found either under their own code as given in this index, or under the code for the work in which they are incorporated. For example, information on anchor bolts should be looked for first under their own code 'Xt6'; then, if necessary, under 'E Cast in-situ work', '(28) Frame', and so on.

Ablutions
Site huts Ab1
Sanitary fixtures (74)
Abutments
Retaining structures (16)
Access floors (33)
Access panels
External walls (31)
Floors (33)
Internal walls (32)
Suspended ceilings (35)
Acoustic barriers
Suspended ceilings (35)
Acoustic telephone hoods (64)
Acrylic based enamels Vv5
Acrylic bonded mortars
Mixes and in general Dr4 or Yr4
Thick coatings Pr4
Acrylic panels
Rigid sheets Rn6
Administration Aa
Admixtures Du2 or Yu2
Aerated concrete
Mixes and in general Dq6 or Yq6
Blocks Ff4
Cast in situ Eq6
Large precast units Gf4
Precasting in general Yf4
Slabs Rf4
Aerials : Parts
Communications installations (64)
Site communications installations (60) or (90.6)
Aggregates
In general Dp or Yp
Aids for the work Ab
Air bricks F
Air conditioning
In general (57)
Air cooled slag Dp2 or Yp2
Air distributed central heating (56)
Air distribution systems space heating in general (56)
Air entrained concrete
see Aerated concrete
Air filters
Parts : Air conditioning (57)
Airing cupboards (75)
Alarm systems
In general (68)
Site (60) or (90.6)
Aluminium
In general Dh4 or Yh4
Foil Lh4
Foldable sheets Mh4
Mesh Jh4
Overlap sheets and tiles Nh4
Paint Vv9
Panels, rigid flat sheets Rh4
Pipes Ih4
Sections Hh4
Special formed units Gh4
Tiles Sh4
Wire Jh4
Anchor bolts Xt6
Angles
Sections H
Anodised aluminium
see Aluminium
Antennas : Parts
Internal communications installations (64)
Site communications installations (60) or (90.6)
Anti-condensation paints Vu6
Anti-corrosive materials
In general Du1 or Yu1
Anti-corrosive paints
In general Vu1
Anti-insect coatings Vu3
Anti-rot coatings Vu3
Anti-static rubber sheets Tn5
Anti-sun coatings Vu5
Appraisal Aa8
Arbitration
Project administration Aa9
Architectural ironmongery Xt7
Armchairs (82)
Armoured glass sheets Ro8
Asbestos cement
Mixes and in general Dq9 or Yq9
Panels : Rigid flat sheets Rf6
Pipes If6
Sections Hf6
Sprayed coatings Pq9
Tiles Sf6
Asbestos fibre
In general Ym1
Cloth Lm1, Um1
Felts, quilts Km1
Pipes Im1
Rope Jm1
Ash
Fill Yp4
Ash trays : Floor mounted (71)
Ash trays : Floor standing (81)
Ashlar
Bricks and blocks Fe

Asphalt
In general Ds or Ys
Blocks Fn1
Thick coatings Ps5
Tiles Sn1
Audio communications
Installations (64)
Audio/visual communications
Installations (64)
Awnings
Site fixtures (70) or (90.7)

Backings
Thick coating P
Baggage conveyors
Internal transportation (66)
Baggage lifts (66)
Bags
Parts : Refuse disposal (51)
Bains marie (73)
Balconies (23)
Ball valves
Parts : Water supply (53)
Ballast
Fill Dp1 or Yp1
Balusters (34)
Balustrades (34)
Bamboo fibres
see Vegetable fibres
Bands
Parts : Internal wall finishes (42)
Bannisters
Parts : Balustrades (34)
Barge boards
Sections H
Overlap tiles N
Barrel-lights
Rooflights (37)
Barrel vault roof (27)
Barriers parts :
Balustrades (34)
External walls (21)
Films V
Internal doors (32)
Internal walls (22)
Site elements (20) or (90.2)
Windows (31)
Bars
Products H
Basalt
In general De1 or Ye1
Blocks Fe1
Formed structural units Ge1
Slabs Re1
Base boarding
Rigid sheets R
Base layer
Floor beds (13)
Bases
Machines : Floors (33)
Pad footings (16)
Basic materials D
Bathrooms
Fixtures (74)
Baths
Sanitary fixtures (74)
Battens : Parts
Ceiling finishes (45)
External wall finishes (41)
Floor finishes (43)
Internal wall finishes (42)
Roof finishes (47)
Battens
Products H
Batteries : Heating and cooling
Parts
Air conditioning systems (57)
Electrical installations (61)
Beads
Sections H
Beams
Ground (16)
Large units (structural) G
Parts : Floor (23)
Parts : Frame (28)
Parts : Roof (27)
Bearers
Sections H
Bed lifts (66)
Bedrooms
Suites (82)
Beds
Floors : substructure (13)
Loose equipment (82)
Bedside cabinets (82)
Beeswax
Surface coatings Vu5
Bell installations (64)
Belt conveyors
Installations (66)
Belts
Parts : conveyors (66)
Benches
Site fixtures (70) or (90.7)
Freestanding (82)
Fixtures (72)

Diaphragm retaining walls (16)
Dictating equipment
Communications installations (64)
Diffusers: Parts
Suspended ceilings (35)
Ventilating and air-conditioning systems (57)
Diminishing pieces
Pipes I
Dishwashers (73)
Dispensers, soap (74)
Displacement (driven) piles (17)
Display boards
In general (71)
Site (70) or (90.7)
Fixtures (71)
Loose equipment (81)
Display cabinets
Refrigeration services (55)
Distemper Vv8
Distribution boards: Parts
Communications installations (64)
Electrical centre (61)
Electrical installations (62)
Lighting installations (63)
Distribution circuits: Parts
Centre (61)
Local (62)
Distribution systems: Parts
Gas and air services (54)
Heating (56)
Refrigeration services (55)
Security installations (68)
Services in general (5–)
Ventilation and air-conditioning systems (57)
Water services (53)
Dome roofs (27)
Domelights (37)
Domes
Parts: Rooflights (37)
Domestic hot water supply
Central (53)
Local (53)
Door bell installations (64)
Door mats
Entrances (81)
Door furniture: Parts
Doors: Internal and in general (32)
Door leaves
Parts: Internal and in general (32)
Door and window combined assemblies
External (31)
Internal (32)
Doors
In general and internal (32)
External (31)
Lifts: Transportation (66)
Dormers (37)
Double glazing units
Glass sheets Ro5
Double leaf walls
External loadbearing walls (21)
Internal loadbearing walls (22)
Double pitched roofs (27)
Dowelling
Sections H
Dowels: Anchorages Xt6
Downpipes: Parts
Drainage (52)
Downshop leads
Parts: Transportation systems (66)
Drainage
In general (52)
External to building services (50) or (90.5)
Internal: Services (52)
Draining boards
Culinary fixtures (73)
Drains, land (11)
Drapes (81)
Draught excluders
Sections H
Drawings
In general Aa3
Dressings
Thin coating V
Dressing tables
Bedroom loose equipment (82)
Driers: Fixtures
Cleaning equipment (75)
Hands (74)
Drinking fountains (74.9)
Drips
Sections: Products H
Driven piles (17)
Drying agents Dw2 or Yw2
Dry risers
Fire fighting (68)
Water services (53.2)
Duckboards (37)
Duct covers
Floors (33)
Ducted warm air central heating (56)

Ducting: Parts
External walls (21)
Internal walls (22)
Flooring (23)
Refrigeration services (55)
Refuse disposal (51)
Roofs (27)
Services in general (5–)
Space heating (56)
Ventilations and air-
conditioning systems (57)
Water services (53)
Ducts
Crawlways (substructure) (16)
Tubes: I
Dumb waiters (66)
Dustbins (51)

Earth Dp1 or Yp1
Earth closets (74)
Earthenware tiles Sg3
Earthing
Security installations (66)
Earthworks (11)
Easy chairs (82)
'Easy clean' hinged windows (31)
Eaves
Parts: Roofs (27)
Edging
Pedestrian pavings (40) or (90.4)
Eel grass
see Vegetable fibres
Effluent disposal (52)
Egg crate ceilings
Suspended ceilings (35)
Elastomers
In general Dn5 or Yn5
Elastomer adhesives Dt3 or Yt3
Elbows
Pipes I
Electric fires
Local heating (56.4)
Electric motors
In general (61)
Electrical central heating (56)
Electrical centre (61)
Electrical installations
In general (6–)
Distribution (62)
Site (60) or (90.6)
Electrical local heating (56)
Electrically heated systems
In general (56)
Centralised hot water supply (53)
Local hot water supply (53)
Warm air central heating (56)
Water and steam distributed central heating (56)
Electro-copper glazed sheets Ro8
Elements
see Primary elements
Secondary elements
Elevated continuous access floors (33)
Embankments
Site works (10) or (90.1)
Emergency lighting (63)
Emergency signs (68)
Emulsifying agents Dw2 or Yw2
Emulsion paints Vv6
Endless belt conveyors
In general (66)
Site installations (60) or (90.6)
Engineering
Electrical installations (6–)
Services (5–)
Entrance fixtures
In general (71)
Epoxides
In general Dn6 or Yn6
Epoxy bonded mortars
Mixes in general Dr4 or Yr4
Thick coatings Pr4
Epoxy resin varnish Vv4
Equipment: Parts
Internal transportation (66)
Equipment: Control and data logging
Parts: Communications
installations (64)
Parts: Transportation (66)
Parts: Security installations (68)
Parts: Space heating in general (56)
Parts: Ventilation and air-conditioning systems (57)
Equipment, fixed.
see Fixtures
Equipment, loose
see Loose equipment
Escalators
In general (66)
Site installations (60) or (90.6)
Internal transportation (66)
Escalator wells
Described separately (24)
Escape stairs
In general (24)
Excavation
In general (11)
Foundations (16)
Site (10) or (90.1)

Exfoliated vermiculite
Aggregates Dp3 or Yp3
Expanded clay
Aggregates Dp3 or Yp3
Expanded metal
Mesh J
Expanded mica
Aggregates Dp3 or Yp3
Expanded perlite
Aggregates Dp3 or Yp3
Expanded plastics
see Cellular plastics
Expanded slag Dp3 or Yp3
Expanded slate
Aggregates Dp3 or Yp3
Expansion joints
Overlap tiles N
Expansion roofs
Pipes I
Expansive cements
Mixes and in general Dq2 or Yq2
Explosion vents (57)
Exterior lighting (60) or (90.6)
External doors (31)
see also (21)
External walls
Elements (21)
Finishes (41)
External works 9
Extinguishers
Fire fighting equipment (68)
Extract: Local
see Local ventilation
Extract hoods
Pipes I
Extract units
Culinary fixtures (73)
Extrusions
Sections H

Fabric
Thin flexible sheets (decorative) U
Thin flexible sheets (non-decorative) L
Fabric reinforcement
Meshes J
Facing bricks F
Facings
Butted tiles S
Faience
In general Dg3 or Yg3
Blocks and bricks Fg3
Overlap tiles Ng3
Slabs Rg3
Tiles Sg3
Fan convectors
Water and steam distributed central heating (56)
Fanlights: Parts
Secondary elements: External (31)
Secondary elements: Internal (32)
Fans
Parts: Ventilation (57)
Fascia boards
Sections H
Thick coatings P
Fascias: Parts
Roof (27)
Fasteners
In general Xt5
Feedback
In general Aa8
Felt backed linoleum sheets and tiles Tn4
Felts
Compressed L
Quilts K
Fences
Site elements (20) or (90.2)
Site protection plant Ab1
Fencing: structural units G
Fibres
Blocks: Products Fj1
Loose fills: Materials Dp7 or Yp7
Impregnated materials Dn2 or Yn2
Minerals: Materials Ym1
Natural materials Dj or Yj
Fibrous plaster (preformed)
Mixes and in general Df7 or Yf7
Mouldings Hf7
Panels Rf7
Tiles Sf7
Figured translucent glass sheets Ro2
Fill
In general: Earthworks (11)
Foundations (16)
Fillets
Roof finishes (47)
Filling
Concrete E
Film projection equipment
Communications installations (64)
Films
Decorative thin flexible sheets U
Thin applied coatings V
Filters: Parts
Air-conditioning (57)
Heating (56)

Sawdust
Aggregate Dp6 or Yp6
Sawdust concrete
Mixes and in general Dq7 or Yq7
Blocks Ff5
Cast in situ Eq7
Large precast units Gf5
For precasting Yf5
Slabs Rf5
Tiles Sf5
Screeding P
Screeds
Parts: Floor finishes (43)
Parts: Roof finishes (47)
Thick coatings P
Screens
Partitions (22)
Visual communications installations (64)
Screen walls
Site elements (20) or (90.2)
Screws
Fastenings Xt6
Scrim
Foils L
Thin coating V
Sealants Dt4 or Yt4
Sealing plates
Pipes I
Seals
Surface coating Vu5
Seats
External fixtures (70) or (90.7)
Internal fixtures (72)
Loose equipment (82)
Secondary cells
Parts: Electrical centre (61)
Secondary elements
In general (3-)
Site (30) or (90.3)
Superstructure (2-), (3-)
Sections
Products, in general H
Security
Installations: Site (60) or (90.6)
Installations: Internal and in general (68)
Semi-rigid frames (28)
Semi-vitreous clay
In general Dg3 or Yg3
Blocks and bricks Fg3
Tiles Sg3
Separating walls (22)
Septic tanks (50) or (90.5)
Service hatches (32)
see also (22)
Service lifts (66)
Services
In general (5-)
As part of superstructure (2-)
Site (50) or (90.5)
Sets
Components X
Settles (fixed benches) (72)
Setts
Bricks and blocks F
Shales Dp1 or Yp1
Shavings
Fills Dp5 or Yp5
Sheet glass Ro1
Sheet piling (17)
Sheets
In general R
Foldable M
Flexible: Decorative T
Overlapping N
Rigid R
Thin flexible, membranes L
Thin flexible sheets (decorative) U
Shelf and cupboard units (76)
Loose equipment (86)
Shell roofs (27)
Shellac
Varnish constituents Dv4 or Yv4
Shellacs
Varnishes Vv4
Shelving (76)
Sherardized steel
see Steel
Shingles
Aggregates and fills Dp1 or Yp1
Overlap tiles N
Shower cabinets (74)
Showers
Parts: Water services (53)
Shredders (51)
Shrubs Dx2 or Yx2
Shutters
In general (32)
Parts: Windows (31)
Rolling: External doors (31)
Rolling: Internal doors and grilles (32)
Side hung doors
In general (32)
Side hung windows and external doors (31)
Sidelights: Windows, doors: Parts
Fixed: In general (31)
Fixed: Internal (32)
Opening see Casements

Signboards
External fixtures (70) or (90.7)
Signs
In general (71)
Illuminated: External (60) or (90.6)
Illuminated: Internal (63)
Not illuminated: External fixed (70) or (90.7)
Not illuminated: Internal fixed (71)
Not illuminated: Internal loose equipment (81)
Silicate of soda Vu5
Silicon bronze
see Copper alloys
Silicone coatings
Water repellant Vu6
Silicone rubber
In general Dn5 or Yn5
Sill plates
Parts: External walls (21)
Parts: Internal walls (22)
Sills
Parts: Windows and external doors (31)
Sink waste disposers (73)
Sinks
In general (73)
Cleaners fixtures (75)
Culinary fixtures (73)
Sintered pulverised fuel ash Dp3 or Yp3
Sintered clay
Aggregate Dp3 or Yp3
Sisal
see Vegetable fibres
Site and building
In general (- -)
Site clearance B
Site only
In general (90)
Finishes (40) or (90.4)
Fixtures (70) or (90.7)
Installations (60) or (90.6)
Loose equipment (80) or (90.8)
Services (50) or (90.5)
Superstructure (20), (30)
Site preparation
Earthworks C
Site slabs (13)
Skeleton frames (28)
Skirting heating
Water and steam distributed central heating (56)
Skirtings
Parts: Floor finishes (43)
Skylights (37)
Slabs
Floors: Substructure (13)
Suspended (23)
Rigid flat sheets R
Slag
Aggregates Dp or Yp
Aggregates: Granulated Dp6 or Yp6
Aggregates: Heavy Dp2 or Yp2
Aggregates: Light Dp3 or Yp3
Slag cement
Mixes and in general Dq2 or Yq2
Slag fibre
In general Dm1 or Ym1
Felts and quilts Km1
Pipes Im1
Slabs Rm1
Tiles Sm1
Slag and lime
see Sandlime
Slaked lime
Mixes and in general Dq1 or Yq1
Slate
In general De5 or Ye5
Blocks Fe5
Paviors Se5
Slabs Re5
Tiles Se5
Slate, expanded
Aggregate Dp3 or Yp3
Slates
Overlap tiles Ne5
Slates: Sections H
Sliding doors
Internal (32)
Sliding windows (31)
Slips
Anchorages Xt6
Slop sinks (75)
Smoke extract (57)
Snow guards
Parts: Roofs (27)
Parts: Rooflights etc (37)
Soakers
Foldable sheets M
Pipes I
Soap dispensers (74)
Sockets
Parts: Power installations (62)
Pipes I
Sodium discharge lamps (63)
Soffits
Ceiling finishes (45)
Stair finishes (44)

Softwood
In general Di2 or Yi2
Blocks Fi2
Overlap tiles Ni2
Panels Ri2
Sections Hi2
Special formed units Gi2
Veneers Ui2
Soil
Stabilised: Foundations (16)
Soil disposal
Drainage (52)
Soldering materials
In general Dt2 or Yt2
Solid floors (13)
Solid fuel heating
In general (56)
Centralised hot water supply (53)
Central heating: Water and steam distributed (56)
Central heating: Warm air (56)
Local heating (56)
Soot blowing equipment
In general (5-)
Sound installations (64)
Sound transmission barriers
Suspended ceilings (35)
Space frames
In general (28)
Roofs (27)
Space heating
Heating systems (56)
With ventilating and air-conditioning (57)
Spacers
Bars H
Spiral stairs (24)
Sponge K
Sports equipment
External fixtures (70) or (90.7)
External loose equipment (80) or (90.8)
Sprayed coating
Thick coating P
Sprays
Horticultural Dw6 or Yw6
Sprinklers
Installations (68)
Sprockets
Sections H
Spruce
see Softwood
Sprung floors
Floor finishes (43)
Stabilised soil
Foundations (16)
Stacks
Chimneys: Building elements
see Chimneys
Staff locating installations (64)
Stages (33)
Stains
Paint constituents Dv2 or Yv2
Stainless steel
In general Dh3 or Yh3
Mesh Jh3
Panel Rh3
Pipes Ih3
Sheets Rh3
Structural units Gh3
Tiles Sh3
Wire Jh3
Stairs
Elements (24)
Finishes (44)
Stanchions
Parts: Frames (28)
Steam central heating (56)
Steam distributed central heating (56)
Steel
In general Dh2 or Yh2
Mesh Jh2
Overlap sheets Nh2
Panels: Rigid sheets Rh2
Pipes Ih2
Sections Hh2
Sheets: Foldable Mh2
Special formed units Gh2
Tiles Sh2
Wire Jh2
Steel alloys
In general Dh3 or Yh3
Panels: Rigid sheets Rh3
Pipes Ih3
Sheets: Foldable Mh3
Tiles Sh3
Steel-backed decorative rubber sheets and tiles Tn5
Step irons (24)
Steps
Site elements (20) or (90.2)
Stiles
Sections H

Diagram 1

Outline Plan of Work

Stage	Purpose of work and Decisions to be reached	Tasks to be done	People directly involved	Usual Terminology
A. Inception	To prepare general outline of requirements and plan future action.	Set up client organisation for briefing. Consider requirements, appoint architect.	All client interests, architect.	Briefing
B. Feasibility	To provide the client with an appraisal and recommendation in order that he may determine the form in which the project is to proceed, ensuring that it is feasible, functionally, technically and financially.	Carry out studies of user requirements, site conditions, planning, design, and cost, etc., as necessary to reach decisions.	Clients' representatives, architects, engineers, and QS according to nature of project.	
C. Outline Proposals	To determine general approach to layout, design and construction in order to obtain authoritative approval of the client on the outline proposals and accompanying report.	Develop the brief further. Carry out studies on user requirements, technical problems, planning, design and costs, as necessary to reach decisions.	All client interests, architects, engineers, QS and specialists as required.	Sketch Plans
D. Scheme Design	To complete the brief and decide on particular proposals, including planning arrangement appearance, constructional method, outline specification, and cost, and to obtain all approvals.	Final development of the brief, full design of the project by architect, preliminary design by engineers, preparation of cost plan and full explanatory report. Submission of proposals for all approvals.	All client interests, architects, engineers, QS and specialists and all statutory and other approving authorities.	

Brief should not be modified after this point.

Stage	Purpose of work and Decisions to be reached	Tasks to be done	People directly involved	Usual Terminology
E. Detail Design	To obtain final decision on every matter related to design, specification, construction and cost	Full design of every part and component of the building by collaboration of all concerned. Complete cost checking of designs.	Architects, QS, engineers and specialists, contractor (if appointed).	Working Drawings

Any further change in location, size, shape, or cost after this time will result in abortive work.

Stage	Purpose of work and Decisions to be reached	Tasks to be done	People directly involved	Usual Terminology
F. Production Information	To prepare production information and make final detailed decisions to carry out work.	Preparation of final production information i.e. drawings, schedules and specifications.	Architects, engineers and specialists, contractor (if appointed).	
G. Bills of Quantities	To prepare and complete all information and arrangements for obtaining tender.	Preparation of Bills of Quantities and tender documents.	Architects, QS, contractor (if appointed).	
H. Tender Action	Action as recommended in paras. 7–14 inclusive of 'Selective Tendering' *	Action as recommended in paras. 7–14 inclusive of 'Selective Tendering' *	Architects, QS, engineers, contractor, client.	
J. Project Planning	Action in accordance with paras. 5–10 inclusive of 'Project Management' *	Action in accordance with paras. 5–10 inclusive of 'Project Management' *	Contractor, sub-contractors.	Site Operations
K. Operations on Site	Action in accordance with paras. 11–14 inclusive of 'Project Management' *	Action in accordance with paras. 11–14 inclusive of 'Project Management' *	Architects, engineers, contractors, sub-contractors, QS, client.	
L. Completion	Action in accordance with paras. 15–18 inclusive of 'Project Management' *	Action in accordance with paras. 15–18 inclusive of 'Project Management' *	Architects, engineers, contractor, QS, client.	
M. Feed-Back	To analyse the management, construction and performance of the project.	Analysis of job records. Inspections of completed building. Studies of building in use.	Architect, engineers, QS. contractor. client.	

* Publication of National Joint Consultative Council of Architects, Quantity Surveyors and Builders.